Handbook
of Copyright
in British
Publishing Practice

Handbook
of Copyright
in British
Publishing Practice

THIRD EDITION

J.M. Cavendish and Kate Pool

CASSELL

Cassell
Villiers House, 41/47 Strand, London WC2N 5JE
387 Park Avenue South, New York, NY 10016–8810

First edition published 1974.
Second edition published 1984.
Third edition published 1993.

Quotations from the Copyright Act 1911; the Copyright Act 1956; the Copyright,
Designs and Patents Act 1988; the International Copyright Convention 1948
(Berne Convention); general letters on the Reproduction and Photocopying of
Crown and Parliamentary Copyright Publications (PU 15/108); a leaflet headed
'Export Licence'; and Copyright and Designs Law: Report of the Committee to
Consider the Law on Copyright and Designs are reprinted by kind permission of
the Controller of Her Majesty's Stationery Office.

British Library Cataloguing-in-Publication Data
A catalogue entry for this book is available from the British Library.

Library of Congress Cataloging-in-Publication Data
Applied for.

ISBN 0-304-32635-6

Typeset by Colset Private Limited, Singapore
Printed and bound in Great Britain by
Biddles Ltd, Guildford and King's Lynn

Contents

Preface: A Word of Caution   xi
Acknowledgements   xiii

1 **Where Are We Now?**   1
2 **What *Is* Copyright?**   2
3 **An Outline of the Copyright, Designs and Patents
   Act of 1988**   5
4 **Geography and the Act**   7
5 **The Subjects Protected by Copyright**   9
   Literary Works – Dramatic Works – Musical
   Works
6 **Who Is the Author?**   15
7 **How Does a Work Qualify for Copyright
   Protection?**   16
   International Protection – UK Protection – Denial
   of Protection to Illegal Works – 'Originality' –
   'Making' a Work – Acceptable Territory – Qualifying
   Persons – Works of United States Origin –
   Recognized International Organizations –
   Governments in the British Sphere
8 **What Is Publication?**   25
9 **Who Owns the Copyright?**   28
   The First Owner: (1) The Author – (2) The
   Employer of the Author – (3a) The Crown –
   (3b) Parliament – (4) The Assignee of a Prospective
   Copyright – Later Owners of the Copyright –
   Reversion of Rights by Agreement – Reversion of
   Rights on Bankruptcy of the Purchaser – Transfer
   of a Publisher's Rights in Works – Reversion of
   Rights under the 25-Year Proviso – Loss of
   Copyright Ownership
10 **How Long Does Copyright Protection Last?**   35
   1 Perpetual Copyrights and Printing Rights –
   2 Copyrights First Owned by Governments in the
   British Sphere – 3 Copyrights First Owned by
   Recognized International Organizations

– 4 Copyrights Not in Categories 1, 2 or 3 –
General Rules for Works Created before and after
1 August 1989 – Pseudonymous and Anonymous
Works and Works of Untraceable Authorship –
Joint Works – Additional Notes

11 **The Extent and Limitations of a Copyright**   44
The Limited Prerogatives of the Copyright
Owner – How Much Can Be Copied Without
Permission? (Substantial Part and Fair
Dealing) – The Rights Controlled by the Copyright
Owner – Infringement – Untraceable Authors

12 **Reproduction in Newly Printed Form**   51
What Is a Copy? – When Is Copying
Privileged? – Copying and Breach of
Confidence – Copying across National Frontiers

13 **Copying by Libraries**   57
What Libraries Are Prescribed? – How Much Can
Be Copied for Members of the Public? – What Can
Be Copied by Libraries and Archives for
Themselves and Each Other?

14 **Copying in and for Education**   60
What Educational Establishments Are Privileged? –
Quotation in Anthologies for Educational Use –
Reproduction and Adaptation for Examinations
– Reproduction and Adaptation in the Course of
Instruction

15 **Reprography: Facsimile Copying**   63
Collective Licences – Reprographic Rights
Organizations Overseas

16 **Using Old Works Without Permission**   65
Copying Old Unpublished Works – Copying
Unpublished Works Made on or after 1 August
1989 – Copying Old Anonymous and Pseudonymous
Works

17 **Using Entire Published Works Without Permission**   68

18 **Using Government Publications and Public Records**   69
Reproduction of Crown and Parliamentary
Copyright Material – Public Records

19 **The Bible**   79

20 **Works in Perpetual Copyright**   80
Peter Pan

21	**Reprinting Extracts: Permission to Quote, Select or Anthologize**	81
	When to Ask Permission to Quote – Applying for Permission to Quote – Acknowledgements – Giving Permission and Charging Fees	
22	**Original Manuscripts**	92
23	**Copying Titles, Ideas, Plots, Slogans, Information and Characters**	94
	Registered Trade Marks	
24	**The Author's Name**	98
	Passing Off – Malicious Falsehood – Choosing a Pseudonym	
25	**Moral Rights**	100
	1 The Right of 'Paternity' – 2 The Right of 'Integrity' – 3 False Attribution of Authorship – 4 The Right of Privacy in Certain Films and Photographs – Assignment and Waiver – Duration	
26	**The Publisher's Copyright in His Typography**	105
	Typefaces	
27	**Collective Licensing**	107
	The Rental Right – The Copyright Tribunal – Organizations Engaged in Collective Licensing	
28	**Performance**	112
	Obtaining Permission for a Performance – The Copyright Tribunal – Performers' Rights – Interviews	
29	**Dramatizing a Literary Work**	116
30	**Translation**	117
31	**Adapting a Work to a Strip Cartoon**	119
32	**Reproducing a Work as a Sound Recording**	120
33	**The Sound Recording as a Separate Subject of Copyright**	122
34	**Broadcasting a Work by Television or Radio**	126
	Cable Television and Satellite Broadcasting	
35	**Broadcasts and Cable Programmes as Separate Subjects of Copyright**	129
36	**Filming a Work for Cinema and Video**	132
37	**The Film as a Separate Subject of Copyright**	133
	Video Recordings	

38 Copyright and Computers: Works in Electronic Form 135
The Protection of Computer Programs –
Computer-generated Work – The Use of
Copyright Works in Electronic Form:
Electro-Publishing – Electrocopying – Delivery of
'Manuscripts' on Disk – The Data Protection Act
1984

39 Public Lending Right 140
40 Submitting and 'Reading' a Work for Publication 143
41 Revising a Text 145
42 Reissuing a Previously Published Text 147
43 Publications with a Supervisory Editor 149
44 Republishing Out-of-Copyright Works 151
45 Deposit Regulations for Publications and Scripts 152
46 Composing the Copyright Notice 155
The General Copyright Notice – The Copyright
Line – Where Should the Line Be
Printed? – Requirements for the Copyright
Line – When to Print a New Copyright
Line – Mistakes – The Symbol – The Name –
The Date – Translations – UK Reprints and
Reproductions – Material for Sale in the
United States

47 A Checklist for the Copyright Page 167
48 Copyright in Artistic Works 170
Moral Rights – Registered Designs and the Design
Right – Export Control of Works of Art

49 Commissioning and Copying Artistic Works 181
Newly Commissioned Works – Permission to
Reproduce Existing Artistic Works – The Object
Reproduced – The Copyright Line, Moral Rights
Assertion and Acknowledgements – Giving
Permission and Charging Fees

50 If a Copyright Owner Dies 188
51 Composing a Contract 190
The Basic Contract – Licences and Assignments

52 Europe – Changes on the Agenda 203
Directive on the Duration of Copyright – The
Software Directive – Directive on Rental and
Lending Rights – Directive Requiring Adherence to
the Berne Convention and the Rome

Convention – Directive on the Legal Protection of
Databases – Directive on Reprography – Directive on
Moral Rights – The Single European Market

53 Copyright and the United States   208
The Manufacturing Clause
54 Copyright and the Countries of the Former USSR   214
55 International Copyright Conventions   216

Bibliography   222
Index   224

For Janet Hurrell and Mark Le Fanu
with respect and affection

Preface: A Word of Caution

This handbook is intended to help where help is most often lacking: in the day-to-day practical problems of book publishing and book writing. It is embarrassing to seek expert opinion on minor points, and as a result too many people muddle through with what they perfectly well know is insufficient knowledge: the author using quotations, the editor cutting a text, the designer commissioning artwork, the director negotiating at Frankfurt. Knowing the basic copyright rules can save a great deal of work and worry, and frequently a lot of money as well.

The advice given in this book is emphatically *not* a substitute for real legal expertise. We have done our best to explain the present law and its relevance to business practice, but areas do exist where, for instance, the meaning of the law has never been precisely resolved, or where a course of action depends on the current law of other countries, or where numerous and complex considerations must be taken into account. To deal adequately with such rarefied matters would need an encyclopedia, as well as a proficiency in legal thinking by the reader which is not assumed in the rest of our text.

If you are at all uncertain of your position, and most especially if court proceedings may be involved, go straight to the expert. He should of course be well versed in publishing matters; an ordinary solicitor, however efficient, is unlikely to be familiar with the practicalities and contracts of the book trade.

If you are an author with an agent, he should be able to tell you if a solicitor is necessary. However, if you have obvious legal problems you may be best advised to start by consulting the Society of Authors (or, for television and films, the Writers' Guild), which offers legal advice to its members and will refer non-members to a firm of solicitors specializing in publishing matters.

The growing problems of deliberate piracy, which affect so many creative works today, are beyond the scope of this book, since in the vast majority of cases the problems exist because no generally applicable way has been found of coping with them. Sometimes they are exacerbated because of inadequate protection under existing law or inadequate enforcement of it. Often they are a matter for international political solution.

The law on these fringes is being slowly but continuously remade, by international agreement, by statute, or by decisions of the courts in particular cases. Combating piracy effectively depends to a very great extent upon how much the legitimate industry is willing to spend on its own protection. In the meantime individual situations have to be handled on an *ad hoc* basis, and your professional association is most likely to know about the latest developments and will be able to offer the best advice.

Acknowledgements

Among the many people who have personally provided informa-tion, assistance and comment for this edition special thanks are due to the following: Charles Clark, Stephen Edwards, Mark Le Fanu of the Society of Authors, Janet Hurrell of the Authors' Licensing and Collecting Society, and Richard Balkwill.

Invaluable help has also been supplied by Jim Parker, Registrar of Public Lending Right, E. O'Byrne of the Department of National Heritage, Chris Scarles of Cambridge University Press, Steve Soderberg of the Library of Congress, David Whitaker and Alan Mollison of J. Whitaker & Sons, Julian Cannon of the British Library, Ian Quarterman of Her Majesty's Stationery Office and O. Whittaker of the Worshipful Company of Stationers and Newspaper Makers.

1 Where Are We Now?

The second edition of this book, published nine years ago, described the bewildering and rapidly developing new technologies that were besetting the media. These days, book publishers produce books about computers, and use computers to compile their books; they issue audio and video recordings of books and with books; they publish electronically, and produce works in electronic form. Copyright infringement has become a way of life among the general public with our tape recorders, video recorders and, most prolific of all, photocopiers. There are new possibilities with interactive CD systems and there is a new threat in the development of electro-copying: a cheap and easy-to-use combination of text-reader, computer and printer, capable of storing, editing, resetting and reproducing text. Cable and satellite TV are established industries. International agreements proliferate but seldom mesh properly, either with each other or with the laws of individual countries. The second edition began with the plea 'What we need now is legislation that will catch up with the reality'. The Copyright, Designs and Patents Act 1988 has at last attempted, with some success, to update the law of copyright to take account of technological developments and to enable the United Kingdom to ratify certain international conventions (notably the 1971 Paris Text of the Berne Convention). It also anticipated European Community legislation, outlined in the European Commission's *Green Paper on Copyright and the Challenge of Technology*, published in June 1988,* although the EC's directives on various aspects of copyright, anticipated in the next few years, may well necessitate changes, by statutory instrument, to the UK's legislation.

This edition is an attempt to outline the current legislation and other developments, in the (no doubt fond) hope that we have at last reached a plateau where technology, and the laws controlling it, have caught up with each other and that copyright legislation

---

Green Paper on Copyright and the Challenge of Technology, Com (88) final, Bll.E.C. 6–1988.

has had the foresight to be applicable to any possible future technological developments.

2 **What *Is* Copyright?**

The main purpose of copyright law is to ensure that authors receive
some share of any money and prestige resulting from the exploitation of their own original work. In general, therefore, it is illegal for
anyone to reproduce an author's work without his* express permission. This means that no one may safely copy or steal it and pass it
off as his own unaided creation because the law defends the real
author's prior rights. It also means that no one may publish a work,
or use it in other ways, without first reaching an agreement with the
author – an agreement which will normally involve payment.

When you write a book, copyright protection begins automatically as soon as you put pen to paper. Nothing more is necessary
to establish copyright in an unpublished work; its mere existence
is enough. Once a work has been published, protection is still
automatic in the United Kingdom and most other developed countries, but in some (notably until recently the USA) protection will
not continue unless all copies carry a formal copyright line.

As a corollary to the protection of authors, the law also safeguards the interests of publishers, since they are able to finance
the production and sale of works with some hope of redress in cases
of piracy, which is becoming ever easier with the developments of
new technology.

Copyright means, simply, 'the right of an author, artist or composer to prevent another person copying an original work which he
himself has created'.* When an author contracts for the publication
of a book, implicit in the agreement is a sharing of this negative,
defensive right. It is as if he was saying to the publisher, 'Until this
moment I could stop you copying my book; now you and I together
can stop anyone else copying it.'

---

* For purely practical reasons, we have used 'he' to stand for 'he or she'
throughout this book.

* Gregory Report on copyright, 1952.

Secondly, copyright is a right of ownership, similar to the ownership of a house. The 'subject of copyright' – the text of a book, for instance – is a perceptible object like the house, and both can be bought, sold, inherited, willed and leased, but in both cases the ownership is an intangible idea.

When a publisher wants to print copies of a book he must first, therefore, obtain the author's general permission to do so. But it is then necessary to establish just how much of the copyright, in its various aspects, is going to be transferred to the publisher.

The author's original absolute ownership of the copyright is almost infinitely divisible. It can be sliced and resliced in five principal ways, each of which limits the other four:

1 BY 'SALEABLE RIGHTS' – THAT IS, BY THE METHOD OF REPRODUCTION

The original complete copyright may be imagined as a number of subordinate rights like sticks in a bundle, each being one possible way of copying the work. A book publisher will naturally want the 'volume rights' (the right to publish the work in book form), but he may well want an interest in others as well: serial, television, radio, film, electronic and so on.

2 BY THE AMOUNT OF CONTROL, OR 'LEGAL INTEREST'

As soon as an author sells any of his rights he must also pass on some measure of legal control so that the purchaser can exercise the rights he is buying. The sale may, for example, be an exclusive licence (where the author retains the copyright but the publisher controls some or all of the methods of reproduction, and can sublicense this control to others) or an 'outright' assignment (where both copyright and control pass to the publisher and the author relinquishes all title to his work). An author can grant rights to one publisher 'exclusively', meaning that he will not grant the same rights to anyone else. Or the grant may be 'non-exclusive', leaving the author free to sell the same rights on the same non-exclusive basis to other publishers.

3 BY TERRITORY

A publisher will at a minimum want the right to distribute a book within the market covered by his own sales force. A Spanish publisher, for instance, will be mainly concerned with selling the book in Spain and the Spanish-speaking countries of Latin America

('Spanish rights'). The author can confine the reproduction rights sold to one such market only, or can give the publisher 'world rights', allowing him to distribute his edition everywhere.

4   BY LANGUAGE

An author can with perfect propriety grant two different publishers exclusive rights within the same territory, provided they are licensed to publish in different languages. Conversely he may sell to one publisher alone the right to publish his book in several or all languages. Here again the word 'rights' is liberally used: English language rights, Japanese rights, translation rights.

5   BY TIME

Some agreements allow the publisher to control the rights he has bought for as long as copyright subsists in the book. Others provide for rights to revert to the author after a specified time (e.g. 10 years), or on a particular occasion (when the book goes out of print) or after the sale of a certain number of copies (an edition limited to 5,000).

Note that the law has nothing to say about money except in one or two special cases. The amount an author is paid for his rights and when he is paid remain matters for individual (or occasionally collective) negotiation.

Of course copyright protection is not confined to books. It covers all kinds of 'Literary' works and also 'Dramatic' and 'Musical' and all varieties of 'Artistic' works. It extends to sound recordings, films, radio, television, works stored in computers and computer programs. Protection is not confined to works which are 'artistic' in the critics' sense. Codes are covered, and so is a child's first drawing.

However, it does not follow that everything one sees, hears or reads in the United Kingdom is protected by our copyright law. A speech is not protectable unless someone records it in some material form. Ideas and titles are not protectable. Moreover, a work may or may not legally qualify for protection, depending on the author's status, the time and place of publication and the essential originality of the work.

'Originality' in copyright law should not be confused with the requirements of patent law. Two people may take identical photographs of Ben Nevis, but as long as both are taken independently and one is not a deliberate copy of the other, both are entitled to copyright protection. Patent law, on the other hand, refuses protection to any work closely resembling one already registered, without regard to other circumstances.

As well as the economic rights of copyright, the Act now includes moral rights, which give authors legal entitlement to credit for their work and control over how it is treated by others.

In the course of their daily work authors and publishers alike tend to see copyright law as a superfluous nuisance and distraction. It is as well to remember that, without such a law, publishing as we know it today could not exist.

3 An Outline of the Copyright, Designs and Patents Act of 1988

Copyright law in the United Kingdom today is governed by the Copyright, Designs and Patents Act 1988 (in the following pages usually called 'the Act'). The principal statute immediately preceding it was the Copyright Act 1956 and before that was the Copyright Act 1911. The formal titles of these Acts are misleading, since none became operative until the following year:

> The 1911 Act came into operation on 1 July 1912
> The 1956 Act came into operation on 1 June 1957
> The 1988 Act came into operation on 1 August 1989

In 1974 a committee was set up under Mr Justice Whitford 'to consider and report whether any, and if so what, changes are desirable in the law relating to copyright . . .' and their eminently readable report (commonly called the Whitford Report) was presented to the government in 1977.[*] By then, the old 1956 Act was very much out of date. A new statute was badly needed, especially to deal with the rapid developments in satellite and cable television,

---

[*] Copyright and Designs Law: Report of the Committee to consider the Law on Copyright and Designs, 1977 (available from HMSO, Cmnd 6732).

---

computer technology and the ease of copying. A new Act was also needed to bring UK law into line with the Paris Text of the Berne Convention (1971) and to pre-empt the changes likely to be imposed by the single European market.

It was not until 1981 that the government responded to the Whitford Report with the publication of its consultative Green Paper on copyright* and then in 1985 a Green Paper on the recording and rental of audio and video material.† A White Paper dealing with copyright, patents and trade mark law was published in 1986‡ and finally, 11 years after the Whitford Report but reflecting many of the points it made, the Copyright, Designs and Patents Act 1988 received Royal Assent.

When the 1988 Act was passed it replaced and repealed the 1956 Act. (The provisions of the Act relating to industrial designs and the small but significant amendments to patent and trade mark law are outside the scope of this book.) In almost all respects the Act is simpler and clearer to understand than previous copyright legislation. Unfortunately, however, in deciding many copyright questions about works existing before 1 August 1989, attention must still be paid to the 1956 Act and sometimes its predecessors also.

The 1988 Act is of course part of a whole network of laws which affect, revise, interpret or implement each other. Others, for instance, set out rules for publishers' deposit copies, govern broadcasting, reflect the aims of the European Community or ratify international conventions.

The 1956 Act dealt with each class of work in turn, setting out the applicable restricted and permitted acts, duration of copyright and a multitude of subsidiary questions. The 1988 Act is more clearly laid out. Part I deals with copyright; Part II with rights in performances; Parts III and IV with designs; Parts V and VI with patents; and Part VII is headed 'miscellaneous and general'. The law relating to copyright, the subject of this book, is contained in Part I, some of Part VII and Schedule I (giving transitional arrangements between the 1956 and 1988 Acts).

---

* Reform of the Law Relating to Copyright, Designs and Performers' Protection, 1981 (Cmnd 8302).

† Green Paper on the Recording and Rental of Audio and Video Copyright Material (Cmnd 9445).

‡ White Paper 'Intellectual Property and Innovation' (Cmnd 9712).

Part I is divided into 10 chapters:

I   the types of work protected by copyright, their ownership and duration;

II what things cannot be done without the copyright owner's permission;

III those acts that are permitted, including new legislation on the rental of sound recordings and films;

IV moral rights;

V   the assignment and transfer of rights;

VI remedies for infringement of copyright;

VII copyright licensing and the bodies that may administer collective licensing schemes;

VIII the Copyright Tribunal (which replaces the Performing Right Tribunal);

IX grounds on which works qualify for copyright protection, by author and place of first publication or transmission;

X   Crown and Parliamentary Copyright as well as 'other miscellaneous provisions'.

4 Geography and the Act

All countries have their own separate copyright laws, just as they have their own laws about taxation, crime and everything else.

Like the other laws, a copyright act is enforceable by the courts only within the country which makes it. The local law, and no other, decides whether, in the home territory, a work is in or out of copyright, what constitutes plagiarism, and so on. The local law has no influence abroad, where the foreign local law is paramount in the same way.

But in order to apply the law, the courts must be told which facts can be admitted as relevant and acceptable. Initially, the law says that these facts can only be things which happen in the home territory: United Kingdom law thus begins by giving copyright protection only to works by UK citizens and residents and to works first published in the UK. So we start with the UK as the only geographical area in which facts of authorship and publication count towards claiming copyright protection. In the pages that follow we call this sort of area 'acceptable territory'.

The area in which a law is enforceable cannot change (except in war) but since the law is free to admit whatever facts it chooses, the 'acceptable territory' can vary widely.

The present UK Act should be seen as related to four broad geographical areas:

1   THE HOME TERRITORY

Since 1 August 1989 the present Act has been the national law in the United Kingdom of England, Scotland, Wales and Northern Ireland. These countries form the basic 'acceptable territory' and within them UK copyright law is enforceable in its entirety.

2   THE 'INTERMEDIATE' TERRITORY

The existence of British colonies, dependencies and protectorates forces the law to take account also of countries which are, as it were, neither completely British nor completely foreign. The Copyright Acts refer to this group when they say that a provision is to be 'extended' to include them.

The intermediate group varies with the contemporary political situation. (On becoming independent a country assumes 'foreign' status, though its law of copyright may continue to be identical with that of the United Kingdom.) At the moment the group contains:

(a) COUNTRIES WHERE THE PRESENT UK ACT IS THE NATIONAL LAW BECAUSE AT VARIOUS DATES IT HAS BEEN SPECIALLY EXTENDED TO THEM. They may modify the Act, but only in certain local circumstances.

(b) COUNTRIES WHERE THE 1911 OR 1956 ACT IS STILL THE NATIONAL LAW BECAUSE THE 1988 ACT HAS NOT YET BEEN EXTENDED TO THEM. These are the Channel Islands, the Isle of Man and all 'intermediate' countries not in category (a) above. They were permitted to modify the 1911 and 1956 Acts in ways similar to category (a) countries.

From the UK point of view the whole of the intermediate group is 'acceptable territory'. The regulations of the Act will be interpreted by a UK court in effectively the same way whether they involve persons and events in the UK or persons and events in an intermediate country, except for rare instances affected by local modifications in the law.

The 'home' and 'intermediate' territories are often grouped together for legal purposes. When necessary we shall refer to all of them at once as 'the British sphere'.

3 FOREIGN TERRITORY

The law for works of foreign origin is distinct from the domestic legislation forming the core of the Act. A 'work of foreign origin' is one whose author is not a citizen or resident of the UK or an intermediate country and which has not been first published there. The authors of works of foreign origin cannot claim copyright protection in the UK unless a special Order has been passed naming their country (or the country where they first publish) as one to which the rules of the UK Act will be 'applied'. This then makes that country 'acceptable territory' and from that date puts the foreign authors in the same position as their UK counterparts. A great many countries (but still by no means all) are now in this position as members of the international copyright conventions.[p. 216]*

4 THE HIGH SEAS

The 1988 Act applies in UK territorial waters as on the mainland, and extends to 'things in the UK sector of the continental shelf on a structure or vessel which is present there for purposes directly connected with the exploration of the seabed or subsoil or the exploitation of their natural resources' – oil rigs, for example. It also applies to things done on British ships, aircraft and hovercraft.

5 The Subjects Protected by Copyright

Chapter I of the Act describes the types of work that are entitled to copyright protection. The main four are Literary, Dramatic,

---

*Superior numbers indicate cross-references to pages in this book.

Musical and Artistic works. The others are: sound recordings, films, broadcasts and cable programmes (none of which receive detailed attention in this book but which are described as necessary in the chapters devoted to them) and the typographical arrangement of the published editions of works.

Literary, Dramatic and Musical works can all be reproduced either in sounds or by written symbols. All three can, for instance, be performed on a stage or printed in a book, and the regulations for all three are similar when they appear in similar forms.

Artistic works, on the other hand, remain subject to their own rules. Each picture (or graph, chart, building, sculpture) is a complete copyright work in itself – and in most cases physically indivisible, which works in the other three categories are not. In many cases legally as well as editorially, Artistic works have to be handled differently from other works. They are therefore dealt with in a separate section of this book, while Literary, Dramatic and Musical works are considered together.

Literary Works

All Literary works are subject to the same general rules, but because of occasional special exceptions they should be divided into:

> Letters (including any type of business communication)
> Speeches (including sermons, addresses, lectures)
> Periodicals and articles for periodicals
> All other literary works, including 'books'

The word 'literary' implies no critical standard, but is used in the same broad sense as it is in the phrase 'sales literature'. To qualify as a protectable Literary work a text must not be music nor in dramatic form (although Literary works do include work which is spoken or sung), and must be recorded 'in writing or otherwise'. The writing can be in letters and/or numerals or in code, shorthand, mathematical symbols, Braille or similar forms of notation. A work can be recorded in any way, such as on tape, film or computer disk. However, until 1 August 1989 a Literary work only qualified when it was 'embodied in the material form of writing'. A Literary work need not have any meaning (a catalogue of type has been protected as a Literary work). Tables, compilations and computer programs are specifically included as Literary works.

Letters are distinguished from most other Literary works by being private or confidential communications addressed to one or at most a limited number of recipients. The publication of a letter or the use of its contents in any way is therefore nearly always limited by general legal considerations as well as by copyright law. The owner of the copyright in a letter is its writer, not the recipient.

Speeches are in a curious position. They are not protectable until they are recorded (in writing or otherwise). It is immaterial whether the recording is made with the permission of the speaker, who has copyright in the speech as soon as it is recorded. There may, in addition, be a separate (dependent) copyright in the version of the speech recorded, belonging to the person who made the recording. This corrects the anomalous situation under the 1956 Act whereby copyright in an extempore lecture, speech or talk belonged to the person writing it down.

Periodicals are mentioned several times in the Act and although they are not formally defined they clearly include magazines, newspapers and any publications reappearing at regular or irregular intervals. They normally contain pieces specially written by many different authors on subjects largely unconnected with one another, both within a single issue and as between consecutive issues. Both the individual articles in a periodical and the periodical as a whole are protectable Literary works. Periodicals are of an ephemeral nature; most of them have a deadline to meet at recurrent intervals; articles in them are frequently unsigned and sometimes unattributable to any particular author.

In some cases it is difficult to say whether a work is or is not a periodical. For instance, a wide variety of publications reappear yearly and are called **annuals**. An almanac, one would think, is a compilation in book form which happens to be published in a revised edition each year, and not a periodical at all. On the other hand an annual scientific journal *is* a periodical. Numerous 'annual' publications, which are certainly books, appear every Christmas for the gift market. **Part works** are exactly like encyclopedias except that they can be bought in separate (often weekly) parts. These parts are bound and designed like magazines, but they build up into complete works of reference and have a definite homogeneity of purpose and content. They are issued 'periodically' until the work is complete, and then sales cease. A part work should, therefore, be regarded as a 'book', not a periodical.

Note that publication in magazine format does not by itself

put a Literary work into the periodical class, and format should generally be ignored when deciding such questions.

All other Literary works fall into an undefined mass which includes advertising copy, blank forms (such as questionnaires), calendars, circulars, coupons, labels, leaflets, lists and tables of all kinds separately published (e.g. prices, games fixtures), prospectuses, registers of voters, rules for games, specifications for inventions, telegrams, timetables – and, of course, books.

To call something a **book** is to imply both a physical format ('paperback book') and a very general branch of literature ('She used to write poetry but is now trying her hand at a book'). The concept is so vague that no one has succeeded in producing a really workable, positive definition, and the Act wisely does not attempt one. Most of us are so accustomed to thinking of books as a special category that it is a mental wrench to see them as part of a legally undifferentiated group. Other important members of the same group are such productions as Braille texts, microfiches, microfilms of text, videotape and filmstrips containing printed text and computer print-outs. It makes remarkably little difference to copyright law in which of these forms a Literary work appears, nor does it make any difference whether the work itself is fiction or non-fiction, prose or poetry, a single paragraph or a multi-volume encyclopedia.

Poetry is a unique form of 'literature' in the critical sense, but not in the eyes of the Act, which has no reason to distinguish it from prose. However, there are some practical differences. You may publish a book of poems which are all new, all by the same poet and which are intended to be read together. But the fact remains that each poem has a copyright easily separable from the others. Choosing one poem for reuse elsewhere does not take the same skill as choosing an equivalent passage from a prose text, and when a poem is reused it is not only an extract from the original book but also complete in itself. Hence reuse of an entire poem is much more strictly controlled than the reuse of an equivalent prose passage.[p. 87] Otherwise, however, poetry should be regarded exactly like prose: it can exist in the form of a letter, a speech, a periodical, a book, or any other Literary work; it can also be used in Dramatic works.

Captions for pictures are Literary works; so is **advertising copy**; and so, very often, are **lyrics** and other **words associated with music**.

Before leaving the consideration of Literary works a few more definitions should be made. The Act offers us its only direct hint towards the definition of a Literary work when it says that such works include '(a) a table or compilation, and (b) a computer program'. **Tables**, of course, are those lists which show facts in a planned spatial relationship (winners of races, trigonometry tables). They must be written; graphs, maps and illustrations such as a diagram of the solar system are drawings and therefore Artistic works.* **Compilations** are an ill-defined category, but plainly must cover material existing already in other forms and newly arranged by the compiler, and would include work stored by electronic means, such as a database.[p. 138]

Computer programs[p. 136] are specifically included as Literary works. They are not defined but appear to include both individual programs and complete software packages.

Common-source books and compilations are those which contain material such as historical, mathematical or geographical information drawn from our common stock of knowledge – which may be in readily available written form. Almanacs, catalogues, most cookery books, directories, some encyclopedias, examination papers, guidebooks, many textbooks and timetables may all be called common-source compilations.

Anthologies are collections of pieces (usually by different authors) quoted exactly. The pieces may be extracts or complete poems, articles, short stories, letters, etc. **Selections** resemble anthologies but there is an implication that all the pieces are drawn from a homogeneous source (a single work, or works by the same author, or the correspondence between X and Y).

Condensations and **digests** shorten previously existing longer works. **Abridgements** do the same thing but with more originality and skill. (See also page 21.)

Collective works are defined as works of joint authorship or works in which there are distinct contributions by different authors or in which works or part works of different authors are incorporated. These would include **encyclopedias, symposia** and **part works**, which consist of individual items newly written by contributors especially

---

*Under the 1911 Act 'maps, charts and plans' were Literary works, but the 1956 Act corrected this anomaly.

---

for them, the general outline of the whole being the responsibility of a supervisory editor.*

Dramatic Works

To qualify as Dramatic, a work must be recorded in writing or otherwise in precisely the same way as a Literary work.[p. 10] The Act states that '"dramatic work" includes a work of dance or mime'. Before 1 August 1989 such works only qualified if reduced to writing, but they are now protected as copyright works when recorded in any form, for example on film or video. **Stage plays, scripts** for television and radio and **screenplays** for films are all Dramatic works. **Words associated with music** will often be Dramatic works also, and the implication is that a Dramatic work must be capable of being performed in a way involving action unlike, for example, a song which is a Literary work.

Opinions and judgements differ as to whether the sum total of a **stage presentation** (including, scenery, scenic effects and the overall 'production' effect) is protectable as a Dramatic work. **Scenery** itself should usually qualify for protection as an Artistic work.

Musical Works

Music and Musical works are not defined in either the 1911 or the 1956 Acts. However, the 1988 Act defines a Musical work as 'a work consisting of music, exclusive of any words or action intended to be sung, spoken or performed with the music'. A Musical work is entitled to protection once it has been recorded, whether in writing or otherwise (and this was also the case under the 1956 Act).

When words are associated with music in any way – however magnificent the fusion – in law the two remain separate. The **libretto** of an opera or musical will therefore be regarded as a Literary or Dramatic work. The **lyrics** of a song will be Literary. For a ballet

---

* Beware of confusion with section 35(1) of the 1911 Act where a collective is defined as '(a) an encyclopedia, dictionary, yearbook . . . (b) a newspaper, magazine . . . (c) any work written in distinct parts by different authors, or in which works or parts of works of different authors are incorporated'. Valuable in context, this definition is altogether too wide a net for practical purposes.

the **choreography** will be a Dramatic work so long as it has been recorded in some way (although until 1 August 1989 the choreography had to exist in some permanent written form to qualify for protection).

6   Who Is the Author?

The author of a Literary, Dramatic or Musical work is the person who creates, i.e. writes or composes it. Someone who contributes an idea without doing any of the actual writing or composing is not an author. Anyone dictating to a secretary is the author of the work dictated, even though the secretary is physically responsible for the writing. A true author's work must also be original[p. 20] so someone who produces pages full of multiplication tables, or who copy-edits a text for the printer, cannot claim authorship. (Note that the definition of an 'author' for Public Lending Right purposes is different.)

The **single author** who originates the whole of one work is the norm. A **contributor** is a single author who writes items for a book or periodical whose overall form is someone else's responsibility.

Collaborations cause some problems. To qualify as a collaborator or co-author each person must meet the definition of a true author above. When the work of each collaborator is clearly separable from the work of the others the relationship of each to their own piece is quite separate, just like the single author's. **Joint authors,** however, are those who produce work 'in which the contribution of each author is not distinct from that of the other author or authors' and consequently joint authors receive much special attention in the Act.

A copyright can be sold (even before the work itself has been made), so the author is not necessarily the same person as the **owner** of the copyright.

The quotation and other use by author A of existing illustrations or text by author B does not make B a co-author with A. If a writer 'ghosts' a book for, say, a famous actor, the writer (who does all the 'original' work) is the true author, though his name may never appear on the book. If the copyright is to be owned by the actor, the author must formally assign it to him. A medium, however, has been held to own the copyright in a work 'dictated' by a spirit.

The author of **computer-generated** works is 'the person by whom

15

the arrangements necessary for the creation of the work are under-taken' (see *Copyright and Computers*[p. 135]).

The work of **editors** is often protected in a manner equivalent to the protection of authors' works. 'Editor' may of course be simply a business title without any necessary copyright relevance. It is what the editor does, not what he is called, that determines his legal interest in a copyright.

Editors (meaning revisers of new editions or supervisory editors of multi-author works, for example, rather than in-house copy-editors) work with text or information (old or new, in or out of copyright) which they have not themselves written. They may rewrite it, abridge it, rearrange it, commission it and/or enlarge it with text newly written by themselves. The law may allow them to claim originality and therefore copyright protection in their arrange-ment of the text depending on the extent of their input.

Editorial revision of a text may be so minor that the revising editor cannot claim authorship, or so extensive that he can qualify as a joint author.

A **new arrangement** of a Musical work – even one which has gone out of copyright – should qualify for a new copyright as long as it is sufficiently 'original', in the same way as an editor's work, and the arranger would be the author of the new copyright.[p. 48]

The **transcription** of a 'traditional' musical air which has never been written down or 'made'[p. 22] before may put it into copyright for the first time.

The author of the **typographical arrangement** of a published work is the publisher of the edition in which it is incorporated.

7 How Does a Work Qualify for Copyright Protection?

International Protection

The rest of this chapter is concerned with how Literary, Dramatic and Musical works qualify for copyright protection in the United Kingdom, BUT it is important to remember that UK publishers sell to markets all over the world and must do what they can to protect their publications outside as well as inside the UK.

Many countries, like the UK itself, adhere to both the Berne and Universal Copyright Conventions, but a number of important ones adhere only to one or the other.[p. 216] To obtain protection under both it is necessary to publish first (or simultaneously[p. 27]) in a Berne Union country *and* to print a UCC copyright line[p. 157] *and* a general copyright notice[p. 156] in every copy of your publication. In practical terms this means publishing first in a country which is a member of *both* Berne *and* UCC – e.g. the United Kingdom.

UK Protection

The Act describes specific standards which all Literary, Dramatic and Musical works must meet before they can claim the protection of UK copyright law. But, of course, the millions of works which are produced every year cannot be submitted to any sort of qualifying examination at their first appearance. Whether any particular work is in fact entitled to protection is a question which normally comes up only if it becomes the subject of a court case.

The rules are:

All works must be 'original'* and must be 'recorded in writing or otherwise'.

An unpublished work will be protected if its author was a 'qualifying person' for at least a substantial part of the time spent 'making' it. (Works made for governments in the British sphere or for recognized international organizations may be protected on other grounds: see below.)

A published work will be protected if:
(a) it was *first published* in 'acceptable territory' OR
(b) it was first published on or after 1 June 1957 on a date when its *author* was a 'qualifying person'. (If the author dies before first publication, the work will still be protected as long as the author was a 'qualifying person' immediately before his death.)
(Works first published by governments in the British sphere or

---

* This and other technical phrases used are explained further on in this chapter.

---

by recognized international organizations may be protected on other grounds: see below.)

Some **rare exceptions** exist to these general rules. (1) Works in existence before 1 July 1912 (when the 1911 Act came into operation) can qualify for protection after 1 June 1957 only if they meet the requirements listed above, but in addition they must have been entitled to protection under the laws existing before 1 July 1912 and have qualified for a continuation of that protection under the 1911 Act. One ought to assume that a work will have so qualified unless it is particularly desirable to prove the contrary. In such a case expert advice should be obtained. (2) Protection may be denied to works which are libellous, immoral, obscene, irreligious, calculated to deceive the public, fraudulent, or infringements (see below). (3) Some titles are still in perpetual copyright.[p. 80] (4) The Authorized Version of the Bible and some other religious texts may be printed by certain firms only.[p. 79] (5) Special enactments may be passed to override the law and deny protection to otherwise qualifying titles (e.g. works of enemy origin) or to protect unqualifying titles (e.g. works of US origin in the World Wars).

Note that these requirements do not include **formal registration**. (UK library deposit has nothing to do with copyright.) Nor do they include any form of **notice**. The symbol © should certainly be used[p. 161] and is often essential for copyright protection abroad, but except as it affects the admissibility of foreign works under the Universal Copyright Convention, the present UK law simply ignores it.

Note also that in effect **copyright status is reassessed at publication**. Where foreign authors or foreign publication are involved it can turn out that a work which is unprotected in manuscript form becomes protected after publication; conversely it may be protected in MS but go out of copyright on publication. For instance, a book written before 27 May 1973 by a Soviet author resident in the then Soviet Union (who was therefore not a qualifying person) was not in copyright in the UK while it remained unpublished – unless it was written for a British-sphere government or a recognized international organization. However, if the book was first published (with the author's consent) in the 'acceptable territory' of France it was then able to claim protection in the UK. The opposite case might be a book by an Englishman resident in the People's Republic of China. If the author was a British citizen (and therefore a qualifying person) when it was written, the unpublished manuscript would be protected in the UK. But suppose the author then took Chinese citizenship. The unpublished book would continue to be protected in the UK. But if it was then first published (with the author's consent) in China before 15 October 1992 (non-acceptable territory) it will have lost its protection in the UK permanently.

An exact definition of **publication** is plainly essential for copyright purposes. If a work is printed and copies are issued to the public for the first time by a publishing firm there can be no doubt that it has then been published and before that time it was unpublished. But what if it has already been serialized, recorded, distributed among friends or otherwise reproduced? If the same work is published at different dates in different countries, which is its 'first' publication? These and related questions are covered in the next chapter, *What Is Publication?*[p. 25]

Denial of Protection to Illegal Works

If the contents of a work are such that publishing it would be a legal offence or could give rise to a civil claim, it cannot depend upon the protection of copyright law. Such a work may be libellous or contravene the current laws on obscenity or immorality.

Theoretically it is illegal to publish works which are blasphemous or unacceptably scandalous, abusive or insulting in relation to the Christian religion, according to the doctrines of the Church of England. These doctrines are statute law, but the present climate of opinion allows an almost infinite latitude to religious discussion in the UK.

A work may be denied protection if it is fraudulent: calculated seriously to mislead the public and/or to obtain money under false pretences. A trade catalogue making important false claims is one example. A work whose authorship is falsely attributed[p. 104] is another.

Publication may be an infringement under the Act. Protection will be denied to editions which have not been authorized by the copyright owner and to proven plagiarisms.

If a work is advertised or published in an illegal way but is itself unobjectionable, its claim to copyright protection will not be affected.

'Originality'

A direct copy of someone else's work (leaving aside its illegality) plainly cannot claim a new and separate copyright for itself. The Act's requirement that a protectable work must be 'original' means, however, a little more than the mere absence of plagiarism, though it does not go so far as to imply novelty or literary merit.

The originality must lie in wording and arrangement, not in subject-matter, ideas or plot. The chief criterion is the quantity of labour, skill and judgement expended by the author.

Completely new works – e.g. new fiction honestly written – qualify without argument.

Compilations may be so skilfully made that the compiler can claim a separate copyright in that arrangement alone. The compiler's 'labour, skill and judgement' are especially important in common-source compilations. A volume containing nothing but columns of figures listed consecutively from 1 to 1,000,000,000,000,000 would not be protected. Printing every tenth number in bold face would make no difference, since that would not affect the wording or arrangement. But arranging these same figures in tables according to their properties (if the author worked them out for himself, and especially if it was a difficult task) would be doing original work. Certain cookery books, directories, fixture lists of football matches and similar compilations have been judged original, but a collection of the ordinary tables found in most pocket diaries has been disqualified.

Anthologies, selections and similar collections may also qualify for a separate copyright in their arrangement, independent of the existing copyright in the material quoted. (A selection from the works of A. Smith, illustrating his gradual conversion to Buddhism, would almost certainly be original, but a collection of his published works in chronological order would not.) Until the copyright in the arrangement has expired it is an infringement to republish the whole of such a collection, even though the individual items may be out of copyright.

A **new version** of a previously existing work may qualify for a new copyright if sufficient skill and labour are employed in its preparation. Minor revision (substituting modern words for occasional archaisms, excising occasional lines, copy-editing) is not sufficient. Major revision, where the result is virtually a collaboration between author and editor, may produce something so different from the original as to qualify for a new copyright in the new text. Updating a previously copyright work such as a travel guide has been held to have the effect of giving a new, later copyright to the entire work, not only to the newly written portions. A new arrangement of an out-of-copyright tune will qualify for a new copyright.[p. 48] So will, say, a version of an opera written for the harp. Of course any work based on another which is still in copyright must not be made without the permission of the owner of the copyright in the existing work. Works produced by computers before 1 August 1989 could sometimes be original enough to qualify for a new copyright. Computer-generated works created since then clearly qualify for copyright protection.[p. 138]

The distinction between a **condensation** which does not qualify for protection separately from its original, and a legally 'original' **abridgement** is made by Copinger and Skone James* as follows:

> To constitute a genuine abridgement, the sense and meaning of the entire work must be preserved, and then the act of abridgement is the product of the understanding, employed in moulding and reducing a large work into a small one. Independent labour must be apparent and the reduction of the size of a work merely by copying some of its parts and omitting others confers no copyright. To abridge in the legal sense of the word is to preserve the substance, the essence of the work, in language suited to such a purpose, language substantially different from that of the original. To make such an abridgement requires the exercise of mind, labour, skill and judgment, and the result is not merely copying.

On these grounds a brief description of a plot will not qualify, but the more nearly it approaches the length and quality of an abridgement the closer it will come to an original work. Of course no abridgement or condensation of a copyright work may be made without the permission of the copyright owner. (For a mere synopsis of the information contained in a work see page 95.)

In works like **encyclopedias** each contribution is separately subject to the test of originality. The overall arrangement will almost always qualify for a separate copyright.

Advertising copy (though not an advertising slogan[p. 96]) can claim copyright protection as long as it is original and not just a string of commonplaces or quotations.

Closely similar or even identical works may each display the

---

* *Copinger and Skone James on Copyright* (see *Bibliography*), 13th edition, para. 3.40. Quoted by kind permission of the publishers, Sweet & Maxwell Ltd.

---

requisite originality. Two surveys of the same farm, two summaries of the same statistics, will necessarily resemble each other but each will be protectable if the authors have each worked out the result for themselves. However, republishing entries taken from an existing directory, even after checking their accuracy and revising them accordingly, is not doing original work.

'Making' a Work

A Literary, Dramatic or Musical work is 'made' when it is first 'recorded, in writing or otherwise'. Writing is defined as including 'any form of notation or code, whether by hand or otherwise and regardless of the method by which, or medium in or on which, it is recorded' – i.e. at the earliest moment when there is solid physical proof that it exists. Before 1 August 1989, Literary and Dramatic works were not 'made' unless recorded in writing, while Musical works could be either in writing or in the form of a sound recording.

Acceptable Territory

What we call 'acceptable territory' at present includes the United Kingdom, the Channel Islands, the Isle of Man and any British colony, and all members of the Berne and Universal Copyright Conventions.[p. 218] The date when a country becomes 'acceptable territory' is governed by the relevant Order in Council extending or applying to it the provisions of the present Act (or the 1911 or 1956 Acts). As time goes on, more and more countries are recognized as 'acceptable' but the recognition is not normally retroactive. There are still a number of countries which are not 'acceptable' in the eyes of our copyright law.

The provisions of the Act are not always extended intact to foreign works: like most countries we generally protect the works of foreigners only when their country protects similar works emanating from the UK. This is especially true for sound recordings, films, broadcasts and cable programmes.

This subject is discussed from a slightly different point of view in *Geography and the Act*.[p. 7]

Qualifying Persons

An individual is a qualifying person if he is either (a) a citizen* of an acceptable country or (b) a person domiciled or resident in an acceptable country or (c) 'a body incorporated under the law of a part of the United Kingdom or of another [acceptable] country'.

Although not specifically defined in the Act, a person's domicile is their permanent home, and whether they are there in person at the relevant time does not matter. Residence implies settled house-keeping but of a more temporary kind.

Joint works are entitled to protection if at least one of the authors is a qualifying person. If authors are **anonymous** or **pseudonymous** it may be assumed that, provided reasonable enquiry[p. 41] can prove them to be qualifying persons, their work will be protected.

Works of United States Origin

Until the United Kingdom ratified the Universal Copyright Convention on 27 September 1957, the US and the UK never belonged to the same copyright union. Consequently before that date works written by American nationals, or published in the USA, could only secure UK copyright protection (or, for that matter, protection elsewhere in the Commonwealth) if they were first or simultaneously[p. 27] published in a Berne Union country. Sensible publishers usually accomplished this by arranging for first publication across the border in Canada. However, UK protection was extended to most works first published in the United States during the First and Second World Wars by special Orders in Council. Note that most works prepared by officers or employees of the US government are not protected by US copyright law.

Recognized International Organizations

Literary, Dramatic, Musical and Artistic works produced by supra-national organizations like UNESCO tend to slip through the meshes

---

*Not necessarily a full citizen. The UK Act includes any class of British citizen, subject or protected person under the British Nationality Act 1981.

---

of UK copyright law. The first difficulty is that as the organizations are not corporate bodies they cannot have clear title in the UK to copyrights they own. The Act deals with this by saying that they shall be treated as if they have 'the legal capacities of a body corporate for the purpose of holding, dealing with and enforcing copyright and in connection with all legal proceedings relating to copyright'.

Secondly, the organizations may own works which are not copyright in the UK because the author is not a qualifying person and (if published) first publication took place in a non-acceptable country. Works like these *which would not otherwise qualify* will be given special protection if they have been made by an officer or employee of, or are published by, a recognized organization and in circumstances which would have qualified them for protection if the author had been a British subject. Note further that to claim this protection an unpublished work must have been made on or after 1 June 1957; a published work must have been first published on or after 1 June 1957.

At present the only recognized organizations are the United Nations (or one of its specialized agencies) and the Organization of American States.

Governments in the British Sphere

Copyright works of all categories which would not otherwise qualify for copyright protection will be protected if they have been made or published (a) by 'Her Majesty or by an officer or servant of the Crown in the course of his duties', or (b) 'by or under the direction or control of the House of Commons or the House of Lords', or (c) by a department or agency of the legislative body of any other country in the British sphere.[p. 8] (The entire copyright in such works automatically belongs to the government unless a specific agreement is made with the author to the contrary.[p. 31]) All unpublished works made in these circumstances will be protected, and published works will be protected as long as they are first published in a country in the British sphere.

Before 1 August 1989 there was no category of Parliamentary copyright. However, Literary, Dramatic and Musical works (but not any other categories of copyright work) made or published by or under the direction or control of the Crown or a government department qualified for Crown copyright protection.

8   **What Is Publication?**

Issuing copies to the public is one of the Acts Restricted by the Copyright [p. 46] in all works. No one may publish a substantial part of any copyright work (or any adaptation of such a work) without the permission of the copyright owner except in the special cases listed on page 54.

The grounds for claiming copyright protection, and in some cases the term and extent of that protection, are not always the same for published works as for unpublished works, particularly for those made before the 1988 Act came into force. And if a work rates as 'published' the grounds, and sometimes the term, depend on the time and place of its 'first' publication. Note that the length of time a work is protected may be affected not only by publication but also by being made available to the public in various other ways. [p. 37]

Once a work has been legally published for the first time it loses its unpublished status permanently. But the definitions below remain useful when (notably in actions for infringement) it is necessary to decide whether a subsequent use of the work is publication or something else. Of course if a work has passed permanently into the public domain copyright law takes no further interest in it. (But see *Europe*, page 203.)

A Literary, Dramatic or Musical work is published only **when authorized copies are issued to the public**, including making the work available by means of an electronic retrieval system (e.g. Teletext). The Act defines copies as reproductions of the work in any material form (not just in writing), including storing the work by electronic means. Until 1 August 1989, the 1956 Act provided that a Literary, Dramatic or Musical work was published only when authorized reproductions in written form (any kind of handwriting, typing or printing) had been issued to the public. A work existing before 1 August 1989 is considered first published after that date if it qualified under the terms of the 1956 Act at 1 August 1989, or if it is published after that date in accordance with the requirements as to first publication as defined in the 1988 Act.

An **authorized** publication is one made with the agreement of the copyright owner or someone to whom the necessary control has been delegated.* If a work is unpublished and in copyright, and is then published without authorization, the law will continue to treat it as 'unpublished' and will only recognize the unlicensed publication in so far as it is grounds for a court action. Similarly, if an unpublished work which is not in copyright is published without the agreement of the author (or his heirs or licensees)† UK law will continue to treat it as 'unpublished'.

More than one reproduction must be made. Making a single copy is not 'publication' (and a letter, of course, is not published by sending it to a recipient). The Act also says firmly that when publication 'is merely colourable and not intended to satisfy the reasonable requirements of the public' a work will not be rated as 'published'.

The **actual text** of the work should be reproduced. Any number of adaptations[p. 47] which qualify for separate copyrights of their own may be published without affecting the 'unpublished' status of the original.

Since 1 August 1989 the reproductions may be in any material form, not just in written form. However, the public performance, broadcasting or cable distribution of a Literary, Dramatic or Musical work do not constitute publication.

The **proportion of the work reproduced** is important. Suppose half of a forthcoming novel is serialized in a magazine during 1984, but the whole novel only appeared in book form in 1985. If you are concerned with whether and how the novel qualifies[p. 17] for UK copyright protection you must judge both halves quite separately, the first rating as 'published' in 1984 and the second as not 'published' until 1985.

One of the commonest ways in which a work is **issued to the public** is when reproductions of it are offered for sale (no one need actually buy a copy), even if it is offered only to a very select group. The issue (offer or delivery) of free copies involves the more difficult question of whether the recipients are 'the public'. This depends partly on their numbers and partly on their relationship to the author and publisher. The issue of presentation, review or booksellers' copies is not publication for copyright purposes. A manuscript can

---

*For collaborations and joint works this agreement should be obtained from all the authors who qualify as copyright owners (see page 23).

† In this case *all* joint authors must give their agreement.

be read by many persons: one copy or numerous carbons or photocopies may be safely circulated among friends and colleagues of the author, professional readers or technical advisers, as long as this circulation is of a definitely private nature. But if a charge is made, or copies of the manuscript (or proof, or printed book) are gratuitously circulated beyond this limited circle, legal 'publication' might be provable, which could affect the duration of copyright protection.

A specific category of **Commercial Publication** was introduced by the 1988 Act (of relevance only in relation to Crown and Parliamentary copyrights). It has a narrower definition than that of publication in that copies must have been 'made in advance of the receipt of orders'.

The **place of publication** is the country where the work is actually put on offer to the public, not the country where it is printed.

A work is **first published**, of course, when for the first time it is reproduced, distributed and offered for sale in accordance with the definition above. If it is first published in two or more different countries on different dates the publications will be regarded as 'simultaneous' if they took place within a period of not more than thirty days.* Thus a claim for protection may be based on any one of a number of publications 'simultaneous' with the first, provided the publication was in acceptable territory.[p. 22] If, however, a work (by an author who is not a 'qualifying person') was first published in, say, China before 15 October 1992 and then not published – in the same language – in an acceptable country until more than 30 days had elapsed, it would lose its UK protection.

It is plain that adhering to a definite publication date can on occasion be crucial to the copyright status of the work published. **'Always publish first in a country which belongs to both Berne and UCC'** is one of the golden rules for international protection.[p. 17]

Book publishers are usually careful to ensure that announced publication dates are honoured by the trade. Booksellers should not offer copies for sale (though they may display them) until the date stipulated by the publisher. Book reviews are not supposed to appear before publication, but a review, whatever its date, does not affect the copyright status of a work.

---

* For works published on or before 31 May 1957 the period was 14 days. The statutory time limit can be overridden by special enactment, and has been in a few cases, as with UK and USA works during the World Wars.

Magazines frequently bear a printed date which is by no means the real publication date, it being general practice to fill newsagents with 'August' issues during July. The real publication date must be ascertained in the rare cases when it is important.

When written proof of publication is necessary it is best obtained in the form of an affidavit from a bookseller or newsagent that he has offered copies for sale on a certain date.

Once published, copies of most works must be deposited with the British Library.[p. 152]

Definitions of publication and 'release' as they apply to Artistic works, sound recordings, films and works on computer are covered in the appropriate chapters.

9 Who Owns the Copyright?

The owner of the copyright in a Literary, Dramatic or Musical work is always either the actual author[p. 15] or someone who has acquired the copyright from the author – directly or indirectly, by agreement or by operation of law.

A copyright can be owned by an individual or a corporation (or jointly by more than one individual or corporation) but UK courts have so far held that unincorporated bodies (except for recognized international organizations[p. 23] and government departments[p. 24]) cannot own copyrights. Incorporated bodies are those incorporated by a special Act of Parliament or by Royal Charter, or companies registered under the Companies Act. When the ownership of copyrights is important, groups which are not incorporated sometimes find it convenient to form incorporated subsidiaries to ensure a clear title to their publications.

Some titles are still in the maverick category of 'perpetual' copyrights and are owned by various universities and colleges.[p. 80] The current Act protects the rights of established owners for a limited period but does not permit any further perpetual copyrights to be created, although a special perpetual non-copyright right has been granted to the Hospital for Sick Children, Great Ormond Street, with respect to *Peter Pan*.[p. 81] The Crown owns the copyright in the Authorized Version of the Bible.[p. 79]

Ownership of a manuscript is in most cases no proof of owner-ship of the related copyright.[p. 92]

The rules stated below will not always apply to the ownership of copyright in **works existing before 1 July 1912**, when the 1911 Act first came into operation. In particular, the performing right in Musical and Dramatic works could devolve separately from the other rights comprised in the copyright. If it becomes necessary to prove title to an old copyright any enquiry should be put in the hands of an expert. Again, rights assigned or licensed before 1 July 1912 often revested in the author at the expiration of the old term of copyright, subject to certain safeguards exercisable by the previous assignee or licensee.

Copyright ownership has two aspects: passive possession of the work as an intangible property, and active control of the ways in which the work can be reproduced. The first copyright owner can transfer to someone else both possession and control, or control alone. So the person of the greatest practical importance is the one who controls the particular rights wanted by a buyer – or illegally used by a pirate. In general, therefore, 'the copyright owner' in the Act and in this book means the controller of the appropriate rights at the relevant time.

Chapter VI of the Act includes, in Sections 104–106, the legal assumptions that will be made about copyright ownership when the actual facts are not known or not questioned.

The most important fact of all, however, is the identity of the very first owner of a copyright: all claims to copyright descend ultimately from that person, and his identity will decide whether a work qualifies for protection at all, and how long its term of protec-tion will be.

The First Owner: (1) The Author

The true author[p. 15] is always the first owner of the copyright in a work unless it was written for a government in the British sphere or under the direction or control of a House of Parliament, or under a contract of service or apprenticeship, or if the author has assigned the prospective copyright to someone else. Apart from these cases, the situation will be as follows.

Co-authors whose contribution to a work is **clearly separable** from the text of their collaborators own the copyright in the text they themselves have written and they have no claim on the rest of the work. **Joint authors** own the copyright together and (in the absence of an agreement between them to the contrary) each has an equal voice in its disposition. It sometimes happens that a collaborator or joint author cannot personally qualify for the protection of UK copyright.[p. 23] In this case a separable contribution by an unqualified author is not protectable, so there is no copyright to own. In the case of joint works the copyright in the whole will be owned by the author or authors who do qualify, and as far as copyright law goes they are the only ones who can sign contracts or otherwise legally deal with their work. (Unqualified authors should protect their rights by contracts with their qualified co-authors.) This difficulty is most likely to affect unpublished works.

Editors of encyclopedias, anthologies, abridgements and similar texts will, if their work is sufficiently original, own a copyright in the arrangement as a whole, separate from and in addition to any copyright subsisting in the parts. (There will be a copyright in an original arrangement even when there is no named editor.)

Contributors own the copyright in their own articles.

Writing **anonymously** or under a **pseudonym** does not prevent authors from owning the copyright in their work but if their identity is too well concealed their work will go out of copyright earlier than it otherwise would.[p. 41]

Translators are in the same position as the author of a completely new work and their ownership of the copyright in their translation (but not the original work) follows exactly the rules given in this chapter.

The First Owner: (2) The Employer of the Author

If an author produces a Literary, Dramatic, Musical or Artistic work under a **contract of service or apprenticeship** and in the course of the employment, the employer will own the copyright unless author and employer agree otherwise. A contract of service is not necessarily a written document; it is a certain kind of relationship between a person and his work and the person or firm for whom he does the work. The author may be a salaried employee or a commissioned freelance. Individual cases differ, but a court will probably hold that you work under a contract of service:

– if your employer closely directs and controls your work. If you are given only a vague brief or none, and the execution of the task is left to your own judgement, you are not under a contract of service but a 'contract for services';

– if your work is done as part of your daily work for the employer (or as overtime). Work unconnected with your duties and done in your spare time will not belong to the employer;

– if the employer can hire or fire you at will and/or if your work is done for a set remuneration;

– if your employer pays your National Insurance contributions.

By special agreement with the author the employer may be entitled to more or less than the general law prescribes.

An **apprentice** does a job with the primary purpose of learning a trade which the employer has agreed to teach. The employer will be the first owner of the copyright in any work done by the apprentice in the course of employment unless they agree otherwise.

The copyright in a **letter** written by an employee is the property of the employer.

The **employees of periodicals** were in a special position between 1 June 1957 and 1 August 1989. During that period, the 1956 Act stated, 'Where a literary, dramatic or artistic work is made by the author in the course of his employment by the proprietor of a newspaper, magazine or similar periodical under a contract of service or apprenticeship, and is so made for the purpose of publication in a newspaper, magazine or similar periodical, the said proprietor shall be entitled to the copyright in the work in so far as the copyright relates to publication of the work in any newspaper, magazine or similar periodical, or to reproduction of the work for the purpose of its being so published; but in all other respects the author shall be entitled to any copyright subsisting in the work.' This exception was not repeated in the 1988 Act and journalists are now treated in the same way as all other employees.

The First Owner: (3a) The Crown

The Crown is the first owner of the copyright in every category of copyright work 'made by Her Majesty or by an officer or servant of

the Crown in the course of his duties', within the British sphere.[p. 8]
Until 1 August 1989, Crown copyright only applied to Literary,
Dramatic, Musical and Artistic works but was wider in application
as it included any such work made by or under the direction or
control of the Crown or a government department. Copyright in a
work commissioned by the Crown and completed before 1 August
1989 belongs to the Crown. If the work was commissioned before but
not completed by then, or commissioned since then, copyright in it
belongs to the author (or his employer) unless specifically assigned
to the Crown.

The Crown also owns the copyright in any work first published
under the direction or control of Her Majesty or a government
department before 1 August 1989, even if Crown copyright would
not otherwise subsist in that work.

The First Owner: (3b) Parliament

The 1988 Act introduced a new category – Parliamentary copyright.
Each House of Parliament (or where appropriate, both Houses
jointly) owns the copyright in any work made under its direction or
control since 1 August 1989 (although the Act says that 'a work shall
not be regarded as made by or under the direction or control of either
House by reason only of its being commissioned by or on behalf of
that House'). It also owns the copyright in works made under its
direction or control before, and still unpublished at, 1 August 1989.

Both Crown and Parliamentary copyright give protection to
works which would not qualify for protection under the normal
rules. By agreement, however, authors may retain the copyright in
their work.

The First Owner: (4) The Assignee of a Prospective Copyright

An assignment of prospective copyright is a document which an
author signs before his work exists, promising that the copyright will
belong to someone else as soon as the work is made. Note, however,
that on or before 31 May 1957 an author could not legally do this;
assignments could only be created after a work was made, so the
author was always the first owner of the copyright.

An assignment of the prospective copyright must be in writing; if it is not, the author will be the first owner although the assignee may have good grounds for demanding a subsequent written assignment. If an author contracts to produce a work in return for a lump sum, a court will almost certainly hold (in the absence of other evidence) that he intended to grant at least some rights (in certain circumstances possibly all) to the contractor, even if there is no written document to that effect.

Later Owners of the Copyright

Ownership of a copyright can be transferred by the first owner to a second, and by him to a third, and so on. The current owner may assign the complete copyright outright, or may sign a partial assignment or an exclusive licence.[p. 200] An assignee or exclusive licensee normally controls the use of the rights transferred while his contract lasts, and anyone interested in these rights must deal with him. If the current owner grants a non-exclusive licence, the licensee cannot normally sublease the rights and anyone else wishing to use the same rights must apply direct to the copyright owner.

Since copyright is divisible, the ownership and control of different rights in a very successful work may be distributed among dozens of people.

If a copyright owner dies, his interest in the copyright passes to his legal heirs.[p. 188]

Reversion of Rights by Agreement

Many licences and partial assignments run for only a limited time, at the end of which control or ownership of a copyright reverts (returns in full) to the previous owner. In such cases both parties to the contract agree on the conditions under which the rights will revert.

Reversion of Rights on Bankruptcy of the Purchaser

If an author has granted an exclusive or non-exclusive licence to a company which goes into liquidation or is wound up, the licence automatically reverts to the author. However, if the entire copyright has been assigned, ownership of the copyright becomes the property of anyone buying the company or, if there is no purchaser, the Crown.

Transfer of a Publisher's Rights in Works

If a publishing company is taken over in its entirety, its contractual rights and obligations become those of the purchasing company.

If only a particular list or imprint or individual titles are sold by a publisher, the relevant authors' consent must be obtained before their contracts can be assigned (if they have granted a licence rather than assigning copyright to the publisher), unless there is a specific commitment by the author in the contract permitting assignment by the publisher. The reference at the beginning of many contracts to the publisher's assigns and successors in business is not relevant in this second case.

Reversion of Rights under the 25-Year Proviso

The 1911 Act contained a proviso under which almost all rights and copyrights licensed or assigned by authors while the 1911 Act was in force would *and still will* revert to their heirs 25 years after the date of the author's death.* (Neither the 1956 Act nor the 1988 Act repeated this proviso.)

The proviso **applies to** all agreements for works (except those listed in the next paragraph) which were (1) made or signed between 1 July 1912 and 31 May 1957 inclusive, *and* were (2) made or signed by the actual author of the work as first owner of the copyright. (When the work itself was made is of no consequence.)

The proviso **does not apply** to: (1) Any assignment[†] of the copyright in '(a) an encyclopedia, dictionary, year book, or similar work; (b) a newspaper, review, magazine, or similar periodical; (c) any work written in distinct parts by different authors, or in which works or parts of works of different authors are incorporated'. (2) A licence[‡] to publish a piece (or part of a longer work)

---

* For joint works the period is 25 years after the death of the author who dies first.

[†] Note that an assignment licensing one of the publications listed in (1), or assigning a contribution listed in (2), will be subject to the proviso.

[‡] As above.

---

in any of the publications just listed. (3) A specific bequest of rights or copyright made in the author's will. (4) Agreements made or signed on or before 30 June 1912 or on or after 1 June 1957.

It is seldom worth anyone's while to invoke this proviso. To publishers it can only mean a loss; to an author's heirs sorting out rights of inheritance via an estate 25 years old or more, it will usually mean legal expenses without any offsetting financial advantage.

However, there are still many authors living today who have signed contracts which will be affected by the proviso 25 years after they die. Living authors can legally sign new agreements covering the residuary period.

Loss of Copyright Ownership

A work which qualifies for UK copyright protection while unpublished can in rare circumstances lose this protection when it is published.[p. 18] Otherwise, it is virtually impossible to lose a copyright in the UK except by voluntarily signing it away to somebody else. Of course, copyright ownership ends when the term of protection expires, and a work may never qualify[p. 17] for protection to begin with.

An owner's right to exercise the copyright may be temporarily suspended (e.g. if he is an enemy citizen in wartime or, in effect, if he goes bankrupt). He cannot lose a UK copyright simply by not exercising it. The concessions in favour of developing countries,[p. 68] which permit compulsory publication in certain circumstances, curtail his control but do not negate the copyrights.

---

10 How Long Does Copyright Protection Last?

By comparison with other forms of property, the copyright in most works is owned for only a relatively short time. At the end of that time the work can be used by anyone in any way without permission – though branches of the law other than copyright (libel or obscenity, for example) may still regulate or prevent its reproduction, and permission to reproduce, say, the only existing copy of a text may have to be obtained from its owner.[p. 92] (See also page 205.)

Naturally no work can have a period of protection unless it qualifies[p. 16] for protection to start with. And even while a work is fully protected it can legally be used in several ways without the copyright owner's permission.[p. 54]

The length of time a work is 'in copyright' (protected by copyright law) is called its 'period of protection', 'duration of protection', 'term of copyright' or simply 'term'. When its term expires a work is said to be 'out of copyright' or 'in the public domain' ('p/d').

Most people today believe that not only authors, but their heirs as well, should have the right to control the use made of their work and to profit from it if they can. On the other hand there is a strong feeling that the public have a kind of natural right to the free enjoyment of Art. The compromise now made by most countries is to protect a work for the whole of the author's life plus a certain limited number of years. In the UK and the USA the most common limit is 50 years after the year of the author's death. Some countries have shorter limits and a few have longer ones.

The EC is proposing from 1 July 1995 to extend the period of copyright for all Community country copyright works to 70 years from the end of the year in which the author dies, with neighbouring rights (sound recordings, broadcasts, performances) protected for 50 years from the end of the calendar year in which they are performed, produced or broadcast. At the time of writing the proposal is still in the form of a draft directive and details are given on page 203.

Until then, under the 1988 Act, copyright in a Literary, Dramatic or Musical work lasts until 50 years from the end of the calendar year in which the author dies. Likewise, if the author died before 1 August 1989 and if the work was made available to the public[p. 37] during the author's lifetime, copyright in that work lasts until 50 years from the end of the calendar year in which the author died.

Unfortunately in addition UK law was until the 1988 Act lumbered with what is now a purely irrational complication. For works created before 1 August 1989 the limited term only started after a work had been either published or made available to the public. Consequently it was possible for a work to stay in copyright indefinitely. This had the singular result of giving the longest period of protection to works which no one considered worth publishing.

The 1988 Act has resolved this problem by providing that if the author died before 1 August 1989 and the work was not made available to the public during the author's lifetime, copyright in that work now lasts for 50 years from the end of the calendar year in which the work was first posthumously made available or until and including 31 December 2039, whichever is the sooner.

The significance of **publication** in this connection varies from one category of work to another, as indicated among the detailed notes below. The definition of publication itself is quite a long one. (See *What Is Publication?*[p. 25])

A work is **made available to the public*** when any version of a work in Column A below is reproduced in any of the ways listed in Column B.

A	*B*
A Literary work (or a dramatization in any language, a translation, or a strip cartoon adaptation of it)	is: – published [p. 25] – performed in public [p. 112]
A Dramatic work (or a non-dramatic version in any language, a translation, or a strip cartoon adaptation of it)	– offered for sale to the public as a record [p. 120] – broadcast [p. 126]
A Musical work (or an arrangement or transcription of it)	– (since 1 August 1989) included in a cable programme [p. 126]

Term is not affected by **changes of copyright ownership**. When the first owner [p. 31] is the Crown or Parliament, or a government or legislative body in the British sphere, or a recognized international organization the normal term is different, but no subsequent change of ownership or control will alter it.

The Act is completely indifferent as to whether a work, once published, is **in print or out of print**. This has no effect on term or

---

*Columns A and B include large concepts defined at length elsewhere, as indicated by the page reference numbers. Note that while the definition of 'publication' in the Act specifically excludes performing or broadcasting a work or issuing recordings of it, making the work available to the public specifically *includes* these actions.

---

anything else except as regards the special concessions allowed to publication in developing countries.

When calculating the duration of UK copyright in any work one of the following four categories must apply. (Examples which may help in calculating expiration dates are given in the 'General Rules': Categories 4(a) and (b).) These four categories contain the rules of the 1911 Act (operating from 1 July 1912 to 31 May 1957), the 1956 Act (operating from 1 June 1957 to 31 July 1989) and the 1988 Act (operating from 1 August 1989). These Acts take much the same view of term, but where differences may still be important they are noted. (See also *Europe*, page 203.)

Immediately **before 1 July 1912** the term for a published Literary, Dramatic or Musical work (provided it qualified for protection at all) was *either* the author's life plus 7 years after death *or* 42 years from the date of first publication, whichever was the longer. Copyright in posthumously published Literary works was 42 years from publication. Unpublished works remained in perpetual copyright. Any work which was still in copyright on 30 June 1912 became entitled to the much longer terms operating from 1 July 1912 (i.e. the terms in the categories below). An expert should be consulted in the comparatively rare cases where it may be necessary to check the subsistence of old copyrights.

1 Perpetual Copyrights and Printing Rights

The Authorized Version of the Bible and some other religious texts are owned in perpetuity by the Crown and may be printed by certain publishers only.[p. 79] Some universities and colleges hold 'perpetual' copyrights in a number of old titles – such copyrights expiring on 31 December 2039.[p. 80] No new perpetual copyrights or printing rights may now be created although the 1988 Act created a non-copyright right in *Peter Pan* in favour of Great Ormond Street Hospital for Sick Children.[p. 81]

2 Copyrights First Owned by Governments in the British Sphere

The Crown and the Houses of Parliament are the first owners of the copyright[p. 31] in virtually all works made for or published by them. However, if by special agreement the author retains the copyright and therefore is himself the first owner, the term for his work will depend on the rules of Category 4 below.

Crown Copyright in works made since 1 August 1989: a Literary, Dramatic or Musical work in this category will go out of copyright 125 years from the end of the calendar year in which it was made or, if it is commercially published [p. 27] within 75 years from when it was made, it will go out of copyright 50 years from the end of the calendar year of first commercial publication.

Parliamentary Copyright in works made since 1 August 1989: Acts of Parliament and Measures of the General Synod of the Church of England remain in copyright until 50 years from the end of the calendar year in which they receive Royal Assent. Copyright in a Parliamentary Bill expires on Royal Assent or at the end of the Parliamentary session if it is withdrawn or rejected. All other Literary, Dramatic or Musical works that are Parliamentary copyright remain in copyright until 50 years from the end of the calendar year in which they were created.

Crown Copyright in works made and published before 1 August 1989: a Literary, Dramatic or Musical work in this category will go out of copyright 50 years from the end of the calendar year in which it was first published.* Crown copyright works made before and still unpublished on 1 August 1989 enjoy the same protection as similar works made since then, or until 31 December 2039, whichever is the longer period of protection. There was no category of Parliamentary copyright under the 1956 Act but such works would have been included in the wider definition of Crown copyright.

3 Copyrights First Owned by Recognized International Organizations Which Would Not Otherwise Obtain UK Copyright Protection

The organizations (e.g. the UN) which can command this special privilege, and the exact conditions under which the privilege is granted, are discussed on page 23. Briefly, to qualify for it a Literary, Dramatic, Artistic or Musical work (but no other category of work)

---

* For works published on or before 31 May 1957 the term was 50 years from the date of publication. If such a work was still in copyright at 1 June 1957 its term was automatically extended an appropriate number of months according to the rule above.

---

must (a) be made or published for or by the organization on or after 1 June 1957 and (b) not otherwise be entitled to UK copyright. Before 1 August 1989 such works had to be made or published after the author had assigned copyright to the organization.

A work in this category will generally go out of copyright 50 years from the end of the calendar year in which it was created (or a longer period if specified by an Order in Council 'for the purpose of complying with the international obligations of the UK'). Works published before 1 August 1989 will go out of copyright 50 years after the end of the calendar year in which they were first published. Works existing but unpublished at 1 August 1989 remain in copyright until 50 years from the end of the year of publication or until and including 31 December 2039, whichever is the sooner.

4 Copyrights Not in Categories 1, 2 or 3 Above

The rules of this category are the most commonly applicable. The first owner of the copyright in Literary, Dramatic and Musical works in this category (including qualifying foreigners[p. 23]) may be the author, or a corporate body, or an individual other than the author, or an international organization if the work it owns qualifies for UK protection under the normal rules – that is, without invoking the special protection described in the preceding Category 3.

(a) GENERAL RULE for works created since 1 August 1989
Copyright in Literary, Dramatic and Musical works lasts until 50 years from the end of the calendar year in which the author dies – whether or not it has been published or made available to the public during that time (e.g. if an author died during 1992, all his works will be in copyright up to and including 31 December 2042. They will be out of copyright on 1 January 2043). (However, see also *Europe*, page 203.)

(b) GENERAL RULE for works created before 1 August 1989
A work made available to the public while its author was alive goes out of copyright 50 years after the end of the calendar year in which the author dies* (e.g. if a book was published in 1965 and its author

---

*Under the 1911 Act the term was 50 years from the actual date (of death or being made available to the public). If a work was still in copyright at 1 June 1957 according to this old rule its term was automatically extended an appropriate number of months according to the new rule.

---

died in 1980 the book will be in copyright up to and including 31 December 2030; it will be out of copyright on 1 January 2031). It follows that all Literary, Dramatic and Musical works in this category by the same (single) author go out of copyright at the same time unless they had not been made available to the public by the time the author died. In other words, where a work has been made available in the author's lifetime the period of copyright protection is the same before and since 1 August 1989.

Where an author died before 1 August 1989 and any of his work was not made available to the public during his lifetime, that work remains in copyright until 50 years from the end of the calendar year in which it is posthumously made available to the public, or up to and including 31 December 2039, whichever is the sooner. (A work first made available to the public after its author's death is called a 'posthumous' work.) (See also *Europe*, page 203.)

(c) PSEUDONYMOUS AND ANONYMOUS WORKS AND WORKS OF UNTRACEABLE AUTHORSHIP

A work is not pseudonymous or anonymous in the eyes of the law if at any time within 50 years from its first being made available to the public 'a person without previous knowledge of the facts' can 'ascertain the identity of the author by reasonable inquiry'. For joint works (see below) it is sufficient to ascertain the identity of any one of the authors. The author's real identity may appear in the copyright line, or in a blurb, or may be common knowledge. 'Reasonable inquiry' should certainly include questioning publishers of the work and perhaps researching some standard reference books or library catalogues. If this yields no information, then:

A Literary, Dramatic or Musical work in this category remains in copyright until it is first made available to the public, with the permission of the copyright holder. Once made available, it goes out of copyright 50 years from the end of the calendar year in which it was made available.

Under the 1956 Act, anonymous and pseudonymous works remained in copyright (unless the author was identified within that time) until 50 years from the end of the calendar year in which they were first published (not made available to the public). Works of unknown authorship created before 1 August 1989 but unpublished at that date now remain in copyright until and including 31 December 2039 or, if made available to the public during that period (i.e. between 1 August 1989 and 1 January 2040), until

50 years from the end of the calendar year in which they were made available. (See also *Europe*, page 203.)

(d) JOINT WORKS

Joint Literary, Dramatic or Musical works **made available to the public before 1 June 1957** may be subject to the rules of the 1911 Act, which were as follows: A work made available to the public before the death of the last surviving author went out of copyright either 50 years after the date of death of the author who died first or when the last surviving author died, whichever was the later date. A work not made available to the public before the death of the last surviving author remained in copyright until the time (if ever) of its first being made available, and then the term ran for 50 years from that date. If under these rules the copyright in a joint work had expired before 1 June 1957 it could not be revived; but if it had not expired before then the work became subject to the new rules, as follows:

Joint Literary, Dramatic or Musical works **in copyright on or after 1 June 1957** follow the General Rules (a) and (b). That is to say, a work goes out of copyright 50 years after the end of the calendar year in which the last surviving qualifying author dies. Where all the authors have died before 1 August 1989, a work not made available to the public before the death of the last surviving author (whether or not qualifying) will go out of copyright 50 years from the end of the calendar year in which it is first made available to the public, or on 1 January 2040, whichever is the sooner. (See also *Europe*, page 203.)

Note also that: (a) If some of the joint authors are **anonymous, pseudonymous** or **untraceable** the 'last surviving author' will be the last among the authors whose identity has been 'disclosed'. An author's identity is disclosed if he writes under his real name or if, at any time within 50 years from the end of the calendar year in which his work was first made available to the public (or, prior to 1 August 1989, first published), his real name can be discovered by 'reasonable enquiry'.[p. 41] If the identity of none of the authors is disclosed then the Pseudonymous rule above applies. (b) Only qualifying authors are relevant in this respect but before 1 August 1989 all the true authors[p. 15] of a joint work had to be considered when calculating term, whatever their status might be for other purposes of the Act. (c) The term for **joint works in Categories 2 and 3** above depends upon the date of publication only, thus avoiding the complications described here concerning names and dates of death.

Additional Notes

In **collaborations where the work of each author is easily distinguishable from that of the co-authors** the term for each author's text is quite separate, following the General, Pseudonymous or Joint rules as appropriate. The same is true of **contributions** specially written for inclusion in a work.

Works of foreign origin (including works of United States origin) may have different terms, even if they qualified for protection in the first place, in accordance with a bewildering number of Orders in Council applying to different cases.

An editor's copyright in his arrangement follows the General Rules if the editor is one person and his name appears on the work, or the 'Pseudonymous and Anonymous' rule if it does not. When two or more editors work on the same book their labour is almost certain to rate as Joint, but if they have worked on quite different sections of a book they will be collaborators only and must be treated separately.

Anthologies, selections and any work which quotes directly from previously existing material will have one copyright which is new when the whole work is put together; this new copyright will be subject to the rules of this chapter. Each quoted passage, however, will have its own separate copyright term which remains unaffected by being quoted in the new work. The quoted passages may go out of copyright before or after the new work as a whole. Similarly the overall copyright in an encyclopedia will have a different term from the terms of the contributions of which it is composed.

The term for **new versions of previously existing material** (e.g. **translations, abridgements, plays based on books**) is in no way affected by the term for the existing work. *The Iliad*, for instance, is manifestly in the public domain but a modern translation will have a copyright term in precisely the same way as an original modern work.

Letters, whether published in the author's lifetime or not, are now protected until 50 years from the end of the year in which the author dies, like other Literary works. Letters written by people who died before 1 August 1989, and unpublished at their death, go out of copyright 50 years from the end of the calendar year of first publication or on 1 January 2040, whichever is the sooner. (See also *Europe*, page 203.)

11 The Extent and Limitations of a Copyright

The Limited Prerogatives of the Copyright Owner

The owner of a copyright does not have absolute control of all the ways in which his work can be used.

The Act takes a three-tiered approach to these rights. On the lowest level is the principle of the Substantial Part: anyone can use a work without permission provided they use less than a certain small amount of it. (Of course in some cases even this may be illegal for reasons outside copyright law.) The owner's right to impose restrictions only begins when at least a substantial part of the work is to be used. (See 'How Much Can Be Copied without Permission?' below.)

On the second level come the Acts Restricted by the Copyright. These include virtually all possible ways of using part of a work (e.g. by publishing or broadcasting it) and over these acts the copyright owner has complete control – legally, though not always nowadays in practice. Doing any of them without permission is an actionable 'infringement' of the copyright. (See 'The Rights Controlled by the Copyright Owner' on page 46.)

But then, on the third level, come the privileged exceptions attached to each Restricted Act: cases where the law allows even a substantial part of a work to be used without the owner's permission. These significantly limit the wide powers granted to him on the second level. Most of these exceptions are made in the public interest; a few are simply practical. (See 'When Is Copying Privileged?' on page 54.)

When the 1956 Act was written, its rules struck a reasonable balance between the public interest and the interests of the copyright owner. Unfortunately technological and social changes since then tipped the scales badly. The establishment of Public Lending Right, the Copyright Licensing Agency and collective licensing schemes, and the introduction in the 1988 Act of the concept of a rental right, are major steps towards redressing the balance.

How Much Can Be Copied Without Permission? – The Principles of 'Substantial Part' and 'Fair Dealing'

Section 16(3) of the 1988 Act makes clear, as did the 1956 Act, that copyright owners can control what is done not only to the whole of their work but also to any substantial part of it. Conversely it means that they cannot control what is done to less than a substantial part of it.

Having said this much, the Act gives us no further clue as to what in fact a substantial part may be. Interpretation is left to the courts.

However, one thing is quite clear: 'substantial' does not necessarily mean 'large'. It means important. A substantial part of a work is much smaller than the phrase itself suggests. It may be one line of a short poem, or a few bars of music which are recognizably part of the tune they came from.

Of course the amount copied is relevant. But quantity matters much less than the quality and contextual value of the copied passages. If an infringer lifts the best part of someone else's work ('best' stylistically, factually or in any other way) he will have copied a more substantial part than if he had lifted other passages of equivalent length but less merit. An extract would constitute a substantial part if it included a summary of the work (or of a part of the work dealing with a specific subject) either in words or, say, in the form of a diagram, graph, statistical or mathematical table or a scientific formula, so that the core of the work (or any specific part of the work) was contained in the extract.

One must also inquire how the lifted passages are used by the copier. Would the work collapse if they were removed? Or are they only used to illustrate the copier's otherwise original work? Does the work perhaps illumine our understanding of the borrowed passages? There is a continuum here from undeniable piracy to a possibly defensible use of the existing work.

Again, a court will be interested in whether the copy competes with the existing work, or otherwise injures the legitimate interests of its owner. This sort of offence is likely to be greater if the existing work is unpublished.

A second concept, **Fair Dealing**, is only mentioned in the Act in connection with the special exceptions made in favour of reproduction for the purposes of research or private study, criticism or review, and reporting of current events. In these cases, a person accused of infringement can claim that, even though it has been established that he has copied a substantial part of the work, the copying is still legal because it is Fair Dealing.

No definition of Fair Dealing is given by the Act. It seems that copying is Fair Dealing if it is reasonable in the circumstances and not prejudicial to the interests of the copyright owner beyond the immediate purpose for which the copy is made. Copying a whole work cannot usually be defended as Fair Dealing, but some authorities still regard this as permissible for 'research or private study'. Note, however, that the *publication* of a text in a school textbook or elsewhere does not qualify as 'research or private study'.

The present ease of photocopying is creating stricter attitudes to what is permissible under the principles of a 'substantial part' and 'Fair Dealing'.

In practice the criteria for deciding whether a substantial part has been used and whether it is Fair Dealing are very much the same, and having the two concepts only leads to confusion. In the United States the law does not differentiate between them but has one concept only, that of 'Fair Use'. One could wish that UK law would follow suit.

The Rights Controlled by the Copyright Owner: the 'Acts Restricted by the Copyright'

No one may use a substantial part of a copyright Literary, Dramatic or Musical work in any of six principal ways without permission from the copyright owner, unless that use falls within one of the specially privileged categories listed on page 54. As indicated below, the restricted acts often cover some or all other categories of copyright work (Artistic works, sound recordings, films, broadcasts, cable programmes and typographical arrangements in published editions). These six 'Acts Restricted by the Copyright' are as follows:

1   COPYING A SUBSTANTIAL PART OF THE WORK
This most basic restriction applies to every description of copyright work. It covers possible loopholes in the Act and makes it illegal to reproduce the work in any material form (e.g. print of any size, video or audio recordings, films) and specifically includes storing the work in any medium by electronic means (including on computer

disk) without permission. 'Copying' extends well beyond verbatim or facsimile copying. (See, especially, 'What Is a Copy?' on page 52.) The 1988 Act introduced a new provision about the rental of copies of sound recordings, films and computer programs to the public (see page 109).

2   ISSUING COPIES OF A SUBSTANTIAL PART OF THE WORK TO THE PUBLIC

This applies to all categories of copyright work and is the first of two methods of making a work available to the public. (See *What Is Publication?*, page 25.)

3   PERFORMING, SHOWING OR PLAYING A SUBSTANTIAL PART OF THE WORK IN PUBLIC

This applies to every category of copyright work except Artistic works and the typographical arrangements of published editions. It is the second of the two methods of making a work available to the public. (See *Performance*, page 112.)

4   BROADCASTING A SUBSTANTIAL PART OF THE WORK OR INCLUDING IT IN A CABLE PROGRAMME SERVICE

This applies to every category of copyright work except the typographical arrangements of published editions. (See *Broadcasting a Work by Television or Radio*, page 126.)

5   MAKING AN ADAPTATION OF A SUBSTANTIAL PART OF THE WORK

This applies to Literary, Dramatic and Musical works only. An 'adaptation' retains the intellectual content and general construction of the original but clothes it in a different outward form. In the specialized vocabulary of the Act, 'adapting' a work means doing one of the following things:

(a) CONVERTING A LITERARY WORK INTO A DRAMATIC WORK. (See *Dramatizing a Literary Work*, page 116.) It does not matter whether the dramatization is in the same language as the original or in a different language.

(b) CONVERTING A DRAMATIC WORK INTO A LITERARY WORK. It does not matter whether the resulting non-dramatic work is in the same language as the Dramatic work or in a different language.

(c) TRANSLATING A LITERARY OR DRAMATIC WORK. Translation involves results of a basically different order from the other kinds of adaptation. (See *Translation*, page 117.)

(d) MAKING A STRIP CARTOON FROM A LITERARY OR DRAMATIC WORK. (See *Adapting a Work to a Strip Cartoon*, page 119.)

(e) ARRANGING OR TRANSCRIBING A MUSICAL WORK. The person who makes substantially a new arrangement or adaptation of a Musical work is entitled to copyright in the new version. As with editing, it is largely a question of degree.

(f) TRANSLATING A COMPUTER PROGRAM. 'Translation' of a computer program includes putting it into a different computer language or code. (See page 137.)

6 COPYING, ISSUING COPIES TO THE PUBLIC, PERFORMING, SHOWING, PLAYING, BROADCASTING OR INCLUDING IN A CABLE PROGRAMME SERVICE A SUBSTANTIAL PART OF ANY ADAPTATION OF A LITERARY, DRAMATIC OR MUSICAL WORK.

Infringement

If you use a copyright work without permission and your use falls within the Acts Restricted by the Copyright in that work, unless you can prove that your use is privileged[p.54] you are said to 'infringe the copyright' and your action is called a direct infringement. A second type of direct infringement is committed by anyone who authorizes the doing of a restricted act when they themselves have not the legal power to do so. Ignorance of wrongdoing is no defence to a charge of direct infringement.

An indirect or secondary infringement is committed by anyone who sells or otherwise deals with a work, knowing or having reason to believe it is an infringement.

An employer is responsible for any infringement committed by employees in the course of their work.

The Limitation Act imposes a time limit on proceedings for infringement: actions must be brought within six years of the date the cause for action occurred.

When the making of an 'article' (such as a book, record or print) is a direct infringement of one of the Acts Restricted by the Copyright in any category of work, then dealing with that article may constitute an indirect infringement of the copyright, as follows:

(a) Importation of an infringing article into any country in the British sphere[p.8] is illegal if (i) the article is imported without the consent of the copyright owner and (ii) the article is imported for purposes other than the 'private and domestic use' of the importer and (iii) the importer is aware or has reason to believe *either* that the article is an infringing copy *or* that it would be an infringement of copyright or breach of an exclusive licence had it been made in the place to which it is imported. However, if an article is in free circulation within the EC it will not be considered an infringing copy.

(b) Anyone who possesses, sells or lets for hire, exhibits in public or distributes the article to such an extent as to affect prejudicially the owner of the copyright, will be guilty of an indirect infringement if (i) he acts without the consent of the copyright owner and (ii) the action takes place within the British sphere[p.8] and (iii) the person concerned knows or has reason to believe that the articles are infringements or (if they are imported) that they would have been infringements if they had been made in the place to which they are imported.

(c) Making or doing any of the secondary acts listed above in connection with an article (e.g. plate, negative, etc.) specifically designed for making copies of a work, knowing or having reason to believe that the article will be used for that purpose, is also an indirect infringement.

(d) Transmitting a work via a telecommunications system (other than by broadcasting it or including it in a cable programme service) – for example sending the work by fax or Telex, knowing or having reason to believe that infringing copies would be made, is an indirect infringement.

(e) Supplying a copy of a sound recording or film which is used to infringe copyright, or supplying apparatus which is used for infringing the copyright in a work by the playing of a sound recording, the showing of a film or the receiving of images or sounds by any electronic means, is an indirect infringement.

(f) When programmes containing copyright material are broadcast in encoded form (e.g. on a cable TV service) anyone who dishonestly receives such a programme commits an offence. So does anyone who makes, trades in or advertises any device specifically designed to circumvent copying protection.

(g) An indirect infringement is also committed by anyone who permits a place of public entertainment to be used for a public performance, where the performance constitutes an infringement of the copyright in any Literary, Dramatic or Musical work. (Whether the work by itself is an infringement does not matter.) A 'place of public entertainment' can be anything from an ordinary theatre or TV studio to premises (e.g. church halls) normally used for other purposes but which 'are from time to time made available for hire for purposes of public entertainment'.

(h) The person who authorizes the use of the premises will be liable (unless he had reasonable grounds for believing that the performance would not be an infringement), as will anyone who supplied the apparatus or the copy of the sound recording or film, or anyone who is an occupier of the premises if he gave permission for the apparatus to be brought onto the premises.

Acts which are not authorized by the copyright owner are ignored by copyright law except in so far as they constitute grounds for a court action. For instance, if an unpublished work is published without the owner's consent, it still rates as 'unpublished' wherever the distinction is important in the Act, but the owner can sue the pirate publisher.

Actions which are lawful at one time do not become infringements retroactively when the copyright position changes. Thus copies of a work legitimately made by licensees while their licence was in force may be legally sold after the licence expires, although the licensees may not make any more of them.

The cost of court action being what it is, the majority of infringements are dealt with by private negotiation. The most serious infringements can be those which are only discovered after a work has been published. Sometimes a publisher will have to withdraw the work from the market, but often it may be more advantageous for the injured party to settle for a pro rata share (or in really indefensible cases the whole) of the royalty or profits.

The penalties and remedies for infringements, who can sue and who is liable are regulated by Chapter VI of Part I of the Act.

Untraceable Authors

It is sometimes impossible to find the copyright owner of a work you want to use, or to get an answer even when you know where he is. For this reason, rights should ideally always be cleared before production starts; injunctions can be costly and so can the payment of 'late' fees.

The Whitford Committee received numerous submissions arguing that in these circumstances, or if clearance is overlooked, some statutory payment should be possible. However, it decided that 'the courts can be trusted to ensure that the genuinely "innocent" infringer is not unduly penalised' and the 1988 Act made no provision for any such statutory payment.

12 Reproduction in Newly Printed Form

This chapter is written from the point of view of printed reproduction when the type is, as it were, newly set for the purpose.

When the 1956 Act was drafted the regulations envisaged only copies made by typesetting, by hand or by typewriter. The 1988 Act is more comprehensive and makes it clear that 'copying' means reproducing a Literary, Musical, Dramatic (or indeed any copyright) work, or any substantial part[p.45] of it, in any material form. This includes writing and all the multitudinous forms of ordinary printed matter (from a single coupon through magazines and newspapers to sheet music, books and encyclopedias), photocopies, video and cassette tapes, and so on. Copying specifically includes 'storing the work in any medium by electronic means' (for example, on computer disk or microfiche).

Illustrations (including graphs) intermixed with text remain complete works in themselves and subject to the rules for Artistic works,[p. 170] though it is sometimes permissible to photocopy them or publish them when it is legal to reproduce the text with which they are associated.[p. 175]

What Is a Copy?

Copyright protection is technically given only to the form and sequence of words or musical notes in the main body of a work and also, in works like anthologies and encyclopedias, to the overall arrangement of the separate items. However, in practice, when judging whether one work is a copy of another, excessive similarity of detail in the development of situations and plots will also be taken into account, though broad plot outlines will not. On the other hand an Artistic or Musical work inspired by, say, a poem cannot be a 'copy' of the words of the poem and so cannot be an infringement of the poet's rights.

An illegal reproduction can be a plagiarism of form and sequence or arrangement, or a verbatim or facsimile copy, an abridgement or a paraphrase, but the word presupposes no change in copyright category between the original and the copy. A book is a non-dramatic Literary work and so can be reproduced only by other non-dramatic Literary works. A play is a Dramatic work and can be reproduced only by other plays and scripts. If there is a change in copyright category (when, for instance, a book is dramatized, translated or turned into a strip cartoon) the Restricted Act technically infringed will be adaptation, not reproduction. However, if an action is brought against a play, say, as being an illegal adaptation of a book, the deciding factor will probably be the extent to which the play has 'copied' the book.

Copying is illegal when: (1) the work reproduced is in copyright, *and* (2) a substantial part [p. 45] of the work is copied, *and* (3) the copy is made without permission from the copyright owner – except in the specially privileged cases listed on page 54.

There is such infinite variety in creative work that no universally applicable test for illegal copying can be devised. In the end, every case must be judged on its own merits. Some general guidance may be found in the section on 'Originality' on page 20. Below are a few notes on the situations where authors seem most likely to go astray.

Your own wording may be freely reused by yourself only when all rights are your own – i.e. none have been licensed or assigned to anyone else. Permission to quote from your own published works must be obtained from whoever controls the quotation rights in the appropriate medium. Recasting or reselling material which has been licensed or assigned previously may be a breach of contract, or fraud.

Parodies are not infringements as long as they are themselves sufficiently original,[p. 20] but if the parody owes its main attraction to the language, sequence of events or anything else in the work parodied, it may be an actionable infringement. This attraction must of course be more than the simple interaction in the reader's mind between the original and the parody, since this is the essence of this type of writing. Parodies and burlesques frequently annoy the owner of the original, but annoyance is not infringement.[p. 96]

Reference works (books of quotations, dictionaries, cookery books, guidebooks, encyclopedias, 'DIY' books) contain information for the reader's practical use, but you should be very careful about reusing it in a book of your own. Sometimes such books contain an implied licence to copy of a limited sort. For example, a book for publishers may include forms of contracts which the author earnestly wishes all publishers would adopt. But the licence does not extend to republication of the forms in another book (such as this one). If you are compiling a reference book you are expected to do all the basic work over again: an author must 'count the milestones for himself'. You may only use previous books as guides to where to go for your information, and to check your conclusions. You must not copy actual entries from a previous work, even if you have checked the facts for yourself.

Translations should be viewed in the same light as any other original work. If the translation itself is still in copyright no substantial part may be quoted or retranslated without the permission of the translator. If the work from which the translation is made is still in copyright, permission to quote or translate must also be obtained from the original author. (See also *Translation*, page 117.)

When Is Copying Privileged? – Exceptions from Protection

A 'substantial part' of a copyright Literary, Dramatic or Musical work (or any adaptation of such a work) may be copied without permission, and without payment to the copyright owner, when the copy is made for any of the following reasons. Where indicated, the privilege extends to other categories of copyright works also:

1. **For research or private study.** This exception also extends to Artistic works and the typographical arrangement of a published edition. Copying for research or private study is permitted as long as (a) the copy is made by or at the request of the person researching or studying and (b) his use of it is Fair Dealing[p. 45] and (c) the copy is for his own or his employer's individual use only, and not for circulation. Free inclusion of passages in a textbook (on the argument that textbooks are for 'private study') is not permitted under this exception. Nor may a person copy material if he 'knows or has reason to believe that it will result in copies of substantially the same material being provided to more than one person at substantially the same time and for substantially the same purpose'. (See also *Copying by Libraries*, page 57, and *Collective Licensing*, page 107.)

2. **For criticism or review.** Any category of copyright work, or any performance of a work, may be copied as long as (a) the use is Fair Dealing[p. 45] and (b) it is accompanied by sufficient acknowledgement. A work may be quoted in a critique or review of itself or of any other work. The review may be an adverse one but the criticism must be real, not just an excuse for reproducing interesting text.

    'Sufficient acknowledgement' in the Act means giving the title of the work and the name of the author (unless the author is anonymous or has requested, or agreed to, the omission of his name) but common publishing usage requires more than this.[p. 85]

    The Society of Authors and the Publishers Association have jointly stated what in their view constitutes the *maximum* length of extract *below which* proprietors would not expect to be asked for permission if the extracts were genuinely used for criticism or review. For a single quotation of prose this maximum would be 400 words. When two or more extracts are quoted from the same prose work the maximum would be 800 words, with no one extract exceeding 300 words. For poetry the maximum would be 40 lines from any one poem, provided that this amounted to no more than a quarter of the poem. For quotations above these limits the user should seek permission; the proprietor should then carefully consider whether, in the individual circumstances, the use is or is not Fair Dealing; if it is, then of course no fee should be charged.

3(a). **For reporting current events** any copyright work (other than a photograph) may be copied as long as the use is Fair Dealing[p. 45] and it is accompanied by 'sufficient acknowledgement'.

3(b). **For reporting current events by means of a sound recording, film, broadcast or cable programme** any copyright work (other than a photograph) may be copied, as long as the use is Fair Dealing.[p. 45] When reported in these media, no acknowledgement is necessary.

4. **For educational use.** There are detailed regulations covering the quotation of any description of copyright work in schools and other educational establishments. (See *Copying in and for Education*, page 60, and *Collective Licensing*, page 107.)

5. **For library purposes.** Under complex regulations, specified libraries and archives are permitted to copy published works for the public and each other. (See *Copying by Libraries*, page 57.)

6. **To make old unpublished works available to the public.** Fifty years after an author's death, even if it is still in copyright his unpublished work may be reproduced in certain circumstances. (See *Using Old Unpublished Works Without Permission*, page 65.)

7. **To copy old anonymous or pseudonymous works of any sort.** Such works, where the author is unknown, may be reproduced in certain circumstances (see page 67).

8. **Interviews.** The use of any record (in writing or otherwise) of spoken words is permitted for the reporting of current events in certain circumstances (see page 115).

9. **Public Administration (1):**
   (a) **For the purposes of judicial or parliamentary**

   proceedings, or a report of those proceedings. Judicial proceedings are 'proceedings before any court, tribunal or person having authority to decide any matter affecting a person's legal rights or liabilities'. Parliamentary proceedings include proceedings of the Northern Ireland Assembly and the European Parliament.

  (b) **For the purposes of a Royal Commission or statutory inquiry or a report of those proceedings if they were held in public.** A statutory inquiry is 'an inquiry held or investigation conducted in pursuance of a duty imposed or power conferred by or under an enactment'.

10. **Public Administration (2):**

  (a) **To copy material open to public inspection.** Material which is open to public inspection under a statutory requirement, or which is on a statutory register (such as the Data Protection Register or the Trade Mark Register), may be copied in certain circumstances (see page 73).

  (b) **To provide copies of material contained in public records.** (See *Using Government Publications and Public Records*, page 69.)

  (c) **To diffuse information contained in most UK government publications.** (See *Using Government Publications and Public Records*, page 69.)

11. **Material Communicated to the Crown** in the course of public business can sometimes be reproduced by the Crown.

12. **If specifically authorized by an Act of Parliament,** works may be copied.

13. **To reproduce works published under compulsory licence.** (See *Using Entire Published Works Without Permission*, page 68.)

14. **To use a typeface.** The use of a typeface in the ordinary course of typing, composing text, typesetting or printing is not an infringement. (See *Typefaces*, page 107.)

15. **Abstracts of scientific or technical articles.** It is not an infringement to copy or issue copies to the public of an abstract or an article on a scientific or technical subject published in a periodical containing both the abstract and the article unless a licensing scheme[p. 64] exists for the granting of licences for the making of such copies.

Copying and Breach of Confidence

If a person is given access to material on the understanding (express or implied) that he will not make it public nor use it himself without the owner's permission, and he then does so, he can be sued for 'breach of confidence' (or 'breach of trust').

A book publisher is thus restrained from making use of or gossiping about the manuscripts offered to him. He may not publish one without first reaching an agreement with its author. Private individuals may not copy, publish or reveal the contents of manuscripts lent to them. An employee may not copy or publish material belonging to his employer, even though he himself collected it. It may be a breach of confidence, and will be a breach of copyright, to publish a private lecture or musical performance.

However, if a second person (usually a publisher but conceivably an author) acquires such material 'for value without notice' – i.e. buys it but has no means of knowing that it constitutes a breach of confidence – he will not be liable for damages. (But if the material infringes a copyright ignorance is no defence.[p. 48])

Copying across National Frontiers

A particular case of copying without permission may be simultaneously illegal in one country and legal in another. It will only be illegal in any given country if (1) the material reproduced comes from a work which is in copyright in that country, (2) copies of the work containing the copied material are published in or imported by way of trade into that country, and (3) the material has been illegally reproduced according to the regulations of the local law.

13 Copying by Libraries

Under the general provisions of the Act it is illegal to reproduce a substantial part of any copyright work. However, prescribed libraries and archives are permitted to copy limited amounts of published Literary, Dramatic and Musical works for members of the public and for each other.* As long as copying is permissible on the grounds outlined below, permission to copy the typographical arrangement of the published edition, and any illustrations accompanying the text, is automatically given by the Act.

Non-copyright material may of course be copied without limit, but if the typographical arrangement is in copyright [p. 105] the publisher's permission should be obtained before a work is reproduced or multiple copies made.

What Libraries Are Prescribed?

Libraries permitted to copy material for the public are, briefly: (1) those which receive deposit copies [p. 152] (some prescribed libraries, notably the British Library, may also offer licensed copying to which these regulations do not apply); (2) the libraries of schools or other educational establishments; [p. 60] (3) public libraries; (4) Parliamentary and government libraries; (5) 'any other library conducted for the purpose of facilitating or encouraging the study of bibliography, education, fine arts, history, languages, law, literature, medicine, music, philosophy, religion, science (including natural and social science) or technology'. However, libraries 'established or conducted for profit' and the libraries of profit-making companies are excluded.

All libraries in the UK are permitted to copy material for other libraries in groups (1)–(5) above, as well as for any library outside the UK which is of a similar class to group (5) above (which may also supply copies if its local law allows). Profit-making libraries and the libraries of profit-making companies may supply copies but not request them.

How Much Can Be Copied for Members of the Public?

A prescribed library may make and supply copies of articles in periodicals [p. 11] or parts of any published Literary, Dramatic or Musical work, and of accompanying illustrations, but only on the following conditions:

---

*The Copyright (Librarians and Archivists) (Copying of Copyright Material) Regulations 1989 (SI 1989 No 1212).

---

1. The copies must be made or supplied by the librarian or a person acting on his behalf.
2. Members of the public requesting copies must be 'persons satisfying the librarian that they require them for purposes of research or private study, and will not use them for any other purpose' and they must sign a declaration to this effect.
3. The applicant must pay for the copies 'a sum not less than the cost (including a contribution to the general expenses of the library) attributable to their production'.
4. Only one copy may be supplied to any one applicant. Furthermore, the librarian must be satisfied that the applicant's requirement is not related to anyone else's requirement to copy 'substantially the same material at substantially the same time and for substantially the same purpose'.
5. When the work required is an article in a periodical, the whole article may be copied but no other article from the same issue of the periodical may be supplied to the same applicant ('article' here includes 'an item of any description' contained in the periodical).
6. Where the work is a published Literary, Dramatic or Musical work (other than an article in a periodical) an applicant may not be supplied with more than one copy of a 'reasonable proportion' of a work. The British Copyright Council suggests that up to 10 per cent of the total work would constitute a 'reasonable proportion'.
7. Illustrations which accompany any work may be copied along with it. If only part of a work is copied this licence extends only to the illustrations which explain or illustrate that part. The Act does not permit illustrations (which include graphs, technical drawings, etc.) to be copied separately, since each is a complete work in itself.

What Can Be Copied by Libraries and Archives for Themselves and Each Other?

1. The librarian of a prescribed library or archive may copy for another prescribed library an article, or the whole or part of a published Literary, Dramatic or Musical work (and accompanying illustrations), as long as (a) no more than one copy is supplied; (b) in certain cases the receiving library gives a statement

that having made enquiries it could not discover a person entitled to authorize the copying; and (c) the applying library must pay for the copies 'a sum not less than the cost (including a contribution to the general expenses of the library) attributable to their production'.

2. A prescribed library or archive may make a copy of a work in its permanent collection to replace or preserve it for its own or another permanent collection or archive which has lost its copy, but only if it is not reasonably practicable to buy a replacement copy.

Certain **unpublished and old anonymous works** may be copied (see page 65) as may items where it is a **condition of their export** (see page 94).

14 **Copying in and for Education**

Some actions which would be infringements of copyright in other circumstances are legal when taken for educational purposes – but the limits are rigid. Free quotation in collections *for* schools has been permitted since 1912 and the rules in the last two Acts covering performance, copying and adaptation *by* schools and other educational establishments are not so much a generous gift as a recognition of common practice.

What Educational Establishments Are Privileged?

To reproduce, adapt or perform copyright material for teaching purposes without charge, an educational establishment must be (a) any school within the meaning of the Education Acts or (b) any other description of educational establishment specified by order of the Secretary of State. In England and Wales a school is 'an institution for providing primary or secondary education or both primary

and secondary education being a school maintained by a local education authority, an independent school, or a school in respect of
which grants are made by [the Secretary of State] to the proprietor
of the School'.* The special privileges allowed under the Copyright
Act extend to extramural work done as part of the instruction given
by a teacher in a school which meets this definition. Other educational establishments specified by order of the Secretary of State[†]
include any university empowered to award degrees and any college
or institution in the nature of a college, in such a university; any
institution providing further or higher education within the meaning
of the Education Acts; and any theological college.

Quotation in Anthologies for Educational Use

An excerpt from a Literary or Dramatic work (but *not* from a
Musical or Artistic work) may be quoted in a collection 'intended for
use in educational establishments' without permission from the
owner of the copyright (and without payment) but only when *all* the
following requirements are met:

1. The quoted work has already been published.
2. The quoted work was not itself published for the use of educational establishments.
3. The quotation is a 'short passage'.
4. The book in which the quotation is to be included is a
   'collection' – i.e. an anthology and not a straight textbook containing incidental quotation.
5. The book is intended for use in educational establishments.
6. The book is 'described in its title and in any advertisements
   issued by or on behalf of the publisher' as being intended for use
   in educational establishments.

---

*Education Act 1944, Section 114. In Scotland, says the Copyright Act,
school 'has the same meaning as in the Education (Scotland) Act 1962, except
that it includes an approved school within the meaning of the Social Work
(Scotland) Act 1968', and in Northern Ireland school 'has the same meaning
as in the Education and Libraries (Northern Ireland) Order 1986'.

[†] The Copyright (Educational Establishments) (No. 2) Order 1989 (SI 1989
No. 1068).

---

7. Apart from the quotation, the book consists 'mainly' of material in the public domain. ('Mainly' is not defined by the Act.)

8. The quotation is accompanied by a 'sufficient acknowledgement'.[p. 85]

9. Not more than two quotations from copyright works by any one author are contained either (a) in the book itself or (b) in any educational collection 'published by the same publisher over any period of five years'.

   The restriction on authorship can be extensive. If we say that X is the author of the first quotation, then the restriction covers other quotations from works by X and from works by X writing in collaboration with anyone else. If the first quotation comes from a work of joint authorship by, say, X, Y and Z, then the restriction extends to other quotations from any works written by X, Y or Z alone, or in collaboration with others.

Reproduction and Adaptation for Examinations

Copyright is not infringed by anything 'done for the purposes of an examination'. Exam questions, communicating them to candidates, and the answers to them, may include copies and adaptations[p. 47] of substantial parts of any copyright work without permission (although the reprographic copying of a Musical work for exam candidates to perform is specifically excluded). However, copies and adaptations of copyright works used for exams may not be published without permission: thus the reproduction in a book or newspaper of papers (and answers) containing copyright material is prohibited.

Examination papers are themselves protected as copyright works.

Reproduction and Adaptation in the Course of Instruction

Anyone giving or receiving instruction in an educational establishment may reproduce substantial parts of any Literary, Dramatic, Musical or Artistic copyright work (but not the typographical arrangement of a published edition) or adapt it and copy the adaptation* without permission as long as (a) these things are done in the course of instruction or preparation for instruction, (b) the copying is done by the person giving or receiving instruction and (c) the copying is not done by means of a reprographic process.[p. 64]

Publication of adaptations or copies of copyright works by educational establishments is specifically prohibited by the Act so, for example, editors of school magazines must not include such copies or adaptations in their pages without formal permission from the copyright owner.

Restrictions on the **performance** of copyright works in educational establishments are described in chapter 28. Licences for the copying and recording of **broadcasts, films** and **cable programmes** for educational purposes are administered by the Educational Recording Agency.[p. 111]

Reprographic copying of published Literary, Dramatic or Musical works, or the typographical arrangements of published editions, by an educational establishment for instruction purposes is not an infringement only:

1.   If no more than 1 per cent of a work is copied in any one calendar quarter;
     and
2.   If licences authorizing the copying are not available. In fact, almost all copying in educational establishments is now covered by licences agreed with the Copyright Licensing Agency. (See page 64.)

---

15 **Reprography: Facsimile Copying**

Many of the machines we commonly call photocopiers are no longer based on photographic techniques, so the term 'reprography' is

---

*The meaning of 'adaptation' for Literary, Dramatic and Musical works is given in chapter 11; Artistic adaptation is not defined by the Act, but see chapter 48.

now used to cover all processes for making facsimile copies. A reprographic reproduction can be a same-size photocopy, an enlarged or reduced version, or a microcopy which cannot be read without the help of a viewing machine. It seems necessary to emphasize that the laws of copyright and contract apply just as much to a microform version of a text as they do to any other copy.

Photocopies are not 'original works' and therefore do not qualify for a separate copyright of their own. Electrocopying may be in a different position.[p. 139]

Reprography is a means of reproducing the written word (or existing illustrations) by a reprographic process defined by the Act as 'a process (a) for making facsimile copies, or (b) involving the use of an appliance for making multiple copies, and includes, in relation to a work held in electronic form, any copying by electronic means, but does not include the making of a film or sound recording'. Since a photocopy is a facsimile of its original, permission to copy must be obtained not only from the owner of the copyright in the text but also from the publisher as owner of the typography copyright,[p. 105] except in certain circumstances where the photocopy is made in a library.[p. 58] If a unique original (e.g. a manuscript or letter) is to be copied, permission must also be sought from the owner of the document.

Infringement by reprography on a massive scale is an international problem. Different countries have approached it in different ways, but the general trend is towards collective licensing schemes[p. 111] and some countries charge a levy on the copying equipment itself. As UK law stands, any copies which may legally be made may be made on photocopiers, although in certain cases such copying is regulated by licensing schemes.

Collective Licences

Licences agreed by the Copyright Licensing Agency (CLA)[p. 111] are in operation covering photocopying in most primary and secondary schools, universities (old and new) and higher and further education colleges in the UK. Licences have also been agreed with the British Library's Document Supply Centre at Boston Spa and the CBI, and negotiations are in progress for the collective licensing of photocopying in a number of other areas. The principal areas where the CLA has or hopes to negotiate licences are education (general, higher and further; charitable and religious); government (national and local government and public bodies); industry (trade, industry, commerce, the professions).

The CLA licences with the Local Education Authorities cover all schools, colleges and resource centres under their control, under certain terms and conditions. The licences only apply to the making of hard copies onto paper and cover the photocopying of up to 5 per cent of a book, one chapter, one journal article or a short story or poem not exceeding ten pages – in one course of study in any one academic year. The number of copies that may be licensed is one for the personal use of each member of the class or tutorial group and one for the teacher. Schools and colleges wishing to copy more than that amount must seek permission from the rights holder (generally the publisher) in the usual way.

Certain categories of work and a few individual publications are not included in the licence. A list of these works, and information on how the licensing operates, are available from the CLA.[p. 111]

Reprographic Rights Organizations Overseas

There are organizations similar to the CLA in many countries and nearly all are members of IFRRO (the International Federation of Reprographic Rights Organizations). The CLA has negotiated reciprocal and bilateral agreements with Australia, Canada, France, Germany, New Zealand, South Africa, Spain, Sweden and the USA. This means, for instance, that individual publishers no longer need to register with the American equivalent of the CLA, the Copyright Clearance Center.

At the time of writing, the European Commission is drafting a Directive on reprography.[p. 207]

---

16 Using Old Works Without Permission

Copying Old Unpublished Works

Under the 1956 Act a Literary, Dramatic or Musical work which qualified for copyright protection but which had never been published remained in copyright indefinitely.[p. 41] Although this is no longer the case (except for unpublished anonymous and pseudonymous works where the author is unknown),[p. 41] as time goes on, tracing the current owner of an old copyright becomes more and more difficult.

The 1956 Act therefore allowed the reproduction of old unpublished copyright works (including letters) either 'for purposes of research or private study' or 'with a view to publication', and the 1988 Act has repeated the provisions, in slightly modified form, in relation to unpublished works created before 1 August 1989. The following conditions must be met:

1. 'The manuscript or a copy of the work is kept in a library, museum or other institution where (subject to any provisions regulating the institution in question) it is open to public inspection.' Note that a privately owned manuscript may therefore be legally reproduced without permission if a copy of it also exists in such an institution.

2. More than 50 years have elapsed from the end of the calendar year in which the author died. (For joint works this means the last surviving author.)

3. More than 100 years have elapsed since 'the time, or the end of the period, at or during which the work was made'.[p. 22]

4. Such an old work may legally be incorporated in a newly written Literary, Dramatic or Musical work and published as part of it, as long as 'immediately before the new work was published, the identity of the owner of the copyright in the old work was not known to the publisher of the new work'.

When the new work has been published, the old work is freed for various other purposes, but if only part of the old work appears in the new one it is only that part which is freed. Any part which has not been published is not freed until all the conditions (1, 2, 3 and 4 above) are satisfied for it separately.

Once freed, the old work may legally be (1) included in any subsequent publication of the new work whether the new work is 'in the same or in an altered form'; (2) broadcast or included in a cable programme; (3) performed in public; (4) recorded. This list does not apparently include adaptation,[p. 47] so that the old work cannot be, say, translated without permission from the legal copyright owner. Nor, apparently, may the old work be published on its own, though it may be broadcast, performed or recorded separately.

'Artistic works provided for explaining or illustrating' the old work may be reproduced along with the text to which they relate. They are then freed for use with that text, but may not be reproduced by themselves.

Copying Unpublished Works Made on or after 1 August 1989

The librarian or archivist of a prescribed library or archive[p. 58] may make and supply a copy of a whole or part of an unpublished Literary, Dramatic or Musical work made on or after 1 August 1989 and deposited in his institution without infringing copyright in the work or any illustrations accompanying it unless, at the time the copy was made, he was or ought to have been aware: (a) that the work had been published before the document was deposited in the library or archive or (b) the copyright owner had prohibited copying of the work.

Such copying is only permitted if (a) the librarian or archivist is satisfied that it is for research or private study; (b) no one person is furnished with more than one copy of the work; and (c) the copying is paid for.[p. 59]

Copying Old Anonymous and Pseudonymous Works

Under the 1988 Act, the only works that can remain in perpetual copyright (other than those listed on page 80) are anonymous works and pseudonymous works where the author is unknown, if they have not been made available to the public with the authority of the copyright owner. Even when they have been made available to the public, it is often hard to trace the copyright owner. The 1988 Act therefore provides that copyright in a Literary, Dramatic, Musical or Artistic work, whether published or not, is not infringed by anything done if (or 'in pursuance of arrangements made at a time when') it is not possible to discover the identity of the author (or, for works of joint authorship, any of the authors) and it is reasonable to assume (a) that copyright has expired (but see also page 205) or (b) that the author (all authors for works of joint authorship) died more than 50 years before the work is exploited. This provision does not include works that are Crown or Parliamentary copyright, or in which copyright belongs to a recognized international organization but, unlike the provisions for using old unpublished manu-scripts,[p.65] Artistic works are included. For photographs made before 1 August 1989, and works which are in perpetual copyright, assumption (a), that copyright has expired, does not apply. If a work was made before 1 August 1989 assumption (b), the require-ment that the author has been dead for more than 50 years, only applies where the work was still unpublished at 1 August 1989.

17 Using Entire Published Works Without Permission

It is generally illegal to publish any work still in copyright without permission from the copyright owner (except in the circumstances listed on page 54) but in accordance with rules in force from 1 July 1912 to 31 May 1957 Literary, Dramatic, Musical and Artistic works which had already been published could sometimes be republished without the owner's consent. **Republication** (but no other use) was permitted as long as: (1) the work had been published before, (2) 25, or in some cases 30, years had elapsed since the author's death or, in the case of works published posthumously, since first publication, (3) copies were reproduced only for sale (not gratuitous circulation), and (4) the intending publisher had given notice to the copyright owner and arranged to pay him a royalty of 10 per cent of the published price. If the proper notice of intention to republish such a work was given on or before 31 May 1957 the republication remains legal under the present Act and will continue to be so for the remainder of the work's term of copyright.

The 1911 Act also permitted the **compulsory republication or reperformance** of Literary, Dramatic and Musical works deliberately 'withheld from the public' by the copyright owner. No one ever made use of this provision and it was repealed by the 1956 Act.

Compulsory licence provisions for developing countries are included in the 1971 'Paris' texts of the Berne and Universal Copy-right Conventions. The provisions cover translations, reprints of works in their original languages (especially the 'world' languages of English, French, and Spanish), and audio-visual materials. The compulsory licensee must pay to the copyright owner 'just compensation that is consistent with standards of royalties normally operating on licences freely negotiated between persons in the two countries concerned'. Governments of developing countries can grant compulsory licences only when quite complicated requirements have been satisfied, and very few have done so.

18 Using Government Publications and Public Records

Anyone wishing to quote, publish or republish material owned by the United Kingdom Government should act just as he would if the material were privately owned. The official attitude to copying and publishing such material is outlined in an HMSO letter* which explains:

Reproduction of Crown and Parliamentary Copyright Material

Introduction

1. This letter revises HMSO's earlier 'Dear Publisher' letter of August 1985 in the light of the Copyright, Designs and Patents Act 1988 (ISBN 0 10 544888 5, available from HMSO). It is intended to clarify the circumstances in which publishers should seek permission before undertaking the reproduction of Crown and Parliamentary copyright material. In recognition of the unique nature of much of this material, considerable freedom is allowed in its reproduction but within the guidance described below.

---

*HMSO also publishes a letter on *Photocopying Crown and Parliamentary Copyright Publications*. Both have the reference number PU 15/108, November 1989, and are available from HMSO, St Crispins, Duke Street, Norwich NR3 1PD.

---

2. Under the Copyright, Designs And Patents Act 1988, a new category of 'Parliamentary copyright' was introduced. It should be noted that HMSO administers Parliamentary copyright on behalf of the House of Lords and the House of Commons in those Parliamentary works published by HMSO but Parliamentary copyright material NOT published by HMSO will be administered by officials of the relevant House of Parliament.

3. For the purposes of defining conditions for reproduction, Crown and Parliamentary copyright material can be divided into the following broad categories:

   (a) Statutory material, including Bills and Acts of Parliament, Statutory Rules and Orders, and Statutory Instruments;
   (b) The Official Report of the House of Lords and House of Commons Debates (Hansard), Lords' Minutes, the Vote Bundle, Commons Order-Books and Commons Statutory Instrument Lists;
   (c) Other Parliamentary papers published by HMSO, including Reports of Select Committees of both Houses (CMND papers, White papers, HC & HL papers);
   (d) Other Parliamentary material not published by HMSO;
   (e) Non-Parliamentary works, comprising all papers of Government Departments – both published and unpublished – not contained in other categories;
   (f) Charts and Navigational publications published by the MOD (Hydrographic Department) and maps and other publications in all media published by the Ordnance Survey.

Statutory Material (Category 3(a) above)

4. There is no objection to the reproduction of extracts (defined for these purposes as being up to 30% of the original publication) provided that the source is acknowledged. Permission is not required unless the official publication is to be used as camera-ready copy.

5. The reproduction of longer extracts (defined for these purposes as being 30% or more of the original publication) or the complete text is NOT NORMALLY ALLOWED during the following embargo periods:

   (i) Bills and Acts of Parliament – 6 months from date of publication;
   (ii) Statutory Instruments, Orders and Rules – 3 months from date of publication.

   However, these restrictions will be waived if the texts are reproduced as part of a book or journal containing SUBSTANTIAL annotations to the text or commentary on it. Permission is not then required unless the official publication is to be used as camera-ready copy. The source should be acknowledged as either Crown or Parliamentary copyright, whichever is appropriate.

6. Outside the embargo periods, there is no objection to the reproduction of this material, and permission is not then required unless the official publication is to be used as camera-ready copy. The source should be

acknowledged as either Crown or Parliamentary copyright, whichever is appropriate.

The Official Reports and House business papers (category 3(b) above)

7. Reproduction is not allowed in connection with advertising.

8. Otherwise, the publications may be reproduced freely. Permission is not required unless the official publication is to be used as camera-ready copy or the extracts form a substantial part of the reproduction. However, please note that:

    (i) the source must be acknowledged as Parliamentary copyright and extracts must be reproduced verbatim;

    (ii) any person or body publishing unofficial reports of proceedings in Parliament, even though they are verbatim reports of speeches as reported in the Official Report, may not enjoy as extensive privilege in proceedings for defamation as the full Official Report would enjoy.

Other Parliamentary Papers published by HMSO (category 3(c) above)

9. There is no objection to the reproduction of BRIEF extracts – which, for this category, may be defined as up to 5% of the whole publication; it is not necessary to seek permission before doing so and no fees are levied. The source should be acknowledged.

10. Longer extracts, or the whole publication, must not be reproduced without the permission of Her Majesty's Stationery Office. The conditions of publication are the subject of formal permission and normally any such permissions would not allow reproduction until 6 months after the date of publication by HMSO.

Other Parliamentary material not published by HMSO (category 3(d) above)

11. This Parliamentary copyright material is administered by officials of the relevant House and application for its use should be made to the appropriate address at paragraph 21.

Non-Parliamentary material (category 3(e) above)

12. This category covers a wide range of material published by HMSO and by Government Departments and Crown bodies. It also covers unpublished material. Neither the whole text nor extracts in this category should be reproduced without the permission of HMSO, or of departments and bodies having delegated authority to grant such permission. The conditions of publication are the subject of formal agreement.

Charts and Navigational publications published by the MOD (Hydrographic Department) and maps and other publications in all media published by the Ordnance Survey

13. The administration of Crown copyright relating to publications in this category is subject to appropriate arrangements for delegation between the

Controller of HMSO and the MOD (Hydrographic Department) and Ordnance Survey. Applications for permission to reproduce such material should be made to MOD (Hydrographic Department) or Ordnance Survey – as appropriate – at the addresses in paragraph 22 and not to HMSO. (Please note that Ordnance Survey maps, map extracts or redrawn maps must not be reproduced without Ordnance Survey permission.)

Camera-Ready Copy

14. As already described, permission is required for the use of the official text as camera-ready copy. Such permission will not normally be refused – subject to the general conditions outlined above relating to embargo periods, etc. – but a fee will be charged.

General

15. The guidance contained in this letter is intended to apply to printed reproduction and to publication within the United Kingdom only. All rights relating to reproduction outside the UK and to reproduction in other media are reserved. Publishers intending to reproduce Crown or Parliamentary copyright material outside the UK or in media other than print (e.g. microform or computer media) must therefore seek HMSO clearance in advance.

16. The Royal Arms and official printing and publishing imprints should not be reproduced. Copies of Acts of Parliament, Statutory Rules and Orders and Statutory Instruments, other than those reproduced by or by the order of Her Majesty's Stationery Office, must not purport to be published by Authority.

17. The reproduction of Crown or Parliamentary copyright material so as to result in unfair or misleading selection, undignified association or undesirable use for advertising purposes is not permitted. In cases of doubt, application must be made to HMSO at the address at paragraph 20 or, as the case may be, to the relevant House at the address in paragraph 21.

18. Although this letter provides the current working guidelines for the reproduction of defined classes of material, all Crown and Parliamentary rights in respect of copyright are reserved and will be asserted in cases considered by the Controller of HMSO or by the relevant House as exceptional.

19. This letter is primarily addressed to publishers, but it also covers the arrangements for any wide-scale reproduction of Crown or Parliamentary copyright material including, for example, by professional bodies.

Contact

20. Further advice may be obtained from:

Her Majesty's Stationery Office
Copyright Section (P6)
St Crispins
Duke Street
Norwich NR3 1PD
Tel: 0603 695506 (Direct dialling)
Fax: 0603 695582

21. Enquiries regarding the reproduction of Parliamentary material not published by HMSO should be directed to:

Chief Clerk   or   Clerk of the Journals
Journal Office   Journal Office
House of Lords   House of Commons
London SW1A 0PW   London SW1A 0AA
Tel: 071–219 3187/3327   Tel: 071–219 3315/3320

22. Other useful addresses are:

Copyright Branch   Hydrographic Department
Ordnance Survey   Finance Section
Romsey Road   Ministry of Defence
Maybush   Taunton
Southamptom SO9 4DH   Somerset TA1 2DN
Tel: 0703 792302   Tel: 0823 337900 Ext 337

Public Records

The copyright in millions of documents is owned by the Crown because they have been written or collected by government employees in the course of their work. Most of these fall into the class of 'public records' which are open to public inspection and are under the care of the Public Record Office: the records of Government departments and courts of law; ships' logbooks; records of censuses, probate, land and so on. Departmental records are usually not released to the public until at least 30 years after their creation. Some public records (e.g. those mainly of local interest) are kept in repositories physically separate from the Public Record Office.

The Act permits single copies of most public records to be supplied to members of the public upon request. Reproducing or publishing them, however, is more strictly controlled. The official view is this:*

5.   HOW DOES COPYRIGHT APPLY TO RECORDS IN THE PUBLIC RECORD OFFICE?

5.1 The holdings of the Public Record Office fall into two categories:
     (a) public records, as defined in the Public Records Act 1958: broadly

---

*Taken from *PRO General Information 15: Copyright*: a leaflet issued by the Public Record Office.

speaking, the records compiled or accumulated by the Crown, central government and the judiciary;
   (b) non-public records.

5.2   Records in both categories contain some works which are Crown copyright, some in which private copyright subsists and some which are no longer in copyright at all.

5.3   Copyright restrictions may affect both the provision of copies by the PRO, and any use which readers may make of either their own transcripts of records or any copies supplied by the PRO.

5.4   Provision of copies

5.4.1   *Public Records*
The PRO is authorised to copy for members of the public, without infringing copyright, any work which forms part of the public records.

5.4.2   *Non-public Records: unpublished literary works*
The PRO may, but is not obliged to, copy such works as follows:
   (a) for purposes of research and private study but *only* upon receipt of a signed declaration form respecting copyright, and if
     either the work is Crown copyright;
     or **both** the following apply:
     – the copyright owner has not prohibited copying;
     – the work was not published before deposit in the PRO
   (b) with a view to publication, but *only* if **all** the following apply:
     – the work was created more than 100 years ago;
     – the author died more than 50 years ago;
     – the work is open to public inspection.
Copyright law makes no provision for the copying of other types of unpublished works in which copyright still subsists. The PRO may provide copies of unpublished artistic works, sound recordings or cinematographic films among non-public record holdings only if the works in question are Crown copyright or no longer in copyright at all.

5.4.3   *Non-public Records: published works*
The PRO may copy for members of the public from non-public records among its holdings any published works in which copyright (including typographical copyright) no longer subsists.
Published works in which copyright still subsists may be copied only in accordance with the provisions of the Copyright, Designs and Patents Act 1988 and the Copyright (Copying by Librarians and Archivists of Copyright Material) Regulations 1989, copies of which are available for consultation at the Reference Desk at Kew and at the Officer's Desk in the Round Room, Chancery Lane. The PRO reserves the right, however, to refuse to make copies of any such work.

5.5   Permission to publish

Publication is defined in law as 'the issue of copies to the public', and thus includes the distribution of copies for non-commercial or non-profit-making purposes, as well as strictly commercial publishing.

5.5.1   *Fair dealing*
No permission is needed to publish or broadcast copyright material when the usage falls within the limits of fair dealing for purposes of criticism or review, or the reporting of current events. There is, however, no legal definition of 'fair dealing', and the staff of the Public Record Office cannot undertake to advise in any particular case.

5.5.2   *Brief quotations from Crown copyright works*
In cases not exempted as 'fair dealing', no permission is needed to publish or broadcast brief quotations from Crown copyright works among records held in the PRO, provided that Crown copyright is acknowledged and the document reference is given. The standard form of acknowledgement in publications is: 'Crown copyright material in the Public Record Office is reproduced by permission of the Controller of Her Majesty's Stationery Office'.
'Brief quotation' cannot be defined, as it depends on the length and nature of the work quoted. In case of doubt, please refer to the Copyright Officer of the PRO.

5.5.3   *Transcripts or facsimiles of works no longer in copyright*
No permission is needed to publish or broadcast transcripts and reprographic or photographic copies of works which are no longer in copyright.

5.5.4   *Transcripts or facsimiles of unpublished Crown copyright works*
Permission to publish or broadcast substantial extracts from, or complete verbatim transcripts, photocopies or facsimiles of, unpublished Crown copyright works among records held in the PRO must be sought in the first instance by written application to the Copyright Officer of the Public Record Office. In certain cases, it will be necessary for the PRO to refer the application to HM Stationery Office.

5.5.5   *Transcripts or facsimiles of published Crown copyright works*
Permission to publish or broadcast substantial extracts from, or complete verbatim transcripts or facsimiles of, published works held in the PRO and in which Crown copyright still subsists must be sought from HM Stationery Office.

5.5.6   *Works in private copyright*
Permission to publish, or broadcast any work in which privately-owned copyright subsists must be sought from the current copyright owner (with certain exceptions: see 'Special cases' below). The PRO cannot undertake to establish the current ownership of copyright in such works, nor to obtain any permission which may be required.

5.6   In case of doubt please refer to the Copyright Officer of the PRO.

6.   HOW TO APPLY FOR PERMISSION TO PUBLISH OR BROAD-CAST CROWN COPYRIGHT MATERIAL IN THE PUBLIC RECORD OFFICE

6.1   Any application for permission to publish or broadcast Crown copyright material among records held in the PRO should state the following details as precisely as possible:

  (a) the full PRO document references of the records, or parts of records, to be used, and the length of the quotations (in words or pages);
  (b) the form in which the material is to be used, i.e. quotation/extract, full verbatim transcript or facsimile;
  (c) the nature of the publication or broadcast, and the name of the publisher or broadcasting company;
  (d) in the case of a facsimile, whether it is to be used as an illustration within a book or journal, or on the wrapper or dustjacket;
  (e) in the case of a facsimile, the proportion of the printed page which it is to occupy (quarter-, half-, three-quarter- or whole page);
  (f) the non-exclusive rights required.

6.2   Reproduction fees may be levied for use in a commercial publication, film or broadcast.

7.   WHAT MAY BE USED IN EXHIBITIONS OR LECTURES?

7.1   The public display of a work may infringe copyright. When a copy of any work among its holdings has been supplied by the PRO, that copy may be used in exhibitions in public institutions, or as an illustration to a lecture, if
either the work is Crown copyright,
or the work is no longer in copyright.

7.2   In such cases, no formal permission is needed for the use of the copy, provided that suitable acknowledgements are made and the full PRO document references are given where appropriate. The use of such material in exhibition catalogues, posters or postcards is, however, subject to the standard provisions concerning publication (see above).

7.3   The PRO is not able to authorise the use in exhibitions or lectures of copies of works in private copyright among the public records. Such use may infringe copyright, unless permission has been obtained from the copyright owner.

7.4   Any doubt concerning the copyright status of a particular work should be referred to the Copyright Officer of the PRO.

8.   MAY PUBLIC RECORD OFFICE COPIES BE COPIED?

8.1   Public institutions and private individuals holding reprographic or photographic copies obtained from the PRO, of works among public or non-public records in the PRO, may make further copies in certain circumstances. Every copy made in accordance with the conditions outlined below should bear the full PRO document reference and, where relevant, a note that the material is Crown copyright and not to be reproduced without permission.

8.1.1   Reprographic and photographic copies, and copies on microfilm and microfiche of works no longer in copyright may be freely reproduced, since no copyright subsists in the copies themselves.

Microforms published commercially may, however, be in copyright as compilations or published editions, and should not be reproduced without reference to the publisher.

8.1.2   Reprographic copies of unpublished works in Crown copyright may be copied to a limited extent, as follows:

(a) for private and non-commercial use;

(b) for use in an exhibition or display;

(c) for members of the public, subject to certain conditions, which must be made clear to all recipients of such further copies:

(i) copies are to be used for study purposes only, and should normally be limited to one copy per page per customer; multiple hard copies for teaching purposes may, however, be made provided that all other conditions are met;

(ii) copies should be provided at cost and not for resale;

(iii) publication of copies or of material from them is subject to the general provisions of current copyright law.

8.1.3   Microfilm or microfiche copies of works in Crown copyright, obtained direct from the PRO (see 8.1.1, above), may be copied *only* as follows:

(a) for the purpose of preservation within a prescribed library or archive which has obtained the film or fiche direct from the PRO; only one copy should be made;

(b) for members of the public, in the form of small quantities of hard copy (not duplicate film), in accordance with the conditions at 8.1.2(c) above; such copyright should be limited to one hard copy per frame per customer.

Microfilm and microfiche copies obtained from the PRO should not be duplicated in any other circumstances without express written permission of the PRO.

8.2   The PRO is not able to authorise the copying of copies of works in private copyright among either public or non-public records in its custody. Such copying may infringe copyright, unless permission has been obtained from the copyright owner.

8.3   In case of doubt, please refer to the Copyright Officer of the PRO.

9.   SPECIAL CASES

9.1   Copies of Prime Ministers' Letters in the Royal Archives (CAB 41)
These may be reproduced on conditions equivalent to those governing Crown copyright material. For use in published works the suggested acknowledgement is: 'Reproduced from photographic copies in the Public Record Office of original letters preserved in the Royal Archives and made available by the gracious permission of Her Majesty the Queen'.

9.2   Duchy of Lancaster Records (DL classes)
These are not public records, but those among them which are in the

copyright of the Duchy itself may be reproduced on conditions equivalent to those of Crown copyright material. For use in published works the suggested acknowledgement is: 'Duchy of Lancaster copyright material in the Public Record Office is reproduced by permission of the Chancellor and Council of the Duchy of Lancaster'.

9.3 Ramsay MacDonald Papers (PRO 30/69)
Photocopying and other restrictions on material in this class are indicated at the front of the class list. Subject to these special conditions, items in which copyright was formerly owned by Ramsay MacDonald or Malcolm MacDonald may be reproduced on conditions equivalent to those for Crown copyright material; for use in published works the suggested acknowledgement is 'Copyright material from the Ramsay MacDonald papers is reproduced by permission of the executrix of the late Macolm MacDonald'.

9.4 British Transport Historical Records (RAIL classes) and British Transport Commission and British Railways Board Records (AN classes). Permission to publish material still in copyright (i) in which the copyright was formerly owned by railway or canal companies which were ultimately nationalised, and (ii) in which copyright is owned by British Rail, must be sought from the Director of Public Affairs, British Railways Board, 222 Marylebone Road, London NW1 6JJ.

9.5 Probate records (PROB classes)
Copyright in a will or codicil is vested in the testator, and passes (unless otherwise assigned) to his heirs. Copyright in the acts of a probate court (such as probate clauses and letters of administration) is vested in the court. In the case of the Prerogative Court of Canterbury and other probate jurisdictions abolished by the Court of Probate Act 1857, no transfer of the ownership of the records was effected, and ownership of surviving copyright remains with the originating authorities or their successors. Acts of courts of probate since 1857 are Crown copyright.

9.6 Public records outside the Public Record Office
Some public records are held in places of deposit (such as local record offices) appointed under s.4(1) of the Public Records Act 1958. The reproduction and publication of material from these records are subject to the same conditions as if they were held in the Public Record Office. Any formal application necessary for permission to publish Crown copyright material among them should be addressed to the Copyright Officer of the Public Record Office, except when such records are held on deposit in another government department, in which case the application should be addressed direct to the department concerned.

9.7 Crown copyright material in non-public records held outside the Public Record Office
Many archival holdings, including the records of local authorities and of families or private individuals, contain both published and unpublished works in Crown copyright. In such cases any permission needed to reproduce or publish the works should be obtained from the Publications Division (Copyright), HM Stationery Office, St Crispins, Duke Street,

Norwich NR3 1PD. Applications should state the exact nature and extent of the material, where or by whom it is now held, and that it is not held under the terms of the Public Records Act 1958.

19 **The Bible**

Translations of the Bible are Literary works, and most of those in common use today are still protected by copyright. All the rules as to term of protection, ownership, privileged quotation and the like are the same for the Bible as for any other Literary work, and permission to use a substantial part of any version still in copyright must be obtained from the copyright owner. However, the **Authorized ('King James') Version*** is in a unique position. It may only be published by very few publishers in the United Kingdom, and enjoys a status akin to perpetual copyright.

When the Authorized Version (AV) was completed under the direction of King James in 1611 only one printer was granted a patent to print it in England. Shortly afterwards the Universities of Oxford and Cambridge became 'privileged' to publish it, by virtue of their royal charters. Today the original patent has descended to Cambridge University Press which, along with Oxford University Press, still publish it 'cum privilegio'. Apart from these 'Privileged Presses' no one may publish the AV in England.

In Scotland the Scottish Bible Board is now the patent holder and anyone wishing to print the AV there must apply to the Board for a licence. The only licence holder for many years has been Collins (now HarperCollins Publishers).

Rights in the AV are owned by the Crown and administered by Cambridge University Press.[†] In Scotland, Crown restrictions now

---

* The Book of Common Prayer, the Administration of the Sacraments, Psalm Books, Confessions of the Faith, the Longer and Shorter Catechisms 'and other rites and ceremonies of the Church of England' are in much the same position as the AV.

† Cambridge University Press, The Edinburgh Building, Shaftesbury Road, Cambridge CB2 2RU.

---

apply only to printing the AV and not to any other right in it, but this distinction is meaningless in practice since anyone wishing to use it in the UK must clear the rights for England, and this means seeking permission from Cambridge University Press.

The Central Board of Finance of the Church of England publishes an extremely useful and comprehensive guide *Liturgical Texts for Local Use – Guidelines and Copyright Information*, available from the Copyright Administrator, Church House, Great Smith Street, London SW1P 3NZ.

20 Works in Perpetual Copyright

Most works go out of copyright eventually[p. 35] but there are a few which are still protected even though they were published a century ago or more.

The position of the Authorized Version of the Bible is described in Chapter 19 above. In addition, the Copyright Act of 1775 gave the Universities of Aberdeen, Cambridge, Edinburgh, Glasgow, Oxford and St Andrews, and the 'colleges' of Eton, Westminster and Winchester the special privilege of owning in perpetuity the copyrights in texts given or bequeathed to them for the purpose of education within them. In 1801 the same privilege was granted to Trinity College, Dublin. This perpetual copyright in a text could be claimed only if the text was registered promptly at Stationers' Hall, and could last only as long as the text was printed by the press of the foundation concerned, for the sole benefit of that foundation, and the rights were neither leased nor sold to any other person or body.

The right of these foundations to own perpetual copyrights was confirmed by every Copyright Act until the 1988 Act which provides that all these works will go out of copyright on 1 January 2040. Until then, a work in perpetual copyright should be treated in exactly the same way as any other copyright work.

Upon inquiry it appears that most of the foundations cannot with certainty claim to hold any current perpetual copyrights. The following titles, now handled by Oxford University Press, were registered* under the provisions of the 1775 Act, though rights in most of these may well have lapsed by now:

Clarendon:	*History of the Rebellion*
	Life, written by himself
Benjamin Jowett:	*The Dialogues of Plato*
	The Republic of Plato
	The Politics of Aristotle
	Thucydides
H. Lee-Warner:	*Extracts from Livy*
	Hints and Helps for Latin Elegiacs
	(and a *Key* to the same)
Bishop Lowth:	*De sacra poesi Hebraeorum*
John Phillips:	*Vesuvius*
	The Geology of Oxford and the
	Valley of the Thames
G. L. Prendergast:	*Concordance to the Iliad*
John Ruskin:	*Lectures on Art*

Peter Pan

The 1988 Act states that the Great Ormond Street Hospital for Sick Children has 'a right to a royalty in respect of the public performance, commercial publication, broadcasting or inclusion in a cable programme service' of J. M. Barrie's *Peter Pan*, or in any adaptation of it, despite the fact that it is now out of copyright.

---

21 Reprinting Extracts: Permission to Quote, Select or Anthologize

When one author wants to quote a substantial extract from another author's copyright work, or a complete item such as a short article

---

*Those by Jowett were registered for Balliol College and the remainder for Oxford University.

---

or a poem, or any line of poetry or lyrics, he must apply to the copyright owner for permission to do so, and he must not use such material without having obtained permission. Transactions like this are called 'Permissions' and a book contract refers to them as 'selection, anthology and quotation' rights. The process of obtaining permission is relatively informal, though detailed and time-consuming.

When a writer is given permission to quote an item his right to do so is non-exclusive. It is understood that though X is told today that he may quote a given passage in one book, Y may be told tomorrow that he may quote the identical passage in another book.

Obtaining ('clearing') the necessary permissions is the responsibility of the author or compiler of the new work which contains quotations. It is his job to contact the owners of all the items quoted and to get their consent to the republication of the items in his book. It is also his job to pay the permission fees. By arrangement, of course, the publisher may take over the paperwork and/or pay the fees.

Anyone who proposes compiling an anthology, and anyone who writes a straight text with much incidental quotation, would do well to estimate permission fees at an early stage. They can be costly, and an author should be particularly wary of undertaking to 'edit' a collection when all permission fees are to come out of a single lump sum paid to him by his publisher.

All quotations should be accurate, down to and including the punctuation. Quotations should be finally checked against the originals at the proof stage.

When to Ask Permission to Quote

The editor of a selection or anthology must obtain permission for *every* piece he includes, however short, unless it is in the public domain[p. 36] or (sometimes) if his collection is for educational use,[p. 61] or if the piece qualifies as 'old unpublished' work.[p. 65] Critics (reviewers and authors of critical works) and journalists are given special quotation privileges by the Act.[p. 54]

An author concerned only with incidental quotation – where passages are quoted as small parts of a larger original work – has to decide his course of action. He can freely use public domain material[p. 36] and material which qualifies as 'old unpublished' work.[p. 65] It is common practice to be able to quote small quantities (say, a few phrases or sentences) from other works without requesting permission from the copyright owner (or, of course, paying a fee) but every such quotation *must* be properly acknowledged at least briefly (see 'Acknowledgements' below).

An author can quote passages without permission if he is convinced that his quotation is less than a 'substantial part' of the original[p. 45] or that his use of it qualifies as one of the specially privileged cases listed on page 54, although he must be prepared to defend his action if necessary.

All quotations from the same source should be considered together. Even when each individual quotation is brief an author may quote from a work so frequently that in the aggregate his borrowing is 'substantial'.

Permission should (with the exceptions above) always be requested for copyright **lyrics** and **poetry** unless the poetry quotation is less than a single line. An author who has **condensed** or **abridged** a quoted passage should obtain permission to quote it in its new form – and from the copyright owner himself, not just from a publisher who controls the quotation rights.

When in doubt the best course is to apply for permission, bearing in mind that obtaining permission is not synonymous with having to pay a fee. For recommended minimum fees and the way in which they may be charged, see below.

Remember that recent translations of the **Bible** and also the **Authorized Version** are not in the public domain and should be approached like any other copyright work.[p. 79]

Public domain works (those unprotected by UK copyright either because their term[p. 36] has expired or because they did not qualify[p. 16] for protection in the first place) may be freely quoted, adapted, rewritten, edited or published in their entirety. Beware of inadvertently quoting from a recently edited version or a new adaptation which can claim a current copyright.

· Remember that a work which is out of copyright in one country may still be protected in another.[p. 36] Remember also that public domain material which has not been published may in rare cases qualify for UK copyright protection subsequently,[p. 17] so it is safer to obtain formal permission to use it. Any use made of such work while it was in the public domain does not retroactively become an infringement, but any use after the date when it acquires protection will be illegal without permission. (See also page 205.)

Notice about permissible quotation is included by some publishers in their books on the copyright page, to the effect that no quotation whatever may be made without permission, or that a certain number of words only may be quoted without permission. When a specific number of words is mentioned in this way without other qualification one can take this as a gratuitous licence to quote up to that number freely. But no publisher can enforce such a quantitative limit when the law's limits are the qualitative ones of substantial part and Fair Dealing.[p. 45]

When quoting from **reference books** it is wise to apply the strictest standards since the information in them is so compact and compartmented. Permission should certainly be requested to quote any complete definition, recipe, guidebook entry or the like.

Paraphrasing someone else's wording may constitute an actionable infringement. On the other hand a mere extract of facts will not.[p. 95]

When a **new edition** of a previously published work is in prospect, check whether permissions received previously will cover the new issue. Fresh applications may have to be made in some cases; in others, further payments may be due.

If a copyright owner is untraceable, or does not answer letters, one must decide whether to omit the desired quotation or to use it and run the risk that the owner will later object. In the case of a person who does not answer letters a reasonable course (though not one in any way supported by law) is to send him a registered or recorded-delivery letter explaining what the situation is and saying that if nothing has been heard from him within, say, four weeks, it will be assumed that he has no objection to the extract being used. A note should certainly appear with the relevant acknowledgement to the effect that efforts have been made – e.g. to trace the copyright proprietor – without success. See also 'Untraceable Authors' on page 51.

Quotation from a **translation** (e.g. an English translation of a play first written in French) may have to be authorized not only by the owner of the copyright in the translation but also by the owner of the copyright in the original. It is worth inquiring whether the owner of the translation is really empowered to grant quotation rights.

For further guidance, *The Extent and Limitations of a Copyright*[p. 44] and *Reproduction in Newly Printed Form*[p. 51] may be helpful.

Applying for Permission to Quote

A request for permission to quote should normally go to the author's agent, if known, or to the publisher of the passage in question, since one of them usually handles quotation rights. Sometimes (particularly in anthologies) the names of the relevant copyright owners can be found on the copyright or acknowledgements page. In some special cases the request should be addressed elsewhere (see *Using Old Works Without Permission,*[p. 65] and *Using Government Publications and Public Records*[p. 69]).

The request should include the title (or provisional title) of the work being written, the names of its author and publisher, its proposed date of publication, a brief description of it (e.g. an anthology of poetry, a novel, a textbook on psychiatry), the expected print run and the territory for which permission is desired. It should also include the title and author of the work quoted from, the edition used and an exact indication of the passage(s) to be quoted, with page references and a rough count of the words quoted. Providing a photocopy of the passage makes matters easier for everybody.

As to territory, if the new work is to be published in both the United States and the United Kingdom it will be necessary to obtain English-language rights in the quotation on both sides of the Atlantic and this will often involve correspondence with both US and UK publishers of the quoted material.

Check whether the permission should cover Europe, Canada and/or Australia. In some cases it may be helpful to ask for US and UK fees to be quoted separately if a single publisher handles both permissions. If translation rights are likely to be sold in the new book it may be as well to clear all languages at the same time if the cost is not prohibitive. (See also page 88 below.)

Acknowledgements

Both the law and publishing custom* require that formal acknowledgement of the source should be made for any quotation used,

---

* In the Copyright Act 'sufficient acknowledgement' is less than the form given here which publishing custom dictates.

---

whether permission has been requested or not. The source of each quotation must be made clear to the reader (implicitly or explicitly) at the point where it appears in the text of the new work.

Incidental and brief quotation can be acknowledged in the course of the text ('As Jo Smith says in *Tyrants of the Mountains* . . .') or by a footnote on the same page. The complete details for such briefly quoted titles can, if desired, be given in a bibliography.

When very long passages or whole items are quoted (for instance in a collection of essays or poetry) and formal permission has been requested and obtained, the acknowledgement can appear as a footnote on the page where the item starts. If, however, this is undesirable for design reasons the details can be relegated to an acknowledgements page. In these cases a copyright line should certainly appear if one exists,[p. 162] and if an item is being published for the first time a copyright line must be specially written for it and included on the copyright page.[p. 157]

It is customary for a full acknowledgement (or an entry in a bibliography or the like) to give title, author, publisher, publisher's city and year of publication. A copyright line should be used in place of the publication date if appropriate or if the owner so desires. Edition numbers, page references, translators' names and other details may be added when necessary.

When a work is published by more than one English-language publisher using the same setting, it is best to give the names of all relevant publishers. (An example might be: *Wheels within Wheels* by Andrew Carson. Tandem Publishing Inc., Chicago, 1990. Bicycle Sport Books Ltd, London, 1991.)

The acknowledgements page (in the permissions sense) is that part of a work which begins with a sentence like 'Grateful acknowledgement is made to the following for permission to reprint copyright material . . .' and goes on to give one or dozens of entries like 'Tandem Publishing, Inc., Chicago, and Bicycle Sport Books Ltd, London, for *Wheels within Wheels* by Andrew Carson. © Andrew Carson 1990'. Ideally these acknowledgements should be on, or at least start on, the copyright page or the page immediately following it. (This is particularly recommended by American authorities for material published in the United States.) The acknowledgements should follow the form requested by the copyright owners, and if they request a particular wording you should follow it exactly. For much good advice on how to handle acknowledgements see Judith Butcher's *Copy-editing*.[p. 222]

Giving Permission and Charging Fees

Before granting (or refusing) any permission it is essential to ascertain whether one has the right to do so. The publisher–author agreement should state clearly who is to deal with the 'selection, anthology and quotation' rights, and what territory and language are covered by the agreement as a whole.

An author should pass all requests for permission on to his agent if he has one. Publishers usually have (and certainly ought to have) one person or department whose duty it is to deal with permissions, and all requests should be referred to this single centre. Many firms receive so many requests for permissions that they have their own standard form which the person seeking permission must complete.

On the whole, **permission to quote** should always be granted unless: (1) The quotation will appear in a context which is undesirable (prejudicial to the reputation of the author, for instance). (2) Another party with an interest in the quoted work (author, co-author, illustrator, publisher) may resent the proposed use. Even if an author's contract gives his publisher *carte blanche* in dealing with permissions, requests from such sources as political organizations should always be cleared with everybody involved. If the applicant wants to abridge a passage, his version should be cleared with the author. (3) The text in which the quotation is to appear will, because it includes the quotation, compete with the original work. (Alternatively, in such a case an unusually high fee may be charged.) (4) The person requesting permission is a bad financial risk.

Remember that quotation of a work (as long as a proper acknowledgement appears, and especially if it appears on the same page as the quotation) is usually a good advertisement for it.

In deciding whether to charge a fee the following points should be taken into consideration: (1) Fees should always be charged for anthology *and* similar use. In doubtful cases it can be important to ascertain the overall shape of the text which will include the quotation. A book on, for instance, sexual customs throughout the world may contain a great many quotations from other works. These may be quite incidental and easily replaceable or removable; or the book may actually be a saleable mosaic of quotations only loosely cemented by a minimum of text. (2) Incidental quotation in long, otherwise original texts will usually be permitted free or for a small fee as long as the extracts are short. Remember, however, that the content of a quotation may be more important than its length.

The recommendations for fees below include units of length against which one can measure actual quotation. (3) The Publishers Association* reminds us that 'Both writers and publishers are likely from time to time to wish to quote another copyright work in the work on which they are currently engaged. Equally, works of theirs will be wanted for quotation purposes by other authors and publishers. In general, therefore, it must pay all concerned to approach the question of granting permissions in a liberal manner.' (4) It is customary to allow quotation in Braille and talking books for the blind and handicapped without charge (but see also page 121).

The amount of the fee is the most difficult thing to decide. Every publisher and agent has his own scale. The copyright owners of musical works and lyrics quote fees which most prospective users find prohibitive, though a little bargaining may sometimes result in substantial reductions.

Any rule of thumb based on nothing but the number of words quoted can be very misleading. Though many publishers have made their own house rules on this basis it is always best to measure them against every individual case.

The Publishers Association and the Society of Authors have given us some much-needed guidance by recommending *basic minimum* fees for English-language quotation and anthology use of copyright material.† The current scale is:

Prose: £82–£96 per 1,000 words for worldwide rights. The rate for the UK and Commonwealth or the UK alone is usually half the world rate. For an individual country (e.g. Canada, Australia or New Zealand) one quarter of the world rate.

Poetry: for publication in the UK and Commonwealth a minimum fee of £30 for the first 10 lines, £1.50 per line for the next 20 lines and £1 per line subsequently. For separate publication elsewhere (e.g. in the USA, Australasia, Europe, Canada) a further fee of not less than half the original fee.

Where the extract is complete in itself (e.g. a chapter, short story or whole poem), publishers sometimes charge an additional fee at

---

* In their pamphlet *Permissions* (long out of print).

† This information is kindly provided by the Society of Authors. The scale of fees and quotations below are from an article in *The Author*, Spring 1991.

half the rate applicable for 1,000 words depending on the importance of the author or scale of territory.

This scale is intended to cover one edition only, 'edition' in this case meaning one type of format issued by one publisher – e.g. a hardback edition published by Bloggs & Co. If Bloggs subsequently issue their own paperback or sublease the rights to another publisher, new fees will be payable. (See 'Future editions' below.)

Some attention should be paid to the current pound/dollar exchange rate.

Working from this base the person giving permission can arrive at an appropriate fee by also taking into account:

1. **Value judgements** affecting the issue, for instance the importance of the author whose work is quoted; the proportion (qualitative as well as purely quantitative [p. 45]) which the quoted passage bears to the existing work as a whole; the value of the quoted passage to the new work.
2. **Special provisions for poetry.** 'It is recommended that poetry rates drop for re-publication in other countries or in a subsequent edition, to encourage the wider sale of anthologies containing the work of new poets. The poetry rate may be reduced by one third if a poem appears in a literary or scholarly journal or an anthology that contains more than 40 poems in copyright or in a book with a print run of less than 1,500 copies although, of course, the rate for established poets may well be significantly higher. Where poetry is being quoted in a work of criticism or review (e.g. a biography) over the limit of Fair Dealing [p. 45] some discount is normally given.'
3. Permission is often given free for **poems that are to be spoken** at speech and drama festivals, but a nominal fee is generally charged for those poems which are included in a prize-winner's subsequent performance.
4. **Whether the new work will compete** with the one from which the quotation comes.
5. **The expected print run and published price.** If either or both of these are high the fee may be increased; on the other hand 'for scholarly works (e.g. theses) with print runs of 1,000 copies or less it is usual to halve the fees'.
6. What **languages** are covered by the permission. One can confine a permission to English-language quotation, and hope that, if and when translation rights are sold in the new work,

someone will remember to ask for the outstanding permission. For quotation in anthologies it is best to reserve translation permissions entirely. But for other works this may not be sensible. If, for instance, the quoted passage is short and used in a run-of-the-mill detective story, or if the basic fee is small anyway, it is probably best to give blanket permission for all languages throughout the world without additional charge. But if the quoted passage forms a valuable (not necessarily long) contribution to a seminal work in genetics which is likely to be translated into many languages, or if the quotation is used in any book likely to do well in translation, the fee should be substantially increased, or a further fee should be payable every time the work is translated into a new language.

7. **Future editions.** Especially when giving permission for an extract to appear in an anthology, or in any context at all resembling anthology use, it is wise to request additional payments on occasions when the anthology reaches, as it were, a new stage in its career. A permission can stipulate that further payments must be made when the anthology appears in a different format, whether printed by the original publisher or by another publisher under sub-licence from the first: paperback after hardback or vice versa, book club, cheap, microform, CD or video editions. Further payments may also be due when any edition reaches a certain multiple of the number of copies in print. For a hardback book this might be every five or ten thousand copies. This sort of recurrent payment is especially applicable in the case of 'good backlist' books, notably educational texts and reference books.

   Recurrent payments of this kind are eminently equitable and their increase is to be encouraged, although most publishers do not like them, partly for costing reasons but mainly because of the difficulty of keying them into the accounting system so that payments will actually be made on the due dates. Anyone requesting such payments should have a means of checking that they have in fact been made in later years. The simplest course is to write a reminder to the publishers concerned at appropriate intervals inquiring whether payment points have been reached or passed.

8. **A pro-rata share of income** may in some cases be preferable to a one-time permissions fee when the quotation appears in an anthology or symposium which includes relatively few

individual pieces, and especially if the borrowed material comprises one third or more of the new work. If this is satisfactory then an agreement should be drawn up with the copyright owner of the text containing the quotation. Ideally this would stipulate that the copyright owner of the piece quoted should receive x per cent of all monies earned by the anthology throughout the world in all languages for the full term of copyright in the work quoted. If there are any reservations to this blanket formula a much more detailed contract will probably be necessary. The agreement must be between the copyright owners since in cases where the copyright in either the work quoted or the work using the quotation is owned by the author and not by his publisher, the author is unlikely to be irrevocably committed to one publisher for the full term of copyright in his work. Having received the money the quoted author can then pay to his current publisher whatever percentage of it may be due under the agreement between them.

9. **Complimentary copies.** In addition to a fee, or as an alternative to it, you can request a complimentary copy of the work using the quotation, to be sent at publication – normally to the author of the quoted passage. These requests should usually be confined to anthology-type permissions and to texts which will be of some use when they are received.

Fees are normally **payable** on publication of the work using the quotations because it is only at publication that everyone will be sure that the quoted passage still forms part of the new work.

The document granting a permission is usually a short letter or form. Two copies should be sent to the person requesting the permission and one copy should be signed and returned by him. Such a document should be formally exchanged whether or not a fee is payable.

The document should contain the following information: (a) The title and author of the work quoted and any other relevant facts such as the edition (e.g. second) quoted from. (b) The quotation used, indicated at least by first and last phrases and a page reference. (c) The title, author, publisher and prospective publication date and price of the new work in which the quotation is to appear. (d) The fee, if any, and when payable. (e) The language and territory to which the permission is limited. (f) Any other limitations or stipulations such as those described in paragraphs 7, 8 and 9 above. (g) The form of acknowledgement desired.

22 Original Manuscripts

A manuscript was defined by the 1956 Act as 'the original document embodying the work, whether written by hand or not'. The abbreviations MS and TS (for typescript) are commonly used.

In the United Kingdom the manuscript of a work and the **copyright** in that work are two distinct forms of property. In the absence of an agreement to the contrary they can be sold separately and owned by different people. Ownership of one does not by itself constitute any legal claim to ownership or use of the other. The only exception is when an unpublished manuscript or any other 'original document or other material thing recording or embodying a literary, dramatic, musical or artistic work' is inherited from the copyright owner (who need not be the actual author). The law now is that in the absence of contrary evidence the bequest of such a manuscript or other material is proof of an intention to bequeath the copyright.

The owner of a manuscript can charge for its **physical use** (e.g. as setting copy) and it cannot be used without his permission – whether or not he also owns the copyright in it, and whether the work it embodies is in or out of copyright.* (This also applies, of course, to any rare copy of a published edition.) Permission to **reproduce** any copyright text (as either a transcription or a facsimile) can only be given by the owner of the copyright in it.†

Letters are of course manuscripts. The physical letter (including the signature on it) belongs to the recipient who may be a private person or a firm, and who may sell it, keep it, throw it away, cut it up and generally dispose of it as he pleases. A letter cannot be reproduced without the consent of the copyright owner (usually the writer but in the case of business letters his employer). A signature is not copyrightable as a Literary work but might be as an Artistic

---

* See also *Europe*, page 205.

† Some exceptions are made for manuscripts over 100 years old. See *Using Old Works Without Permission* on page 65.

one, so permission should be obtained before reproducing the signature by itself.

Abroad, close attention must often be paid to Article 14 *ter* of the Paris text of the Berne Convention, which describes the right known as the **'droit de suite'**:

> (1) The author, or after his death the persons or institutions authorised by national legislation, shall, with respect to original works of art and original manuscripts of writers and composers, enjoy the inalienable right to an interest [i.e. a share in the profits] in any sale of the work subsequent to the first transfer by the author of the work.
>
> (2) The protection provided by the preceding paragraph may be claimed in a country of the Union only if legislation in the country to which the author belongs so permits, and to the extent permitted by the country where this protection is claimed.

Droit de suite, usually applied only to Artistic works sold publicly, is a fruitful source of complex litigation. It is not recognized under UK law so it does not affect British authors or works by foreign authors within the UK (although it is possible that in the future the European Commission might introduce a droit de suite throughout the Community).

The **export of old documents** is closely controlled by the Export Licensing Unit of the Department of National Heritage. An EC Directive on the Movement of Works of Art was adopted in November 1992. At the moment a licence* is needed for the export of:

1. 'articles recovered from the soil of the UK, the bed of a stream or area of water in the UK or UK territorial waters, other than a coin and other than any article concealed for less than fifty years';
2. 'any photographic positive or negative or any assemblage of such photographs' more than 50 years old and valued at £6,000 or more;
3. 'archives, documents and manuscripts (not being printed

---

* More detailed information can be obtained from the Department of National Heritage, Export Licensing Unit, 2-4 Cockspur Street, London SWIY 5DH. The quotations come from their leaflet headed *Export Licence* (1992). They also provide a much longer *Notice to Exporters: Export of Antiques, Collectors' Items, Etc (Including Works of Art, Archaeological Material, Documents and Photographs)*.

---

matter); architectural, scientific or engineering drawings produced by hand' that are more than 50 years old and of any value;

4. paintings that are more than 50 years old 'of British historical personages' valued at £6,000 or more. A 'British historical personage' means 'any person, living or dead, in respect of whom an entry appears in the *Dictionary of National Biography* (or any supplement thereto), *Who's Who* or *Who Was Who*'.

5. 'any other work of art, antique or collectors' item' more than 50 years old and valued at £35,000 or more.

An applicant may in a tiny minority of cases be refused an immediate licence because of a specific exclusion, e.g. at the time of writing exports to Iraq, or because the article is 'a work of national importance'. A copy may have to be made of any such document before it is exported, so that researchers in the UK will not be wholly deprived of the work. Most documents which have to be photocopied will be unpublished and therefore still in copyright, and strictly speaking the permission of the copyright owner must be obtained before the photocopy can be made. However, the Act does permit the copying of a work of cultural or historical importance or interest if it cannot lawfully be exported until a copy has been deposited in the appropriate library or archive.

23 Copying Titles, Ideas, Plots, Slogans, Information and Characters

Titles – of books, films, magazines, paintings, newspapers, songs or anything else – are held to be unprotected by copyright* because

---

* But it is possible to register periodical and some book titles as trade marks.

they are too short to display the necessary originality[p. 20] of wording and arrangement and do not form a 'substantial part'[p. 45] of a creative work. Since there is no foolproof way of checking whether titles have been used before, their non-copyright status is a practical advantage.

However, the owner of an existing work can invoke the principle of **passing off**[p. 98] to prevent the reuse of his title as long as his own work enjoys an established reputation in a similar field and the title is deliberately reused in such a way that the public connect the original work with the subsequent one or mistake one for the other. Whether he succeeds in a passing-off action will also depend on how imaginative his own title is. The author of *Birds of the British Isles* could hardly complain if the same title was used by someone else, but if his book was called *Songsters of the Sceptred Isle* he would have a much better case. The protection of the passing-off principle is particularly valuable to publishers of periodicals, multi-volume works and individual volumes published under the same series title.

Ideas and information cannot be owned like a copyright because in themselves they cannot exist in a material form.[p. 17] The person who, for instance, contributes an idea for an advertisement, proposes the subject for a book, or tells his life story to a journalist, has no copyright grounds for claiming remuneration or demanding alterations unless he has come to an agreement with the author covering these points. For provisions about the recording of spoken words (such as interviews) for reporting current events see page 115.

In general, anyone may use published ideas and facts provided he does not copy[p. 52] the wording in which they are expressed, but the detailed information in compilations like guidebooks may not be copied wholesale, as the skill and labour expended by the original author have been held to be protected by the law of copyright. In such cases the second writer is expected to check all facts again at source. (For database use see page 138.)

Synopses, precis and **digests** are not infringements of copyright as long as they describe only ideas and information and do not use extracts from the original text, but plainly the distinction between a permissible synopsis and the actionable infringement of an author's original arrangement is a delicate one.

To **communicate** ideas or information may, however, be a **breach of contract, breach of confidence**[p. 57]or illegal under the Official Secrets Act. The communication or publication by an employee of his employer's secrets or the conduct of his employer's business will be a breach of confidence or contract, though the employee is entitled to use his accumulated trade know-how for his own purposes. To disclose the contents of a letter, an unpublished manuscript or an unpublished scientific paper, or any similar communication of information given confidentially, is to commit a breach of confidence.

Plots in works of fiction, and the **development of the argument** in non-fiction, are in general unprotected by copyright for the same reasons as ideas. To describe the mere outline of a plot or argument is permissible as long as doing so is not a breach of confidence. An argument may be reproduced in detail if the actual language is not copied or paraphrased. But with plots there is a line beyond which an action for infringement may succeed. Even when no single phrase is the same, a court will take into account how far the individual incidents and characters, and the dramatic development as a whole, are reproduced in the construction of another work.

Advertising slogans are considered to be unprotected by copyright for the same reasons as titles. (But for advertising copy see page 21.)

Fictitious names are not copyright but may be protectable under the law on passing off.[p. 98]

Characters like James Bond are in an awkward position. The Whitford Report (para. 909) rejected the proposal to introduce a 'character right', noting that 'there would be a very real difficulty in defining exactly what a "character" is, i.e. in deciding what are the essential features that make the character distinctive and which are therefore worthy of protection'. Characters are protectable by and large 'against reproduction of the literary or artistic form' but two members of the Committee felt that 'there should be the possibility of an action for infringement without having to identify any particular artistic representation as having been copied'.

No character right was introduced in the 1988 Act although some characters are now registered as trade marks (see below).

A useful discussion of the problems involved in protecting characters is given in *A User's Guide to Copyright* by Michael Flint (see *Bibliography*).

Prequels, sequels and **spin-offs** may well give rise to an action for passing off [p. 98] or infringement of the copyright in the original work, and great care should be taken if you are writing a work that derives from one that is protected by copyright.

Registered Trade Marks

It is not within the scope of this book to give coverage of the complex subject of trade marks but the following general comments may be useful.

A Patent Office leaflet *Basic Facts: Registered Trade and Service Marks*** describes a trade mark as 'an identification symbol which is used in the course of trade to enable the purchasing public to distinguish one trader's goods from the similar goods of other traders'. At the time of writing, there are discussions within the European Community about introducing a 'Euromark', but at present the laws governing trade marks are the Trade Marks Act 1938 and the Trade Marks (Amendment) Act 1984.

Trade mark protection is given for specific classes of goods (of which there are 34, including 'paper and printed matter') and service mark protection for specific services (of which there are eight, including 'education and entertainment'). It is an infringement of the trade mark to make unlawful use of it within the class for which it was registered – but only if you are using it as a trade mark yourself. It would be a defence to show that the word had become generic (for instance, if it has a generic definition in the Oxford English Dictionary). To be registered as a trade mark, the identification symbol (written or designed) must be distinctive. The Patent Office booklet says that it is not possible to register a trade mark 'which consists of, or is confusable with, words and/or the symbols which other traders may reasonably want to use in the course of business' nor one 'which would be likely to confuse or deceive the public about the nature of the goods'. There must be some evidence that, when the mark is used, the public associates the goods with the manufacturer, and the mark must actively be used (it is not enough for it only to be registered).

Individual book titles have generally been held not to be registerable although some series titles (such as 'Grove' music directories) are trade marks. Characters, illustrations and even a signature have been registered as trade marks, but qualification varies very much according to the individual circumstances. A useful discussion of

---

* This and a more extensive booklet *Registering a Trade or Service Mark* are available from the Marketing and Publicity Unit, the Patent Office, Cardiff Road, Newport, Gwent NP9 1RH.

trade marks is given in *Intellectual Property* by David Bainbridge (see *Bibliography*).

---

24 **The Author's Name**

The name used by the author of a Literary, Dramatic, Musical or Artistic work may be his own, or a pseudonym, or initials representing either.

There is no copyright in an author's name and no means of registering it, but when necessary his name can be defended as his own property via the principle of 'passing off' or the Act's provisions about false attribution of authorship,[p. 104] and his right to have his own name appear on his own work can be defended by an action for malicious falsehood.

The introduction in the 1988 Act of **moral rights** clarified the law considerably, ensuring that an author can insist on his name appearing on his own work and prevent the work being altered to the detriment of his reputation. (See page 100.)

Passing Off

If A is an established author and B writes a book under the same name as A, with the intention *and* effect of deceiving the public, A can apply for an injunction against B's work on the grounds that B is passing himself off as A.

For a passing-off action to succeed there must also be some reason why a reader should mistake B's work for A's. So the author who sues must have acquired a prior reputation under the name in question, and the two authors must share a common field of activity – e.g. both must be historical novelists or writers of popular songs. (It has been held that rights in a pseudonym established on a radio programme were not infringed by the use of the same name on a breakfast cereal.) A similarity of format can also be taken into account – for instance, if a book by B is published with a jacket closely resembling those regularly used on A's books.

A special situation is that of the newspaper or magazine columnist who makes his reputation under a pseudonym. It has been held that, in the absence of a specific agreement to the contrary, the columnist will have the exclusive right to continue using the pseudonym if he stops writing for the periodical, and he can prevent the periodical using it over the work of some other writer.

Malicious Falsehood

An author's work might in rare circumstances be published under someone else's name, without the author's consent. One means of redress in this situation would be an action under the Defamation Act for malicious falsehood: a difficult legal concept where he must be able to prove not only damage to his reputation but 'malice' on the part of the offender (the act could also be a breach of contract or an infringement of moral rights[p. 104]). The courts have interpreted 'malice' very variously, from its common usage to a simple intention to deceive the public. An action can be brought whether or not the author still owns the copyright, but only during his lifetime.

Choosing a Pseudonym

The best name for an author to put on his work is his own. Correspondence and other records tying a real name to a pseudonym are easily lost; memories are short except for the most famous names. If an author cannot be traced he cannot be consulted about the quotation or other use of his existing work, and if any money falls due to him he will not receive it. The term of copyright protection for a pseudonymous work whose author is untraceable is shorter than usual.[p. 41] Minor problems may arise over the wording of the copyright line[p. 161] on a pseudonymous work.

In any case, before committing himself to a particular pseudonym an author would do well to recall the law on passing off and check the index of a big library for any previous use of the same name by someone else.

Sometimes of course there is a real need for a pseudonym. An author who writes both scholarly works and lurid thrillers may not want to put the same name on both; an author's real name may resemble or be identical to that of an established author, or his real name may be unsuitable for the material he writes. In these cases a line of communication can be kept open by ensuring that the copyright line[p. 157] carries his real name.

If it is essential to conceal his true identity an author must employ cloak-and-dagger tactics. He must not only write under a pseudonym but ensure that his connection with it is unknown. He must remember that the publishing business thrives on gossip and that publishing firms do not necessarily instil the virtues of secrecy into their staff. Even institutions like banks are not proof against deliberate attempts to acquire information. The last and greatest stumbling-block will be the tax man.

25 **Moral Rights**

Article 6 *bis* of the Berne Copyright Convention requires that, independently of his copyright or 'economic rights' and *even after the transfer of those rights*, an author should have the right to claim authorship of his work and to object to any distortion, mutilation, modification or other 'derogatory' action in relation to his work which would be prejudicial to his honour or reputation. The 1988 Act introduced three moral rights into UK copyright law for the first time, in addition to the right to object to false attribution of an author's work, which already existed (in slightly different form) under the 1956 Act.

Other than the right of an author not to have work falsely attributed to him, moral rights do not apply to anything done before 1 August 1989, nor to any Literary, Dramatic, Musical or Artistic work where the author died before then, or to any film made before then. They do not apply to anything done under an assignment of copyright or licence granted before 1 August 1989 and they do not apply to anything to which the person entitled to the right has consented.

1. The Right of 'Paternity'

This is the right to be identified as the author of a Literary, Dramatic, Musical or Artistic work or any part of or adaptation of such a work. The right extends to a translator (who is the author of the translation as an adaptation of a Literary or Dramatic work) and the director of a film (who is not necessarily the same as the 'author' for the purposes of determining the first owner of copyright in a film).

The author or director has the right to be identified whenever his work is published commercially (including by means of an electronic retrieval system); performed, shown or exhibited in public; broadcast or included in a cable programme service; or included in a film or sound recording that is issued to the public.

The authors of works of architecture, sculpture and works of artistic craftsmanship[p. 171] also have the right to be identified on the original as well as in graphic works[p. 170] or photographs of their work that are issued to the public.

The identification can be in the form of a pseudonym, initials or 'any reasonable form of identification' if the author prefers. It should appear on every copy of a Literary, Dramatic, Musical or Artistic work and the identification must be clear and reasonably prominent.

A tiresome formality is that the right of paternity must be 'asserted by the author'. No particular form of words is required, but the assertion must be in writing. The Society of Authors and the Publishers Association recommend that assertion take the form of a clause in the publishing contract:

> The Author asserts his/her moral right to be identified as the Author of the work in relation to all such rights as are granted by the Author to the Publisher under the terms and conditions of this Agreement.
>
> The Publisher hereby undertakes:
> – to print on the verso title page of every copy of every edition of the work published by him/her in the United Kingdom the words 'the right of [the author] to be identified as author of this work has been asserted by him/her in accordance with the Copyright, Designs and Patents Act 1988'
> – to make it a condition of contract with any licensee concerning any edition of the work to be published in the United Kingdom that a notice of assertion in the same terms as above shall be printed in every edition published by such licensee
> – to set the name of the author in customary form with due prominence on the title page and on the binding, jacket and/or cover of every copy of the work published by it and to make it a condition of contract that a similar undertaking is made in respect of any editions of the work licensed by it.

Where Artistic works are publicly exhibited, the Act says that assertion should take the form of identification of the author 'on the original or copy, or on a frame, mount or other thing to which it is attached' or by a written statement by the author that he asserts the right to be identified if the copy is exhibited in public.

EXCEPTIONS TO THE RIGHT OF PATERNITY

The right of paternity does not apply:

(a) to any use where acknowledgement is not necessary (see page 54): reporting current events by means of a sound recording, broadcast or cable programme; incidental inclusion in an Artistic work, sound recording, film, broadcast or cable programme;[p. 121] public administration;[p. 55] in the use of design documents or models;[p. 178] where an Artistic work is copied by making articles of any description after 25 years from when authorized articles are first made by an industrial process and marketed;[p. 180] where the work is anonymous or pseudonymous and the author is unknown;

(b) to anything done with the consent of the owner of the copyright (whether that is the author or his employer);

(c) to works in which the copyright belongs to the Crown, Parliament or a recognized international organization;

(d) where the work is published in a newspaper, magazine or similar periodical;

(e) where the work is published in an encyclopedia, dictionary, yearbook or other collective work of reference;

(f) to any work made for the reporting of current events;

(g) to computer programs, computer-generated work or the design of a typeface.

2. The Right of 'Integrity'

The author of a Literary, Dramatic, Musical or Artistic work, or the director of a film, has the right to object to 'derogatory treatment' of his work. 'Treatment' is defined as 'any addition to, deletion from, or alteration to or adaptation of the work' (other than a translation or, in the case of Musical works, a change of key or register). Treatment is derogatory if it amounts to 'distortion or mutilation of the work or is otherwise prejudicial to the honour or reputation of the author or director'. This right does not have to be asserted.

The right of integrity is infringed if a derogatory treatment of a copyright work, or part of a work, is published commercially; performed, shown or exhibited in public; broadcast, or included in a cable programme service; or if copies of a film or sound recording of, or including, a derogatory treatment of a work are issued to the public. The right of integrity is also infringed if a graphic work [p. 170] or photograph of a derogatory treatment of the model for a building, a sculpture or a work of artistic craftsmanship [p. 171] is published.

The extent to which a work can be altered before the 'treatment' is 'derogatory' has yet to be tested in the courts. However, it does seem that, as far as copy-editing is concerned, a work would probably have to be savaged or given an unwarranted bias before the treatment could be said to be 'derogatory'. Less excessive editing could still, however, be a breach of copyright or contract. The people most likely to have their right of integrity infringed are film directors and visual artists (for example, if a character has been airbrushed out of a photograph). The derogatory treatment must be of the author's work. It is not certain, for example, that the inclusion within the text of inappropriate or bad illustrations would be an infringement. While cropping or other alteration of an Artistic work probably would be an infringement of the right of integrity, it seems that the total destruction of a work of art by its owner would not.

EXCEPTIONS TO THE RIGHT OF INTEGRITY

The right of integrity does not apply:

> in the instances listed at (b) and (c) above for the right of paternity – even if the author is identified, as long as in that case there is a disclaimer that the author had not consented to the act;
> in any of the instances listed at (d), (e) and (f) above – or to any subsequent use of the unmodified version of the work as already published;
> as listed at (g) above;
> to changes made for the purposes of avoiding the commission of an offence (e.g. altering libellous text);

to changes made to comply with a duty imposed by or under an enactment;

in the case of the BBC, if alterations are made to avoid the inclusion of 'anything which offends against good taste or decency or which is likely to encourage or incite to crime or to lead to disorder or to be offensive to public feeling'.

3. False Attribution of Authorship

This moral right resembles the law of passing off but is differently angled in its application. It applies to anyone – not just established authors and directors. A broadly similar right existed under the 1956 Act.

A person has the right not to have a Literary, Dramatic, Musical or Artistic work, or a part or adaptation of it, falsely attributed to him and a director has the right not to have any part of a film falsely attributed to him. False attribution means any statement, express or implied, as to who is the author or director, and includes false representation that a copy or altered version of an Artistic work (e.g. perhaps a coloured version of a black and white picture) is by the artist.

The right not to have work falsely attributed applies when a work is published, performed, shown or exhibited in public, or when material containing the false attribution is issued to the public or publicly displayed.

An author may also be able to make a claim for passing off,[p. 98] libel and/or breach of contract if a work has been falsely attributed to him.

4. The Right of Privacy in Certain Films and Photographs

Since 1 August 1989, the copyright in a commissioned film or photograph belongs to the person taking the film or picture, unless there is an agreement to the contrary. However, anyone who commissions a film or photograph for private and domestic purposes has a right of privacy in it. (See page 177.)

Assignment and Waiver

Moral rights are **not assignable** but it is possible to **waive** them. Publishers may sometimes want to seek a limited waiver of the right of integrity so that, for example, a condensed version of a book can be published without it being an infringement of the author's moral rights. A waiver must be in writing. It might be related to a specific use of the work and it can be conditional or subject to revocation. Film companies almost always insist on waivers, but in general publishers have not found it necessary to seek a waiver of moral rights, which are really no more than an extension of good publishing practice.

Where a work is made by more than one author, each joint author must assert and/or waive his moral rights individually.

Duration

The moral rights of paternity, integrity and privacy last for as long as copyright subsists in the work (and belong to the author whether or not he has assigned his copyright to someone else). The right to object to false attribution of authorship lasts until 20 years from the end of the year in which the author dies. While moral rights cannot be assigned, the rights of paternity, integrity and privacy can be willed to another person or organization on the author's death. If there are no specific instructions to the contrary in the author's will, his moral rights will pass to the inheritor of his copyright.[p. 188] The right not to have work falsely attributed is, after the death of an author, enforceable by his personal representatives.

26 The Publisher's Copyright in His Typography

The publisher's permission must be obtained before making a facsimile of any substantial part[p. 45] of the typographical arrangement of a published edition 'by any photographic or similar process' except in the ways listed in Chapter 11.* This includes copies which are enlarged or reduced in scale. Typographical arrangement means the design, layout and typeface on a printed page. The material printed may be any number or combination of Literary, Dramatic or Musical works. Individual illustrations are not part of the typographical arrangement and may be photographed from any edition as long as the necessary permission has been obtained from the owners of the original.[p. 182]

The Act's provisions were designed mainly to protect the originating publisher against other publishers who might offset from his edition without paying for the privilege. However, the principle is also applicable to individual photocopying, and there is a special exemption for libraries, which are allowed to copy copyright typography without permission when their copying is otherwise legal.[p. 58] Under CLA photocopying licences,[p. 64] the payment of the licence fee covers the copyright in both the wording and the typography.

A publisher can only claim the protection of the typographical copyright for his edition if (a) the edition was first published[p. 27] in the UK or elsewhere in the British sphere[p. 8] OR its publisher was a qualified person[p. 23] at the date of its first publication, and if (b) the edition was first published[p. 27] on or after 1 June 1957. An edition which contains the same work and the same typographical format as one published before that date is not protected.

A typographical copyright lasts for 25 years from the end of the calendar year in which the edition containing the arrangement was first published. The copyright is owned by the publisher (who may be an individual or a company) and is independent of the copyright in the work reproduced: ownership of one constitutes no claim to ownership of the other. The typography is protected whether the work itself is in or out of copyright.

Note that a publisher is only protected against quick-and-easy reproduction. Anyone may 'copy' a style of arrangement as long as he expends as much care and labour on his edition as the first publisher spent on his – provided of course that there is no intention of passing off.[p. 98]

When a work is in the public domain and can therefore be

---

*There appears to be no similar restriction under United States law.

published by anybody, typographical copyright is a valuable protection: a publisher can go to the expense of designing a good-looking book with the assurance that (piracy apart) no competitor can undersell him with an edition cheaply photographed from his own. (See also *Europe*, page 205.)

If a publisher does allow his typography to be photographed for any reason he is entitled to charge an appropriate fee.

Typefaces

The design of a typeface is an Artistic work. However, it is not an infringement of the copyright in that Artistic work to use the typeface in the ordinary course of typing, composing text, typesetting or printing, nor to do anything in relation to material produced by such use. Where an article (e.g. a mechanical or laser printer) is specifically designed or adapted for producing material in a particular typeface, copyright in that typeface is not infringed by the making, selling or hiring of other articles 25 years from the end of the year in which the article was first marketed. Where such an article was first marketed before 1 August 1989, it is protected until and including 31 December 2039.

27 Collective Licensing

Ideally, every time a copyright work is used its owner should receive a reasonable sum, the exact amount of which is negotiated direct with the user. Sometimes, however, this is impossible, and the areas in which it is impossible have expanded enormously in recent years.

Collective licensing seems to be the only practicable means of enforcing, or partially enforcing, the claims of copyright owners in cases where, for instance, each individual infringement is itself very small (as with photocopying), or undetectable (audio and video taping in the home) or just prohibitively cumbersome to sort out. There is of course the huge problem of outright piracy, but by definition no licensing schemes can help there (except by adding one more truncheon to our legal armoury); they are of most use where copyright is infringed by more or less well-intentioned people who have no easy legal alternative.

There may also be a long and complex chain of copying, coding, broadcasting or rebroadcasting between the original author and the person who ultimately sees or reads his work, and in these circumstances it would be extremely difficult to enforce rights by way of a chain of contracts of the traditional kind. (We have enough trouble even keeping track of what happens when there are only two or three contracts between the author and the final publisher within the same media, e.g. when the author's original publisher sublicenses a paperback.) It is in this sort of situation that collective licensing, and/or the monitoring of material at the point of 'reception', really comes into its own.

Very generally, collective licensing works like this: a group of copyright owners, whose works are used in similar ways, set up a licensing, collecting and distributing society to act as their agent. As members of the society they may pay a regular subscription, though the society itself is non-profit-making. The society identifies distinct areas in which its members' works are used but where normal contracts are difficult to arrange or enforce – for instance, the playing of records in jukeboxes or the photocopying of texts in schools.

The society then negotiates with the users (jukebox operators or education authorities) and establishes an annual fee, on payment of which the user has permission to use any work by any registered member of the society without further bother – thus relieving the user and the copyright owner of the legal and commercial necessity, but practical impossibility, of correspondence and bargaining over each seperate use.

For collective licensing to work properly all or nearly all copyright owners in a given field need to join as members of the licensing body. Sometimes the licensees are expected to keep records of the works they use; sometimes a sampling procedure has to be instituted to discover whose works are in fact being copied so as to distribute the fees equitably after they have been received. Licensees (and non-licensees) must be monitored to make sure all is proceeding correctly. And, of course, it is essential that the users of the copyright material agree to be licensed in the first place. These four areas involve the most complex considerations, and even in countries where licensing agencies are backed up by the force of law their experiences have not been by any means straightforward.

A **licensing body** is defined by the Act as 'a society or other organisation which has as its main object, or one of its main objects, the negotiation or granting, either as owner or prospective owner of copyright or as agent for him, of copyright licences, and whose objects include the granting of licences covering works of more than one author'. Licensing bodies may either provide separate licences to individual users or closed-membership groups, or operate licences or a licensing scheme for broad categories of use.

An alternative to collective licensing is a levy at source on the hardware, where the manufacturer or retailer pays an agreed or specified fee per machine sold (as with Germany which has statutory royalty schemes for audio and video recording equipment and for reprographic equipment). Another variation is for government funding to provide the 'fee' (as with Sweden's library photocopying arrangements and our own Public Lending Right). There is of course nothing to stop the three approaches being mixed.

Schemes of this kind are generally subject to government control of fees and terms, approval of the licensing bodies and arbitration between them and their licensees. The statutory body overseeing licensing bodies under the present UK Act is the Copyright Tribunal.

Collecting and distributing societies link up with other similar organizations in other countries and eventually, if they are viable, they form international networks through which permissions and fees flow relatively easily. Since the societies can usually deal only with each other, for administrative or legal reasons, the establishment of a society in your own country is a prerequisite for collecting money available to your own nationals through societies abroad.

Library lending, which in the UK is a maverick category outside copyright law, has been dealt with by the Public Lending Right Act.[p. 140]

The Rental Right

The Act provides that if specified by the Secretary of State, or under a licensing scheme, the rental of sound recordings, films and computer programs is permitted – subject to a reasonable royalty or other payment being made to the copyright holder.

There is a European Directive on rental and lending rights as described on page 205.

The Copyright Tribunal

The statutory body overseeing the long-established performing rights societies was the Performing Right Tribunal. Under the 1988 Act the Tribunal was replaced by the Copyright Tribunal, with limited power in relation to performers but with greatly extended powers over licensing schemes to prevent licensing bodies abusing what is becoming a potential monopoly in their dealings with licensees. The Act describes the Tribunal and its powers in great detail and devotes the whole of Chapter VIII to it.

The Copyright Tribunal is empowered to confirm or vary proposed licensing schemes, and to arbitrate in disputes arising over existing licensing schemes. It also has control over the licensing of copyright works in other areas (schemes for reprographic copying by educational establishments, the rental right in respect of sound recordings, films and computer programs) and determines the royalty payable to the Hospital for Sick Children at Great Ormond Street for *Peter Pan*.[p. 81]

A pamphlet giving clear and concise information on the complicated and extensive provisions in the Act for the Copyright Tribunal is available from the British Copyright Council.*

Organizations Engaged in Collective Licensing

The Authors' Licensing and Collecting Society (ALCS), 33 Alfred Place, London WC1E 9DP. The ALCS represents writers (some subscribe individually; members of the Society of Authors and the Writers' Guild of Great Britain are automatically members) where their interests are best (or can only be) administered collectively. At present, the ALCS collects money for its members from reprography; retransmission by cable; Public Lending Right from countries with which the UK has reciprocal arrangements; off-air and private recording (through ERA); and, through agreements with overseas societies, fees from rental, private copying and public reception of broadcasts.

The Publishers Licensing Society (PLS), 90 Tottenham Court Road, London W1P 9HE. PLS administers rights for publishers where they can only be exercised collectively (for example, collecting

---

* *The Law of Copyright and Rights in Performances* by Denis de Freitas.[p. 222]

and distributing income from the licensing of reprography through CLA).

The Copyright Licensing Agency (CLA), 90 Tottenham Court Road, London W1P 9HE. The CLA is a licensing body, formed in 1982 and owned by the ALCS and PLS. It licenses copying in the UK from books, journals and periodicals (but not music or newspapers). Since its formation the CLA has collected and redistributed, through ALCS and PLS, more than £10m to individual rights owners.

The Design and Artists' Copyright Society (DACS), St Mary's Clergy House, 2 Whitechurch Lane, London E1 7QR. DACS represents visual artists and licenses use of their work in any medium.

The Educational Recording Agency (ERA), c/o 33 Alfred Place, London WC1E 7DP. ERA represents the interests of the ALCS, DACS, MCPS and the British Phonographic Industry Ltd as well as the BBC, Channel 4, S4C, the Independent Television Association, Equity and the Musicians' Union. It issues licences to educational establishments for the off-air recording of broadcasts and cable programmes for purposes of educational instruction. These came into effect on 30 May 1990 and cover all broadcasts except those by the Open University, which licenses the recording of its own programmes.

Other licensing organizations in the UK are:

The International Federation of Phonographic Industries (IFPI), 54 Regent Street, London W1R 5PJ. IFPI licenses the performance, broadcasting and cable distribution of certain (mainly foreign) sound recordings.[p. 122]

The Mechanical Copyright Protection Society (MCPS), Elgar House, 41 Streatham High Road, London SW16 1ER. MCPS represents composers, authors and publishers of music and licenses use of their work as far as the original recording of it is concerned (e.g. by recording companies, radio and TV, film and video companies).

The Performing Right Society (PRS), 29/33 Berners Street, London W1P 4AA. PRS represents composers, lyricists and music publishers with respect to performing music, either live or by playing a recording (on a record or CD, or via TV or radio).[p. 113]

Phonographic Performance Ltd (PPL), Ganton House 14–22 Ganton Street, London W1V 1LB. PPL licenses the public performance, broadcasting and cable distribution of sound recordings.[p. 114]

Video Performance Ltd (VPL), Ganton House, 14–22 Ganton Street, London W1V 1LB. VPL licenses the public performance, broadcasting and cable distribution of music video recordings.

28 **Performance**

Performance is one of the Acts Restricted by the Copyright in all Literary, Dramatic and Musical works. No one may perform a substantial part[p. 45] of any such work (or an adaptation of one) in public without permission from the copyright owner, except in the special cases mentioned below.

The Act reminds us that, in addition to acting on a stage, 'performance' includes 'delivery in the case of lectures, addresses, speeches and sermons', and 'in general includes any mode of visual or acoustic presentation, including presentation by means of a sound recording, film, broadcast or cable programme of the work'.

Literary works can only be performed by 'straight reading' or 'delivery' – direct to an audience or via television, radio, records, tapes or films. Any other performance of a written work presupposes that it is in or has been adapted into a dramatic form.

It is only necessary to obtain permission to perform a work if the performance is given 'in public' – which means *anywhere* outside the domestic circle. Performance anywhere else (whether live or through the media of television, radio, sound recordings, films or videos) – even including private clubs, and certainly including hotels and shops – needs permission. The owner of the premises or the promoter of the entertainment should apply; it is not up to the performers themselves to do so.

The possession or purchase of a musical score, TV or radio set, sound recording or dramatic script does not by itself entitle its owner to perform the work it contains in public. Separate permission must always be obtained.

Indirect infringements of this right are similar to those described on page 48.

The Act permits the public performance of a substantial part of a work without permission in a few special cases, as follows:

1. 'The reading or recitation in public by one person of a reasonable extract from a published literary or dramatic work', if accompanied by a sufficient acknowledgement.[p. 85]
2. The making of a sound recording, or the broadcast or inclusion in a cable programme service, of such reading or

recitation provided the recording, broadcast or cable programme consists mainly of material which does not rely on that reading or recitation.

3. 'Fair dealing with a work for the purpose of criticism or review, of that or another work or of a performance of a work', if accompanied by sufficient acknowledgement.

4. Fair dealing with a work (other than a photograph) for the purpose of reporting current events, if accompanied by sufficient acknowledgement (if by means of a sound recording, film, broadcast or cable programme, acknowledgement is not necessary).

5. The incidental inclusion of a public performance in a sound recording, film, broadcast or cable programme.[p. 121]

6. The performance of a Literary, Dramatic or Musical work before an audience consisting of teachers and pupils at an educational establishment[p. 60] and of other people directly connected with the establishment. (The performance must be by a teacher or pupil in the course of the activities of the establishment or by any person as long as it is for the purposes of instruction at the establishment.)

    The Act clearly says that 'A person is not for this purpose directly connected with the activities of the educational establishment simply because he is the parent of a pupil at the establishment'. So performances in the course of an ordinary class, or given by one class to another, are permissible without limit. But a performance given by a visiting celebrity, or productions attended by friends and parents, are not privileged.

Obtaining Permission for a Performance

Permission for public performances can often be obtained direct from the author or publisher, but Musical works are generally handled by the Performing Right Society.* The PRS can grant licences for specific works but its invaluable function is as a licensing body[p. 112] which represents 'virtually all British and Irish composers, authors and music publishers whose works are publicly performed

---

* 29/33 Berners Street, London W1P 4AA. The quotations in this section are from a booklet issued by the Society, *What Is PRS?* See also page 115.

to any appreciable extent' and which also represents the interests of 'more than 700,000' foreign musical copyright owners either directly or through its reciprocal links with similar organizations all over the world. The PRS is concerned only with 'non-dramatic performances of musical works (including lyrics or other literary works when set to music)', and sometimes with music specially written for the soundtrack of a film (the 'synchronization right') but not with music played in conjunction with acting, dancing and so on.

Where music is performed in the UK via the medium of a sound recording a licence may also have to be obtained from Phonographic Performance Ltd.[p. 111]

The Copyright Tribunal[p. 115]

The terms set by the PRS and PPL and other licensing bodies are subject to the scrutiny of the Copyright Tribunal, which has replaced the Performing Right Tribunal. When a case is brought before it (but not otherwise) the Tribunal has power to confirm or vary the prices and other terms fixed by licensing bodies (but not by individuals) for the public performance of Literary, Dramatic and Musical works, television and radio programmes and sound recordings, originating within the UK or abroad.

Performers' Rights

Under the 1988 Act, qualifying performers have a civil right of action when performances in which they have an interest are used in various ways without their consent. This right is separate from and in addition to any restrictions imposed by copyright. It is known as the Performer's Right and restricts the doing of the following acts, unless with the performer's agreement:

1. Making a recording of the performance.
2. Broadcasting the performance live or including it in a cable programme service.
3. Using an unauthorized recording to broadcast, distribute by cable or give a public performance of the performer's work.
4. Importing or trading in unauthorized recordings.

Film and record producers who have recording rights have a similar right of action when recordings in which they have an interest are used in various ways. Their permission is necessary before (1) a recording is made of a performance; (2) the recording is presented in public, broadcast or included in a cable programme service; or (3) unauthorized copies are imported or traded.

The performers' and recording rights last until 50 years from the end of the calendar year in which the performance took place (but see also page 203). There are a large number of exceptions, and some useful information on performers' rights is given in *The Law of Copyright and Rights in Performances* by Denis de Freitas (see *Bibliography*).

Interviews

The restricted act of 'performance' covers 'any mode of acoustic presentation' and includes recording the spoken word, whether or not the record is made with the permission of the speaker. Since 1 August 1989, it is the person speaking, rather than the one writing down or recording the words, who is the owner of the copyright in the words as a Literary work.[p. 11] However, the Act makes special provision in the case of interviews given for the purpose of reporting current events. It is not an infringement of the copyright in the record of such words (in writing, on tape or video film, etc.) to use any material taken from it for the purpose of reporting current events – and the material may also be broadcast or included in a cable programme service – as long as four conditions are met:

> '(a) the record is a direct record of the spoken words and is not taken from a previous record or from a broadcast or cable programme;
>
> (b) the making of the record was not prohibited by the speaker and, where copyright already subsisted in the work, did not infringe copyright;
>
> (c) the use made of the record or material taken from it is not of a kind prohibited by or on behalf of the speaker or copyright owner before the record was made; and
>
> (d) the use is by or with the authority of a person who is lawfully in possession of the record.'

29 Dramatizing a Literary Work

No one may dramatize a substantial part[p. 45] of any Literary work without permission from the copyright owner except in the special cases listed below. Dramatization is one of the Acts Restricted by the Copyright in all Literary works and is one of the three so-called 'adaptations' (the others being translation and making a strip cartoon version of a work).

Dramatization is described by the Act as 'a version of . . . a non-dramatic work in which it is converted into a dramatic work'. A Dramatic work will normally be a play for performance in the live theatre, a script for a TV or radio programme, a screenplay for a film (or video), a work of dance or mime, or words associated with music. (See also page 14.)

A substantial part of a work may be dramatized without permission when the dramatization is (1) Fair Dealing[p. 45] for purposes of research or private study, (2) Fair Dealing for purposes of criticism or review, whether of that work or another work or a performance of a work, if accompanied by sufficient acknowledgement, (3) Fair Dealing for the purpose of reporting current events if accompanied by sufficient acknowledgement (if by means of a sound recording, film, broadcast or cable programme acknowledgement is not necessary), (4) in the course of educational instruction or for the purposes of an examination.

The term 'dramatic rights' used in publishers' contracts does not unfortunately carry the same connotation as the term 'Dramatic work' used in the Act. Dramatic *rights* are, or should be, confined to the preparation of a play for, and the performance of it on, a theatre stage. Much unnecessary worry has been caused by this confusion and the resulting failure of people to define their terms when granting rights.

It is theoretically quite possible to grant to X the right to adapt a novel, say, into a stage-play plus the right to perform the play on the stage (dramatic rights) while granting to Y the right to adapt the same novel into a television script for performance on television (television rights) and similarly with dramatic adaptations for radio and film. In a case where the dramatic rights (play plus stage performance) have been granted to a playwright, and a television company then comes along and wants to perform his play on television, the company must apply back to the copyright owner for the television rights as well.

When granting someone the right to dramatize a Literary work one must therefore specify which or how many of the possible types of Dramatic work he will be permitted to make. One must also specify whether *or not* he has the right to reproduce his dramatization in volume form – and if he has, what payment is due to the original copyright proprietor on such an edition. (Volume rights cannot of course normally be granted in such a case without the consent of the publisher of the original Literary work.)

Once a Literary work has been dramatized, the resulting dramatization is entitled to a new and separate copyright of its own, and becomes subject to all the rules given throughout this book for Dramatic works.

---

30 **Translation**

Translation is one of the Acts Restricted by the Copyright in all Literary and Dramatic works and is one of the three so-called 'adaptations' (the others being dramatization of a non-dramatic work or the reverse, and making a strip cartoon version of the work). However, because of its results, translation is not really comparable to other restricted acts, and attempts to treat it like the others only cause difficulties.

It is more realistic to take a different approach and to think of any written work as potentially existing in every known language, each language having its own separate and complete set of Acts Restricted by the Copyright (reproduction, publication, performance, etc.) and sales packages (book rights, television rights, etc.). The work of the translator then becomes merely the necessary bridge between languages.

Seen from this point of view language is a limitation on the grant of a copyright exactly equivalent to the limitations by time and by territory. Indeed, the three appear together in most publishing agreements, where rights are granted, for instance, 'in all languages throughout the world for the legal term of copyright in the Work'.

No one may translate a substantial part of any copyright Literary or Dramatic work without the permission of the copyright owner, except in the course of educational instruction,[p. 62] in examinations, or when a compulsory licence[p. 68] is granted.

In many ways a translation is quite separate from the work on which it is based. It is a new work (Literary or Dramatic) and is entitled to its own new copyright, regardless of the copyright status of the original. It qualifies for copyright protection, or does not, entirely on its own. The translator is the legal author; publication of a translation does not constitute publication of its original and vice versa. The copyright term for a translation is computed in the same way as the term for completely original works. A translator is also entitled to the same moral rights[p. 100] as any other author of a Literary or Dramatic work.

However, translations can never completely sever their connection with the parent original. Anyone wishing to use a substantial part of a translation must be sure that he has permission not only from the owner of the copyright in the translation, but also from the owner of the copyright in the original. He may have to approach both owners, but in some cases the owner of the translation will have a licence from the original owner to sublease some or all rights.

Suppose a French publisher wishes to publish a French translation of a book first written in English. He must of course get permission to make the translation itself, from the owner of the copyright in the English book, but he cannot use his translation in any way until he has also been granted an appropriate part of the complete copyright vested in the English owner. So a translation agreement* will convey the basic right to print, publish and sell the book in the French language. (If it does not also, for instance, convey the right to televise the book in French, the French publisher cannot sell television rights in his translation.)

The French publisher then engages someone to translate the book into French, and the copyright in this translation is and remains the property of the French translator (or his publisher). Translation agreements are often of short duration. When all rights

---

*Forms for agreements with foreign-language publishers and translators, and a discussion of the 1976 UNESCO recommendation for upgrading the status and earnings of translators, appear in *Publishing Agreements* by Charles Clark (see *Bibliography*). See also *Composing a Contract* on page 190.

in our imaginary French translation revert to the English owner the physical translation will still exist, but no one will legally be able to use it.

If our English owner has previously sold French translation rights to someone else, he *must* give the new publisher notice of all the details before signing a new contract. (The new publisher may find it worth his while to buy or lease the previous translation from its first owner.) Subject to this essential notice there is, theoretically, nothing to prevent an infinite number of French translations being made as long as our English owner has retained or regained the legal right to license each one. Each such translation would be entitled to its own separate copyright.

When a work is translated into more than one foreign language the copyright situation for each version is totally separate. You can, for instance, lease identical rights to German and French publishers with the sole difference that the rights are granted in the German language only in one case and French only in the other.

Before selling translation rights, check that any quotations and/or illustrations are yours to license. If they are not, the foreign publisher will have to pay permission fees all over again. Before buying translation rights a similar enquiry is very desirable.

It is customary – and common sense – for any translation to be made from the first, original work. A German publisher wishing to print a German edition of our English book would normally have it translated from the English, not from the existing French translation. Should it ever be desirable to translate a work which is itself a translation special permission to do so must be obtained from the copyright owner of the original.

31 **Adapting a Work to a Strip Cartoon**

Strip cartoons (or comic strips) are works, the Act says, 'in which the story or action is conveyed wholly or mainly by means of pictures in a form suitable for reproduction in a book, or in a newspaper, magazine or similar periodical'. The pictures are protectable as Artistic works (drawings or photographs as the case may be). The text is protectable as a Literary work.

Since 1 June 1957 making a strip cartoon version has been one of the Acts Restricted by the Copyright in all Literary and Dramatic works. It is one of the three restricted acts called 'adaptations' (the others being dramatization of a non-dramatic work or the reverse, and translation). It is now an infringement to base a strip cartoon (with or without words) on a substantial part of an existing Literary or Dramatic work without obtaining permission from the owner of the 'picturisation' rights – except when this is done in the course of educational instruction[p. 62] or for examinations or, presumably, if it falls within the special exceptions outlined on page 54.

For remarks on the protection of cartoon characters see page 96.

32 **Reproducing a Work as a Sound Recording**

Reproduction in any material form is one of the Acts Restricted by the Copyright in all works and one kind of material form is a sound recording.*

The Act defines 'sound recording' as '(a) a recording of sounds, from which the sounds may be reproduced, or (b) a recording of the whole or any part of a literary, dramatic or musical work, from which sounds reproducing the work or part may be produced, regardless of the medium on which the recording is made or the method by which the sounds are reproduced or produced.'

Soundtracks of films are not excluded from the definition (under the 1956 Act they were included in the copyright of the film) although a new copyright does not subsist in a sound recording that has been copied from a previous sound recording or film. A sound

---

*In practice the music and book publishing industries are almost totally separate. Much useful information from the music industry's point of view can be found in *Music Business Agreements* by Richard Baghot (see *Bibliography*).

recording can appear in the form of an LP or compact disk, as a master tape, an audio cassette, a dictaphone tape or disk, the audible part of an audio-visual package or film and so on. The recording of noises (for example, of birdsong) is included but the sounds have to have meaning to the human ear. A computer program, for example, on which a Literary work has been recorded but which it is not possible to play back with the sound meaning anything is not a 'sound recording'.

No one may reproduce a substantial part of any copyright work (or any adaptation of a copyright work) in sound recording form without the permission of the copyright owner except:

(1) for research or private study, criticism or review, or reporting current events, provided the reproduction is 'fair dealing'; [p. 45]
(2) if it is incidentally included in another sound recording, film, broadcast or cable programme. However, the Act emphasizes that 'A musical work, words spoken or sung with music, or so much of a sound recording, broadcast or cable programme as includes a musical work or such words, shall not be regarded as incidentally included in another work if it is deliberately included';
(3) for public administration; [p. 55]
(4) to enable an authorized broadcast to take place; [p. 126]
(5) in the course of or preparation for instruction or for exams (the rules are the same as those for written reproduction as far as they are applicable). [p. 62]

Statutory licence provisions permitting the re-recording of Musical works which had been recorded once already, on payment of a fixed royalty, were repealed by the 1988 Act. The Mechanical Copyright Protection Society (MCPS) [p. 111] is the licensing body for the recording of Musical works (but not for their transmission or subsequent reuse) as sound recordings or as part of a film, video, CD, cassette, audio-visual tape, broadcast, etc.

'Talking books' are records or tapes containing straight reading of texts. When made for use by the blind or handicapped they are usually licensed free of charge or for a nominal fee, but in such cases it is essential to ensure that the recording can only be played on special machines made for the handicapped and not on publicly available commerical machines. Other important con-tractual points are recommended by Charles Clark in *Publishing Agreements*. [p. 222]

A sound recording of **folksongs** (the words of which must be unpublished and of unknown authorship) may be made for archival purposes, as long as no other material on the recording – for example, any accompanying music – is in copyright.

Once a sound recording has been made it is entitled to a copyright of its own, separate from the work(s) it embodies and subject to different rules. These rules are outlined in the following chapter.

33 The Sound Recording as a Separate Subject of Copyright

Since 1 June 1957 sound recordings have been entitled to copyright protection quite separately from any copyright that may subsist in the Literary, Dramatic or Musical work they contain.* The actual sound need not in itself be a work protectable by copyright; a recording of birdsong qualifies equally with a symphony, but the sounds must have meaning to the human ear. The recording can be made by any method and in any medium. It is not within the scope of this book to treat sound recording copyright in detail, but the following outline of the present law may be useful.

A recording (published or unpublished) will **qualify for UK copyright protection** if its maker was a qualified person[p. 23] at the time the recording was made, or if it was made by an officer or servant of the Crown in the course of his duties or under the direction or control of Parliament. A published recording will also qualify for protection if its first authorized publication took place in acceptable territory.[p. 8] **Publication** is 'the issue to the public of records embodying the recording'.

The **author** of a sound recording is the person or organization by whom the arrangements necessary for the making of the recording

---

*Sound recordings are defined on page 120. The 1911 Act protected sound recordings but only 'in like manner as if such contrivances were musical works'.

are undertaken. The **first owner of the copyright** is the author unless he has made an agreement to the contrary, or he worked for the Crown or Parliament (when in the absence of an agreement to the contrary the recording will be Crown or Parliamentary copyright).

The situation was slightly different for sound recordings made or commissioned before 1 August 1989, when the first owner of the copyright was the 'maker' of the recording i.e. the person or firm owning the master record (the physical material) at the time that the recording was made. Copyright in sound recordings that were commissioned before 1 August 1989 belongs to the commissioner, even if the recordings were not actually made until after then.

The **term of protection** expires 50 years after the end of the calendar year in which the recording was made or, if it is released within that period, 50 years from the end of the year of authorized release (see also *Europe*, page 203). This applies equally to sound recordings that are Crown or Parliamentary copyright. The definition of 'release' is much wider than that of 'publication': it covers not only publication but also the authorized broadcasting of the sound recording or its inclusion in a cable programme service or, in the case of a film soundtrack, its first authorized playing to the public. The period of protection for a sound recording made between 1 June 1957 and 1 August 1989, and published before 1 August 1989, expires 50 years after the end of the calendar year in which the sound recording is published. Sound recordings existing but unpublished at 1 August 1989 are protected until 1 January 2040 or, if published (not released) before then, until 50 years from the end of the calendar year in which they were published. The copyright in a sound recording made before 1 June 1957 lasts until 50 years from the end of the calendar year in which it was made, whether or not it has been published (or released).

The **Acts Restricted by the Copyright** in a sound recording are:

(1) **Copying** the recording (including re-recording it or storing it by electronic means). The 1956 Act contained legally prescribed date mark conditions, but these were not repeated in the 1988 Act. (Note that the widespread practice of taping recordings at home – whether directly or from a broadcast – is strictly illegal unless done temporarily for time-shifting purposes; see below.)
(2) **Issuing copies of the recording to the public.**

(3) **Playing** a recording (or showing a film including a copyright soundtrack) in public.*

(4) **Broadcasting the recording or its inclusion in a cable programme service.*** However, the Act provides that 'the showing or playing in public of a broadcast or cable programme to an audience who have not paid for admission to the place where the broadcast or programme is to be seen or heard' does not infringe the copyright in any sound recording included in it.

(5) **Renting** a recording to the public.

Licences for the broadcasting and public performance of sound recordings are issued by Phonographic Performance Ltd.[p.111] When the recording contains copyright music a licence is also required from the Performing Right Society.[p.111]

As far as the performance of a recording constitutes the performance of the work it contains, it must also be exempt from infringement proceedings under the exceptions listed on page 112.

Indirect infringements are as listed on page 48 for Literary, Dramatic and Musical works.

Exceptions from protection, when the sound recording may be used without permission from the copyright owner, are:

(a) for criticism or review or the reporting of current events, if the use is Fair Dealing;[p.45]

(b) including it in another sound recording, or a film, broadcast or cable programme as long as the inclusion is only incidental;[p.121]

(c) copying it by a person teaching or receiving instruction in the making of a film or film soundtrack;

(d) anything done for examinations;

(e) playing it to an audience of teachers and pupils at an educational establishment for the purposes of instruction;[p.62]

(f) using it in connection with public administration;[p.55]

---

* Causing a recording to be heard in public and broadcasting it are not restricted acts for recordings originating in countries which do not offer the same protection to UK recordings.

    (g) playing it as part of the activities of or for the benefit of a club, society or other organization whose main objects are charitable;

    (h) renting it to the public under a compulsory licence and subject to payment of an agreed royalty.^{p. 109}

See also the acts permitted in relation to broadcasts, on page 131.

Illegal copying of audio recordings (and of video recordings and broadcasts) has reached epidemic proportions. Attempts to deal with outright piracy for profit are being made at national and international levels, but this apart the problem is most acute in private homes. The Whitford Report concluded that the only viable way of making domestic users meet their legal obligations was to impose a levy on the manufacturers of all audio and video recorders. This has been done for some time in Germany, where the proceeds are distributed among all registered copyright owners (composers, lyricists, performers, record companies, etc.) through the collecting society ZPU. Although the concept of a levy on blank tapes was rejected when the 1988 Act was drafted, it is possible that such a measure may be introduced via the EC in due course.[p. 207]

Education is another field where recording is frequent, and it is also necessary. Licences exist allowing educational establishments to record off-air broadcasts and cable programmes for purposes of instruction (see page 65).

The **copyright notice** (as distinct from trade mark notices) on a sound recording or its packaging commonly includes some variation of the statement 'All Rights Reserved. Unauthorized copying, public performance and broadcasting prohibited.'

Instead of the C-in-a-circle, the notice must also include the symbol ℗ (for phonogram), with the name of the copyright owner and the year(s) and country of first publication. This is sufficient for international protection among countries adhering to the 1961 Rome Convention for the Protection of Performers, Producers of Phonograms and Broadcasting Organizations. The United States Copyright Revision Act 1976 requires the form ℗ 19— Copyright Owner (or as the third portion 'a generally known alternative designation of the owner'); the Copyright Office [p. 208] must be consulted for exact instructions.

34 **Broadcasting a Work by Television or Radio**

The Acts Restricted by the Copyright in any work (other than a typographical arrangement) include broadcasting a substantial part of it or including it in a cable programme service.

A **broadcast** is defined as 'a transmission by wireless telegraphy of visual images, sounds or other information which – (a) is capable of being lawfully received by members of the public, or (b) is transmitted for presentation to members of the public'. 'Wireless telegraphy' is further defined as 'the sending of electro-magnetic energy over paths not provided by a material substance constructed or arranged for that purpose'. This includes TV (and teletext) and radio and even encrypted transmissions.

A **cable programme service** is 'a service which consists wholly or mainly in sending visual images, sounds or other information by means of a telecommunications system, otherwise than by wireless telegraphy, for reception – (a) at two or more places (whether for simultaneous reception or at different times in response to requests by different users), or (b) for presentation to members of the public'. There are a number of exceptions to these provisions mainly concerned with private cable services belonging to businesses or individuals (further information is given in *A User's Guide to Copyright* by Michael Flint[p. 222]).

A Literary work can be broadcast or transmitted in its original wording in 'straight reading' or 'narrative' form when the text is simply read aloud, or if the printed text is directly photographed. When novelists sell television rights or sound broadcasting rights in their books they are usually selling the right to turn the novel into a script for broadcasting: part of the restricted act of converting a non-Dramatic work into a Dramatic work. Dramatic and Musical works can be broadcast direct, as it were, though it is possible to give a straight reading of a play as well as a full-scale performance of it.

'Television rights' must be regarded as including the restricted acts mentioned above. (Further distinctions are made in the chapter on *Dramatizing a Literary Work*, page 116.)

No one may broadcast or include in a cable programme service a substantial part of any copyright work, or any adaptation of it, without permission except in the circumstances listed on page 131. The Act makes a special concession to practicality (the 'ephemeral right') by providing at Section 68 that

> where by virtue of a licence or assignment of copyright a person is authorised to broadcast or include in a cable programme service –
>
> (a) a literary, dramatic or musical work, or an adaptation of such a work,
> (b) an artistic work, or
> (c) a sound recording or film'
>
> they will be 'treated as licensed by the owner of the copyright in the work to do or authorise any of the following for the purposes of the broadcast or cable programme –
>
> (a) in the case of a literary, dramatic or musical work, or an adaptation of such a work, to make a sound recording or film of the work or adaptation;
> (b) in the case of an artistic work, to take a photograph or make a film of the work;
> (c) in the case of a sound recording or film, to make a copy of it'
>
> on condition that 'the recording, film, photograph or copy in question –
>
> (a) shall not be used for any other purpose, and
> (b) shall be destroyed within 28 days of being first used for broadcasting the work or, as the case may be, including it in a cable programme service.

Fees for broadcasting existing material (not for television dramatizations) are agreed annually with the BBC (but not with independent broadcasters) by the Publishers Association and the Society of Authors.

Some **hospitals** run their own internal broadcasting stations as well as relaying normal broadcasts to patients' headphones. *Publishing Agreements*[p. 222] recommends a modified commercial approach to requests from such stations.

Cable Television and Satellite Broadcasting

Radio and television have always had to to deal with the fact that their broadcasts can be received beyond their own national boundaries, but these problems are greatly increased by the expansion of cable TV and satellite broadcasting. The two are in many ways interlinked. Cable is often the distribution system for satellite broadcasts from the point on the Earth's surface where they are received, and both cable and satellite involve important international considerations, forcing UK law to take account of supranational agreements. The type of copyright protection (if any) given to broadcasts, cable transmissions and satellite broadcasts varies greatly between countries. The EC is currently drafting a Directive on cable and satellite broadcasting in an attempt to harmonize protection within the Community.[p. 207]

Cable television for the public at large is now a considerable venture in the UK, and from both the copyright and commercial points of view has to be treated separately from broadcasting. Cable TV channels reach the homes of paying subscribers through continuous wire or optical fibres, in contrast to the traditional channels whose transmitters broadcast signals through the air to receptor aerials.

In **satellite broadcasting** a ground station transmits material to an orbiting satellite (the 'up-leg' signal) and the satellite rebroadcasts it down to Earth again (the 'down-leg' signal).

In point-to-point satellite systems the down-leg signal can only be picked up by special receiving stations which then rebroadcast the material, or transmit it to subscribers via a cable service, or use a combination of both methods. In a direct-broadcasting satellite ('DBS') system the down-leg is received directly by any individual who owns the correct receiving apparatus.

Satellite broadcasting greatly extends the audience which can be reached by one transmitting station, since signals beamed from a satellite can reach a much wider 'footprint' area before they are faded out by the curvature of the Earth. The footprint may cover many different countries, in Europe especially, and this creates overspill: the signals may be received in countries for which they are not intended and which pay nothing for the privilege.

The **commercial problems** for copyright owners are how to license material for international cable and, even more, satellite broadcasting, and how to enforce the licensing. The appropriate rights in any given work may be controlled by totally different people in the different receiving countries. Payments may be arranged through the formation and international linkage of licensing and collecting bodies (for example, payment to authors for transmission of BBC broadcasts through the extensive cable system in Belgium is now forwarded by the Belgian collecting society SABAM to the ALCS in London for distribution to individual rights owners[p. 110]).

Existing cable and satellite systems carry a high proportion of reruns: films or TV programmes which have already appeared in cinemas, or been broadcast on television and/or issued on video. Sales of relevant rights should distinguish between the various methods of performance and, for cable and satellite at least, should probably be on a non-exclusive basis with restrictions as to the time of release.

35 Broadcasts and Cable Programmes as Separate Subjects of Copyright

Before 1 June 1957 television and radio programmes could only claim copyright protection via the original material they contained. Thus the script of a radio play was protectable as a Dramatic work but the complete programme – with actors, sound effects, etc. – was not protectable unless it was pre-recorded, in which case it would have been protected by the copyright in the sound recording it contained. If the programme consisted of something unprotected by copyright it was not protectable at all.

Any television or radio broadcast made since 1 June 1957 can claim copyright protection quite separately from any copyright that may subsist in the works which it may use or contain, although until 1985 there was no copyright in cable programmes.

It is not within the scope of this book to treat radio and television copyright in detail, but the following outline of the present law may be useful.

According to the Act, a programme is any item included in a broadcast. A broadcast or cable programme will **qualify for UK copyright protection** if its author was a qualified person[p. 23] or if it was sent from a place which is either in the UK or in a country to which the relevant provisions of the Act extend, or a country to which they do not extend but an order extending them has been made. This means any, not only the first, transmission, so would include an authorized repeat transmitted from acceptable territory. In the case of a satellite transmission, the place from which the transmission is made is the place from which the signals carrying the broadcast are transmitted to the satellite (i.e. the up-leg). Programmes made before 1 August 1989 only qualified if they were first broadcast by the BBC or the Independent Broadcasting Authority (now the Independent Television Commission) from any place in the UK or from a place in a number of dependencies and ex-dependencies of the UK. Since 1 August 1989 broadcasts by other broadcasters are also protected. This includes, for example, independent television companies which are broadcasters in their own right, and anyone up-linking to a satellite from acceptable territory.

The **author and first owner of the copyright** of a broadcast is the person or organization who is responsible for the content of the programme and who transmitted it or made the arrangements necessary for its transmission. The author and first owner of the copyright in a cable programme is the person who provided the programme service[p. 126] in which the programme was included. However, the owner of the copyright in broadcasts made before 1 August 1989 is the BBC or IBA (now ITC), or another firm or person to whom the BBC or IBA assigned or licensed the copyright. If the programme is made by an officer or servant of the Crown, or for or on behalf of a House of Parliament, the Crown or Parliament is the first owner of the copyright.

The **term of protection** for a broadcast or cable programme is 50 years from the end of the calendar year in which the broadcast was made or the programme was included in a cable programme service. The copyright includes protection of any repeat (if the repeat qualifies for protection, even if the original did not) whose copyright expires at the same time as the copyright in the original. The term of protection applies equally to broadcasts or cable programmes which are Crown or Parliamentary copyright.[p. 31] (See also *Europe*, page 203).

The **Acts Restricted by the Copyright** in a broadcast or cable programme are: (1) copying the work. This includes re-recording it, or making a photograph of a substantial part of any image which is part of the broadcast or cable programme (but see below); (2) issuing copies of the broadcast or cable programme to the public; (3) playing or showing them in public, including the playing of a television or radio in public (but see below); (4) broadcasting the work or including it in another cable television service.

Indirect infringements are the same as those listed on page 48 for Literary, Dramatic and Musical works.

Exceptions from protection, when a broadcast or cable programme may be used without permission from the copyright owner, are:

(a) using it for criticism or review (with acknowledgement) where the use is Fair Dealing;[p. 45]

(b) using it for news reporting where the use is Fair Dealing;[p. 45]

(c) including it in a sound recording, or other broadcast or cable programme as long as the inclusion is incidental;[p. 121]

(d) copying it by a person teaching or receiving instruction in the making of films or film soundtracks;

(e) using it in any way for examinations;

(f) playing it at an educational establishment for the purposes of instruction or making a recording of a cable programme, or a copy of such a recording, for the educational purposes of that establishment under the terms of a certified licensing scheme;[p. 107]

(g) using it for purposes of public administration;[p. 55]

(h) the 'ephemeral right';[p. 127]

(i) recording it for the supervision and control of programmes by the BBC, ITC, Radio Authority or Cable Authority;

(j) recording it at home so a broadcast or cable programme may be viewed or listened to at a more convenient time;

(k) taking a photograph of an image in a television broadcast or cable programme, for private and domestic use;

(l) showing or playing a broadcast or cable programme in public, and any sound recording or film contained in it, if the audience has not paid for admission to the showing (the definition of what constitutes a paying audience is described in detail at Section 72 of the Act);

(m) the reception and immediate retransmission by a cable programme service of a broadcast under certain circumstances;

(n) copying broadcasts or cable programmes and any works contained in them for the handicapped in certain circumstances or under the terms of a certified licensing scheme – this would include, for example, subtitled broadcasts.

The Broadcasting Act 1990 provides that publishers may reproduce information about the times and titles of programmes which are to be broadcast, under a licence from and with payment to the person providing the programme service (e.g. the BBC).

36 Filming a Work for Cinema and Video

The first step in making a film or a video recording from a non-dramatic Literary work is to turn it into a screenplay. This is the restricted act of dramatization. Thereafter, making a film of any Literary, Dramatic or Musical work involves the two further restricted acts of recording it and of performance in public. Anyone who sells 'film rights' in their work will usually be giving permission for the buyer to do all these things (limited to their application for the cinema and/or video), and no one can legally make a film of a substantial part of any copyright work until they have this permission. It is also possible simply to photograph a printed text onto a moving film. (In fact, the buyer will almost certainly seek extensive rights, and expert advice should be sought from your professional organization or agent if you are negotiating a film deal.)

No one may perform a substantial part of any copyright work by the projection of a film without permission except in the circumstances listed on page 112.

Note that it is only copyright works which are protected by law against indiscriminate filming. People and events have no such protection in the UK (except that access may be subject to agreed terms) although where an individual has commissioned a film for his own use he has a moral right of privacy in the resulting work.[p. 177]

Films are films whether they are made for exhibition in a cinema or for use in a video recorder (see 'Video Recordings' on page 135). If an older contract has licensed the cinematographic film rights it may well be assumed that the licensee also has video rights, though discussion and clarification may be in order. Contracts now should cover the various possible 'windows' for film, with the time of release for each type: 'theatrical' exhibition (i.e. in a cinema), video rental and sales, cable TV, traditional or 'network' TV and satellite broadcasting. None of these methods of exploitation should be sold without taking the others into consideration.

Normally the buyer of film rights will also want to acquire television rights[p. 126] in the same work.

See also *Performance* (page 112), *Dramatizing a Literary Work* (page 116), and *Broadcast and Cable Programmes* (page 129).

---

37 The Film as a Separate Subject of Copyright

Since 1 June 1957 a film as a whole has been entitled to copyright protection quite separately from any copyright that may subsist in the Literary, Dramatic, Musical or Artistic works that it contains.

The 1988 Act defines a film as 'a recording on any medium from which a moving image may by any means be produced'. The soundtrack of a film has a separate copyright as a sound recording (see page 120).*

It is not within the scope of this book to treat film copyright in detail, but the following outline of the present law may be useful.

A film **qualifies for UK copyright protection** if its author was a qualified person[p. 23] for the whole or a substantial part of the period during which the film was made, or if (since 1 August 1989) it was made by an officer or servant of the Crown in the course of his duties, or under the direction or control of Parliament.[p. 31] A published film will also qualify for protection if its first authorized publication took place in acceptable territory.[p. 8] Playing or showing a film in public does not constitute publication, and nor does broadcasting it or including it in a cable programme service. **Publication** means the issuing of copies of the film to the public.

The **author** of a film is the person by whom the arrangements necessary for the making of the film are undertaken: normally this would be the producer and not, for example, the camera operator. (But see *Europe*, page 204.)

---

*Films made between 1 July 1912 and 31 May 1957 were and are protected as a series of still photographic works, and the soundtrack as a 'contrivance by means of which [a] work may be mechanically reproduced'.

The **owner of the copyright** in a film is the author unless he has made an agreement to the contrary, or if he made the film as an officer or servant of the Crown or under the direction or control of Parliament when (in the absence of an agreement to the contrary) the film will be Crown or Parliamentary copyright.[p. 31]

The **term of protection** for films made since 1 August 1989 is 50 years from the end of the calendar year in which the film was made or, if it is released within that time, 50 years from its first release (this applies also to films that are Crown or Parliamentary copyright). A film is 'released' when '(a) it is first published, broadcast or included in a cable programme service, or (b) . . . the film is first shown to the public', provided the release is authorized by the copyright holder. Where a film was created before 1 August 1989, and published or registered (under the provisions of the Films Act) before that date, protection lasts until 50 years from the end of the calendar year of publication or registration; where the film was unpublished and unregistered at 1 August 1989, copyright protection lasts until 1 January 2040 or, if the film is published within that time, until 50 years from the end of the calendar year in which it was published (not released). However, see also *Europe*, page 203.

The **Acts Restricted by the Copyright** in a film are (1) making a copy of it (including making a photograph of a substantial part of any image forming part of the film); (2) issuing copies to the public, including any rental of copies to the public; (3) showing a substantial part of it in public; (4) broadcasting it, or including it in a cable programme service.

Indirect infringements are as listed on page 48 for Literary, Dramatic and Musical works.

Exceptions from protection, when the film may be used without permission from the copyright owner, are: (a) using it for criticism or review or the reporting of current events (if the use is Fair Dealing);[p. 45] (b) its inclusion in another film, broadcast or cable programme if the inclusion is incidental;[p. 121] (c) copying it in the course of, or preparation for, instruction in the making of films or film soundtracks, provided the recording is done by a person giving or receiving instruction; (d) using it in any way for examinations; (e) playing it before an audience of teachers and pupils for purposes of instruction;[p. 113] (f) using it for public administration;[p. 55] (g) renting it under a licensing scheme (subject to payment of a royalty).[p. 109]

Video Recordings

Videos are included in the definition of a film.[p. 133] However, note that while video *recordings* have to be translated to your TV screen with the help of a video recorder, the entertainments called video *games* are computer programs and have to be translated with the help of a computer. Matters are becoming increasingly complicated because video games may or may not also include copyright Literary, Artistic or Musical works, sound recordings or films in their make-up.

38 Copyright and Computers: Works in Electronic Form

This is probably the area in which the greatest changes have taken place since the last edition of this book. The enormous extent to which computers have become part of life for everyone was impossible to foresee when the 1956 Act was drafted, and consequently that Act made no reference to them at all.

Work in electronic form covers everything from a business letter stored on disk to databases, CD-ROM (compact disk read-only memory – a computer-based CD), CD-I (interactive CD) and computer programs themselves. 'Electronic' is defined by the Act as meaning 'actuated by electric, magnetic, electro-magnetic, electro-chemical or electro-mechanical energy' and 'in electronic form' means 'in a form usable only by electronic means'.

A **program** is a set of instructions which, when introduced into a computer, will tell the computer how to perform a particular task (add columns of numbers; produce typed documents; search for specified information; present this information in a predetermined form; and so on ad infinitum). The instructions are in electronic code, though they are communicable between programmer and computer and between computer and user, in a form more like human language.

A distinction must be made between two sorts of works produced by a computer with the assistance of a program. First, a program may instruct a computer to act simply as a typewriter (word processor), with the end product being, for example, a letter, a speech, a novel. The same goes for much accounting material, where a number-crunching program has been used, but the input and the output could have equally well been achieved manually, though much more slowly. This first category shades off into a second: works which simply could never have been produced at all without a specific program and a computer with sufficient capacity to carry out the program: complex spreadsheets, or projections based on the manipulation of complex data (as in the famous illustrations of chaos theory or the solutions for three-dimensional problems in aerospace technology). For this second category the Act's provisions for computer-generated work are directly and uniquely relevant.

The Protection of Computer Programs

Computer programs are specifically included in the 1988 Act* as Literary works, though the Act does not define 'program'.

As with other Literary works, copyright exists as soon as a program is first recorded (for example, saved on a floppy or hard disk or chip, or printed out), provided it satisfies the Act's requirements as to originality.[p. 20] A computer program qualifies for protection if the author is a qualifying person[p. 23] or if the program was first published in acceptable territory.[p. 8] First publication in this respect includes making the program available to the public by means of an electronic retrieval system. Likewise, a copy of a computer program includes one that is stored electronically.

The **author** and **first owner of the copyright** in a computer program is the person who created it. When a program is created in the course of the author's employment, copyright in it belongs to the employer; the first owner of the copyright in a program created by an officer or servant of the Crown in the course of his duties, or for or on behalf of one of the Houses of Parliament, belongs to the Crown or Parliament and, as a Literary work, a computer program that would not otherwise qualify for protection will do so if it is created by a recognized international organization (which would own the copyright[p. 23]).

Copyright in a computer program lasts until 50 years from the

---

*Following the Copyright (Computer Software) Amendment Act 1985.

---

end of the calendar year in which the author died (see also *Europe*, page 203). The term of protection cannot be extended simply by the addition of insubstantial amounts of work and, at least until the EC devises a standard for originality, such judgements will be a question of degree. However, 50 years from the end of the calendar year in which they are first issued to the public in electronic form, it is not an infringement to rent copies of a program. Within the 50 years, rental is only permitted under a licensing scheme and subject to payment of a royalty.[p. 109]

The **Acts Restricted by the Copyright** in a computer program are as for all other Literary works,[p. 46] and include reproducing the program in a computer or in transient form (such as displaying it on a VDU). Making unauthorized back-up copies of a program or any work in a form usable only by electronic means is also an infringement. However, where a copy of such a work has been purchased on terms which 'expressly, impliedly or by virtue of any rule of law' allow the purchaser to copy the work or to adapt it or make copies of an adaptation in connection with the purchaser's use of it, it is not an infringement for the purchaser, or anyone to whom he sells the work, to make such use of it.

The restricted act of adaptation when applied to a computer program means translating it from one computer language into another. However, this has been overridden by the EC's Software Directive (which came into effect on 1 January 1993).* The Directive permits the user of a computer program to load, run, translate, adapt, arrange, alter or copy it when – but only when – it is necessary for the use of the program. The user is also permitted to make a back-up copy (in case, for example, the original is lost), but only for archival purposes. He may alter a program to correct errors but not to update or enhance it. Reverse engineering is also permitted – in other words a program can be decompiled into a form in which its coding and structure can be analysed – although, again, this is only permitted in order to achieve inter-operability or net-working with other information suppliers and only if the amended form of program is not readily available from other sources.

Indirect infringements are as described on page 48 for other Literary works.

---

* At the time of writing, the UK's law is being amended to reflect the different specifications of the Software Directive.

Although they are Literary works, computer programs do not benefit from the protection afforded by moral rights.

Computer-generated Work

Computers are used to produce (among other things) new diagrams, reference works (largely by cannibalizing other reference works), digitized maps, music, databases and more computer programs.

Where a work is generated by computer in circumstances such that there is no human author, the 'author' is held to be 'the person by whom the arrangements necessary for the creation of the work are undertaken'.

Such works are now protected for 50 years from the end of the calendar year in which they were made, but it seems that there is no copyright protection for computer-generated works made before 1 August 1989.

The Use of Copyright Works in Electronic Form: Electro-Publishing

A **databank** or **database** is basically a collection of material like an encyclopedia, specialist library, bibliography, filing system or other information reference system. Once provided with an 'index' of cross-references and with appropriate text, the computer acts as researcher and bookshelf combined. Preparing a database is sometimes a long and costly procedure, but after that, getting the facts the user wants ('information retrieval') is virtually instantaneous.

With a computer database it is possible for only one original to exist, while millions of copies are made of it and supplied on-line to users throughout the world. This copying can be of whole works but is commonly of extracts or abstracts, and the copy can be a 'hard copy' (printed out) or ephemeral, appearing on a screen only as long as the user wants to read it.

When contracting for database use one should bear in mind the enormous impact it may have on book sales through the full range of possible copying, and a basic input fee should be agreed on this basis and, if possible, a per-use fee for output. Ideally, to prevent further unauthorized use of material, the database should include individual copyright lines, or at least a general notice, on every print-out or VDU use. In addition, the author's moral rights[p. 100] should be respected – notably the right not to have his work subject to derogatory treatment – important in a medium in which it is very easy to manipulate text. Providing it has sufficient originality[p. 20] a database is entitled to copyright protection itself, separately from the copyright in any works contained in it. The EC is drafting a Directive on the protection of databases (see page 206).

Where the original of a work is only available in a computer memory rather than, for instance, on paper, it is an electronic publication. Specialist reference works in particular (medical and chemical journals, engineering manuals, financial services, complete dictionaries, etc.) are now available and electronic publications may be delivered through the whole range of electronic media (CD-ROM, on-line, videotext, audiotext, etc.). Even though print-outs are inferior to bound books, and reading work on a screen one frame at a time is tedious, novels and other long continuous works are being published in electronic form, and CD-ROM systems are being installed in most British schools. **Multi-media** packages are being aimed at the education and leisure markets and are another rapidly expanding form of reproducing work. A multi-media system (such as a CD player linked to a computer, or CD–I) can mix text, sound, graphics, photographic images, videos and sophisticated computer games. All can play audio CDs and many can play photo CDs, and all the various components in the system can be manipulated.

Technology is moving so fast that there is bound to be some confusion as to whether the rights acquired by publishers under old contracts include the right to issue a version in the form of a video game, a database which can be accessed by subscribers, on disk, cassette, CD, CD-ROM or CD-I, but unless the author assigned all rights under the contract it is probable that electronic rights are not automatically included in most old contracts. *Publishing Agreements*[p. 222] includes a chapter on electronic media rights agreements.

Electrocopying

This is a dangerous area indeed, including reproduction by disk copying, fax, e-mail and database downloading. The problems of 'electrocopying' are similar to those posed by photocopying, but considerably more difficult to detect. Many word processors and desktop publishing systems include a scanner and optical character recognition facility, with which a work can be scanned and stored and then the typeface, design and text manipulated until the original is unrecognizable. Anything approaching an effective way of policing electrocopying has so far proved elusive, but electrocopying depends on a computer so at least in theory one possibility should be to program the computer to keep a record of the copies it makes.

Delivery of 'Manuscripts' on Disk

Copyright protection applies as much to an author's work delivered on disk as it does to one in the form of a manuscript or typescript. Editorial changes on a disk can be harder to spot so they should be clearly flagged, and approved by the author, and his moral rights respected. Full information for authors and publishers on producing and working with material on disk, as well as a checklist of rights in the form of a detailed 'conditions of use' list that can be included on the disk envelope, are given in *Writing on Disk* by Jane Dorner. (See *Bibliography*.[p. 222])

The Data Protection Act 1984

If you collect information about living individuals in electronic form and it is possible to retrieve, categorize or otherwise process the individual's details – or if the individual is identifiable from the information held – you must register as a Data User under the Data Protection Act. Registration forms and further information are available from the Post Office.

---

39 **Public Lending Right**

For over 30 years a considerable number of influential, vocal and tenacious people argued that it was unfair to pay an author only one unit of royalty on a copy of his book bought by a library. The author's earnings should, they said, be related in some way to the number of times the book was actually lent to the public – hence the principle became known as Public Lending Right (PLR).

A Public Lending Right Act for the United Kingdom was passed by Parliament in 1979* and the first payments to authors were made in 1984, based on a loan sample taken in 1983. The total number of loans from UK public libraries in recent years has been declining as local authorities close branch libraries, reduce opening hours and cut book funds to save money, but loans in 1990–91 were still a substantial 563 million. PLR is not covered by the Copyright Act and its definitions are different. Registration forms and beautifully lucid explanatory pamphlets are available from the Registrar, PLR Office, Bayheath House, Prince Regent Street, Stockton-on-Tees, Cleveland TS18 1DF.

Very briefly, the UK system works as follows. Authors are eligible for payments (whether or not they own the copyright) if they and their books meet a number of requirements and if the books are then formally registered. As an **author** you must meet *all* of the following qualifications:

1. You have contributed to the book as writer, illustrator, compiler, editor, reviser or translator. (Illustrators include photographers.) Compilers or editors (including revisers and abridgers) only qualify if in receipt of a royalty payment for that book or if they have written more than 10 pages of text or 10 per cent of the book's contents.
2. Your name is on the book's title page or you can prove authorship by some other means (e.g. receipt of a royalty statement).
3. You are resident in the UK (not including the Isle of Man or the Channel Islands) or Germany.
4. You are alive at the time of registration (even if a co-author or illustrator is dead or cannot be located).

Your **book** is eligible if it meets *all* of the following qualifications:

(a) it has an eligible author (or co-author) *or* it is a translation;
(b) it is printed and bound (paperbacks counting as bound);

---

*The text of *The Public Lending Right Act 1979* and *The Public Lending Right Scheme 1982*, with later amendments (SI 1988 No. 2070), are available from HMSO. The whole subject is covered by Brigid Brophy in *A Guide to Public Lending Right* (see *Bibliography*).

(c) copies of it have been put on sale (i.e. it is not a free handout and it is already published);

(d) it is not a newspaper, magazine, journal or periodical;

(e) the authorship is personal (i.e. not a company or association) and the book is not Crown copyright;

(f) it is not wholly or mainly a musical score;

(g) it has an ISBN.[p. 168]

Your book or books must be formally **registered** on an application form supplied by the Registrar. Co-authors must agree percentage shares and each of them may then complete one or separate application forms for their own share. Editors and compilers are eligible for a fixed 20 per cent share and translators for a 30 per cent share. The fixed share can be increased in proportion to the editor's or compiler's contribution to the book. As loans data for each ISBN is collected and calculated separately you must register all editions of each title. The PLR loans year runs from 1 July to 30 June, and payments are made to authors in the following February. Completed forms, duly notarized by, for example, a solicitor or JP if it is the author's first application, must reach the Registrar not later than 30 June in any year to qualify for PLR payments for that year. You register each edition only once (hardback and paperback must be registered separately); thereafter it remains on the PLR computer. However, if the ISBN changes (for example, if the publisher is taken over by another firm) the new ISBN must also be registered.

Payments continue yearly until 50 years after the author's death. An annual sum (£4.75m in 1992) is provided by the government to fund administration and authors' payments, which are calculated on a loan sample from 30 regional library authorities (a third of which change each year) scaled up to an estimated national figure. There is a top limit of £6,000 per author. In 1990–91 the average payment to authors who got anything was £223, with 81 out of the total 22,203 authors registered earning the maximum £6,000. Note that payments are made by the PLR administration to authors, not to publishers.

An author's right to PLR can be **assigned** or **bequeathed** to other individuals or firms, without restriction as to nationality or residence.

Abroad, PLR systems of various sorts exist in Australia, Canada, Denmark, Finland, Germany, Holland, Iceland, New Zealand,

Norway and Sweden, and the possible introduction and harmonization of PLR schemes throughout Europe is currently under discussion within the EC.[p. 205] Most of the existing systems make payments only to their own nationals, but the German one pays UK authors and vice versa, under a reciprocal arrangement. Proceeds from the German scheme are distributed to British authors registered with the ALCS.[p. 110]

---

40 Submitting and 'Reading' a Work for Publication

The text and arrangement[p. 20] of virtually every unpublished Literary, Dramatic or Musical work is protected by copyright,[p. 16] and on the rare occasions when it is not, any unauthorized use of it will almost certainly constitute a breach of confidence.[p. 57]

Sending a letter or an article to a periodical is equivalent to giving the periodical an immediate licence to publish it (on the standard terms, whatever they may be, in the case of an article) unless, for instance, you specifically state that the letter is *not* for publication or that you hope to receive an acceptable offer for the publication of the article.

Sending a manuscript to a book publisher does not imply a licence to publish but is only an offer to negotiate terms.

No publisher or agent is under any obligation to preserve or return **unsolicited material** sent to him,* nor is he liable for its loss, and some publishers and agents wisely print a notice to this effect on their stationery and, in the case of periodicals, on each issue.

Titles, plots and the development of an argument are not nearly as well protected as the actual wording of a text. Though redress is available in proven cases of unauthorized use,[p. 98] bear in mind that legal proceedings, however soundly based, are tedious and expensive.

---

*However, there remains a moral obligation to do so, which most publishers and agents recognize. Authors of unsolicited material should always enclose stamps for return postage, and keep a copy of anything they send out.

Although an author's nervous imagination may lead him to see infringers behind every bush, very few people ever really do use someone else's unpublished material. Plots of fiction are most unlikely to be expropriated since after all what makes or breaks a book is the calibre of the writing. Reputable publishers and agents are too busy and too sensible to bother with lifting plots from unpublishable manuscripts.

But non-fiction, especially when its subject or viewpoint is new, can be in a little more danger – particularly from other writers in the same field. The author should therefore exercise reasonable prudence about the people he allows to read his unpublished work or to become privy to his developed ideas. The best course for most non-fiction writers, whether or not they fear plagiarism, is to sign a contract with a publisher on the basis of an outline and sample chapter. This can save a lot of time and effort and allows discussion about the ultimate shape of the book before, not after, it has been written. By the time an author has completed the manuscript his book is already scheduled for publication, leaving little enough time for the most determined infringer to get another book out first.

Original ideas of a marketing nature (a new angle for a TV programme, an unusual theme for an anthology, new subjects for books) are the most liable to hijacking, which in some quarters has become virtually a basic management skill. Common sense is the best protection here.

If it seems really vital to establish proof of your claim to authorship you can deposit a copy of the material with a bank, witnessed as to the date. Most Literary, Dramatic and Musical works can be registered at Stationers' Hall.* If an unpublished work is very widely circulated a copyright line should appear on all copies.[p. 157]

The author, his agent and the publisher's reader should all be wary of material which may, for instance, be libellous, blasphemous, obscene, in contempt of court, in contravention of the Official Secrets Act or in breach of confidence. The possibility of negligent mis-statement (e.g. misleading investment advice; an explosive combination in a chemistry textbook) should be noted and appropriate safeguards planned. It is worth checking the names even of fictional characters to a reasonable extent: a real 'Dr Cloudesley Dunderhead

---

*Enquiries, with a stamped addressed envelope, to the Registrar, Stationers' Hall, Ludgate Hill, London EC4M 7DD.

of Putney' might sue because his fictional namesake indulges in abhorrent behaviour. Perhaps the text should be checked by an expert in the subject of the book before an offer is made for it, or it may have to be submitted to a specialized legal reader before publication. Note that a disclaimer[p. 155] is not necessarily any protection against legal action.

A valuable attribute in a reader or agent is the ability to recognize infringement when he sees it, realizing that the work is a plagiarism of something he has seen, heard or read before or, as sometimes happens, a copy of an old published piece by the same author.

Attention should be paid to the quotations, illustrations or other matter which are to be included in the work; they may cost more in permission fees than the likely profit or royalties will cover.

---

41 **Revising a Text**

Most published Literary and Dramatic texts are not exactly the same as their manuscript originals. The degree to which they have been reworked varies from a copy-editor's polishing-up to wholesale rearrangement and rewriting.

If a publisher feels that substantial revision of a work is necessary his ideal course is to have all alterations made by the author, or at least with his approval. But when is a publisher *obliged* to refer to the author?

It makes no difference how old a work is when changes are made, as long as it is still in copyright. If it has gone out of copyright anyone can alter it in any way provided there is no intention of misleading the public.[p. 98] If the alterations are sufficiently 'original' the resulting new version may qualify for a new copyright.[p. 20]

Book publishers have the customary right to copy-edit a manuscript, to the extent of making it conform to 'house style' in punctuation, capitalization, and so on, and correcting typographical errors and errors of syntax. However, some authors feel strongly about these matters and it would seem common sense in such cases to follow the author's usage if it is reasonable and consistent.

More major alterations may or may not have to be submitted to the author, depending upon (1) his contract with his publisher and (2) whether his name appears on the work.

The first step is to consider the author–publisher contract. If it has been signed after the publisher has seen and accepted a complete manuscript the author is not obliged to alter his text in any way* – unless he has already agreed to do so, verbally or in writing. The author is in much the same position when a contract has been signed before the manuscript is completed – for instance, when it has been 'commissioned' on the basis of an outline plus sample chapter, or of an idea only. But in this sort of case the publisher can demand alterations (and even sometimes reject the MS entirely) if he can show that the text as delivered is not the text he was expecting. It is therefore in the interest of both publisher and author to agree at the time a text is commissioned on at least the general lines it is to take. Any such agreement should certainly be in writing and, ideally, incorporated in the contract ('. . . as outlined in X's letter to the Author of 11 April 1992 which is appended as a Schedule to this agreement').

Again, there may be a clause in the author–publisher contract which says, for instance, 'the Publishers shall make no alterations to the Work except by agreement with the Author'. This kind of statement, or the reverse of it, can settle the question immediately. Beyond that, if the contract is only a licence[p. 200] the publisher will most probably be expected to reproduce the work virtually unaltered. If it is an assignment[p. 201] (especially an assignment for an outright fee) one would at first think that the publisher, being now the sole owner of the copyright, should be able to do what he pleases with his own property.

It is at this point that the use of the author's name becomes particularly important. If his name appears in connection with the work alterations must still be very carefully made. If they are made without his permission and change, for example, the character, sense or style of the work the author may be able to sue on grounds of injury to his reputation. An author can also object if alteration to his work infringes his moral right of integrity[p. 102] or false attribution.[p. 104] However, if an author has assigned his copyright and his name is *not* attached to his work (for instance, if he is one of a

---

*Except for portions covered by the 'warranty clause' under which the author promises that his text will be original and not previously published nor libellous nor obscene nor an infringement of copyright, etc. A publisher can certainly insist on the alteration of any text which is in violation of this undertaking.

team of writers producing entries for a guidebook) or if his work has been done anonymously under a contract of service,[p. 30] there is practically no limit to the changes permissible.

For periodical publishers the situation is much the same. They have by custom the right to alter unsigned contributions without the author's consent, but not signed ones – except perhaps for unsubstantial cuts dictated by layout difficulties, and even these should be checked with the author unless it is known that he has no objection to such cuts being made.

Each case should be judged on its merits and when necessary expert advice may have to be taken. (An amicable personal settlement of any disagreement is likely to cost less in the end.) On the whole, cuts (unless they change the sense of the work) are most likely to be unobjectionable, whereas changes or additions should be very carefully scrutinized. Publishing custom – and therefore the judgement of any court that must take custom into consideration – is growing more considerate of authors' rights, so it is as well for a publisher to err on the side of the angels.

The copyright status of a work may be altered by revision. The person responsible for the revision may qualify under copyright law as a co-author.[p. 15] A revised version of a previously published or out-of-copyright text may qualify for a new copyright.[p. 20] In such cases the copyright line[p. 157] may be changed, or the insertion of some other 'sentence'[p. 165] on the copyright page may be appropriate.

When describing and advertising a revised text a publisher must be careful not to mislead the public. For instance, an abridged or condensed version must not appear to be the original full-length work; a text should not be called 'revised and up-dated' if only minor changes have been made.

See also *Reissuing a Previously Published Text* (below).

42 **Reissuing a Previously Published Text**

Terms like 'new edition', 'reprint', 'reissue' or 'republish' are often used when it is not at all clear whether they indicate (1) a new print run with the same text and format* as before or (2) a new format (e.g. paperback instead of the previous hardback) with or without resetting but with the same text as before or (3) a revised text, in the same or a new format. (It is also possible for 'new edition' to mean the release of a few more thousand copies from previously printed stock, but this is not good practice since it verges on misleading the public.)

When such terms are used it is important to define them carefully. The most complex misunderstandings can otherwise result with regard to territory, royalties, termination and other matters which can be dependent upon the issue of 'editions'. In translation agreements a definition is imperative.

When an unaltered reprint of a work is to be published the publisher (and author) should first check the rights position. In rare cases a publisher's rights may be limited to the publication of a limited number of copies. If the author–publisher agreement was signed between 1 July 1912 and 31 May 1957 inclusive, and 25 years have elapsed since the author died, all rights may have reverted to his heirs under the '25-year Proviso'.[p. 34] And if, for instance, the first edition was in hardback and it is now proposed to publish it in paperback, the publisher may not have the paperback rights. Then again, does the agreement stipulate that the author is obliged to revise his text when it is reprinted, or that he must be given the opportunity to revise it if he wishes? And what about quotations and illustrations: do previous permissions cover use in this reprint or do some have to be cleared again, or are additional sums payable at this point?

Changes may have to be made in the copyright line,[p. 157] or in the form of notice[p. 156] used, though the only likely change will be a statement that this is the *n*th edition (with the date) or, in the case of a licensee publisher, that this edition is published by arrangement with such-and-such a publishing firm.

If a text is revised before it is reprinted, all the above considerations apply. In addition, if the revisions are made by someone other than the author the publisher may have to submit them to the author.[p. 145] A new copyright line[p. 157] will almost certainly be advisable. Statements to the effect that this is a 'new and revised

---

* 'Format' of course is another vague word. Here it means the overall appearance of a publication: the design, type, paper, binding, size and so on.

edition' will be appropriate on the title page, copyright page, blurb, jacket and advertising matter. If substantial revisions are made by someone other than the author his name ought perhaps to be added to the title page (usually only with the main author's consent). Library deposit[p. 152] of the new version should not be forgotten; a new ISBN[p. 168] should be obtained and authors should notify the PLR Office.[p. 141]

See also *Revising a Text* (page 145).

43 Publications with a Supervisory Editor

Many Literary works are composed of items written by several authors (sometimes hundreds of authors) whose contributions have been commissioned or chosen and arranged and generally supervised by a single editor.* Such works include anthologies, encyclopedias, symposia, part works, guidebooks, directories, almanacs, dictionaries and newspapers, magazines and other periodicals.

The typical situation is one where a publisher contracts with an editor to produce a specific book or periodical, and the editor then proceeds to commission contributors to write new items specially for it. If the book is an anthology containing nothing but extracts from previously published material the editor's responsibility for commissioning new work is replaced by his responsibility for clearing permissions.[p. 82]

There are two distinct types of copyright in works of this sort: the editor's copyright in his arrangement[p. 20] and the numerous copyrights in the material he arranges. When the new work is a selection or anthology the copyrights in this material remain the property of the original owners, and all that the editor obtains is a non-exclusive licence ('permission') to publish the material within an agreed territory. When the new work contains a large number of items newly

---

*A very small number of Dramatic works, and even sometimes Musical works, may also fit this pattern, e.g. revues with sketches and tunes written by different people.

---

written by contributors for it, it may make sense for each contributor to assign the copyright in his material outright to the editor or publisher. When the work contains only a small number of items or has few contributors the copyright in the contributed material may or may not be assigned outright.

The editor's relationship to the publisher may be that of an employee under a contract of service[p. 30] like the permanent editor of a periodical or an executive overseeing the production of an encyclopedia. Or the editor may be a freelance under contract to prepare one particular book or series.

The copyright in the overall arrangement vests in the editor unless he works under a contract of service,[p. 30] or works for a government department,[p. 31] or assigns his copyright to someone else.[p. 32] If (as is often the case) the publisher wishes to control the complete copyright in a projected work he must ensure that the editor assigns[p. 201] to him the copyright in the arrangement plus the copyright in anything (preface, article, etc.) which the editor may himself write for the work. Whatever the arrangement between publisher and editor it is best to embody it in a signed document.

A contributor of new work is most likely to be commissioned by the editor or the publisher, or to work under a contract of service for the publisher. He will very seldom be the direct employee of the editor. The contributor controls the copyright in his article unless he is under a contract of service, or works for a government department, or assigns his copyright to someone else (the editor or the publisher).

If the editor is independent he must, if necessary, get a written assignment of copyright from each contributor for each item contributed. Whatever his arrangement with his contributors his wisest course is to sign a formal agreement with each of them so as to avoid later misunderstanding.

If the editor assigns the copyright in his arrangement to the publisher he will usually have to ensure that each contributor assigns his copyright to the publisher also. In such a case the publisher will be best advised to handle the contractual arrangements with the contributors direct, working from information supplied by the editor.

The payment of contributors is a vexed question. The simplest course is to pay each contributor a lump sum (generally a standard amount for each thousand words commissioned) for all rights in the contribution. Authors and agents, however, argue that contributors often do not receive a fair return under this method, and that they should be paid a higher fee per thousand words and/or additional sums from time to time according to the sales of the work as a whole. Contributors to books which contain only a small number of contributions are sometimes paid a pro-rata royalty. Publishers object to continuing payments of this kind, not so much on principle but because when the contributions run into dozens or even hundreds, making the suggested payments every time the overall work is sold in a new market would be a time-consuming business and one expensive in itself.

The publisher's insistence on having an assignment of all rights in contributions is another source of complaint. What is important is that the rights acquired from all contributors should be identical, so that the publisher can confidently sub-license rights in the work without constant reference to individual special conditions.

See also *Reprinting Extracts* (page 81); *Revising a Text* (page 145); *Composing the Copyright Notice* (page 155).

44 Republishing Out-of-Copyright Works

When a publisher prints an edition of a work which is in the public domain he is free from any obligation to pay royalties. This advantage is however, offset by the competition, for at present there is then no limit to the number of publishers who can print editions of the same work. See, however, *Europe* on page 205.

The term of protection for published Literary, Dramatic, Musical and Artistic works is usually 50 years from the end of the calendar year in which the author died, but particularly for works created before 1 August 1989, there are considerable variations. Works which have not been published or otherwise made available to the public will still be in copyright. Some works are in perpetual copyright. (See *How Long Does Copyright Protection Last?* on page 35.)

If an unpublished work is in the public domain because it does not qualify for UK copyright protection, publication may give it copyright status later on.[p. 18] A new translation of an old work qualifies for a new copyright of its own.[p. 117] In a continually revised work, like an almanac, those parts which have survived unchanged may still profit from the protection afforded to the newest version, and one cannot assume that it is safe to reprint an old work of this kind if a copyright version is in existence.

The term of copyright protection varies from country to country. Just because the term for a given work has expired in the UK it should not be automatically assumed that it has expired everywhere else as well.

Having established that a work really is in the public domain a publisher must beware of accidentally setting from a newly copyrightable version. If a text has been recently edited, abridged or rearranged with sufficient originality the result may qualify for a new copyright.[p. 20] (On the other hand, a copyright line of recent date on the copyright page may only cover a new introduction or footnotes.)

The typography of an edition first printed since 1 June 1957 cannot be photographed without the permission of its publisher for 25 years afterwards.[p. 105]

If a manuscript or other original document, however old, is used for facsimile reproduction, setting copy or any other purpose, permission must be obtained for its use from the owner of the manuscript.[p. 92]

Illustrations which accompany a public-domain text may not have gone out of copyright. If a publisher wishes to use them he should check them out separately. This is true also of incidental quotations from other works which may appear in the text. And in the case of collections like anthologies, the editor's copyright in the arrangement may expire long before, say, a poet's copyright in a poem in the anthology – or vice versa, depending on who died when.

See also *Composing the Copyright Notice* (page 155).

---

45 Deposit Regulations for Publications and Scripts

In the United Kingdom, as in other countries, publishers are obliged to deposit copies of their new publications with the national archives so as to provide scholars with a complete and historically continuous reference source. Those deposited with the British Library are listed weekly in the *British National Bibliography* or the *British Catalogue of Music* (and are on-line through the information service BLAISE and through computer tape and CD-ROM services), providing librarians at home and overseas with information for book selection and ordering.

All United Kingdom publishers* must deliver one copy of each new publication to the Legal Deposit Office of the British Library (Boston Spa, Wetherby, West Yorkshire LS23 7BY; newspapers go to the Newspaper Legal Deposit Office, The British Library, Unit 3, 120 Colindale Avenue, London NW9 5LF) within one month of its publication. (The Legal Deposit Office does not accept unpublished material.) In return the publisher receives a written receipt. The deposited copies become part of the British Library and are used by the British National Bibliography.

Note that in the United Kingdom deposit – or failure to deposit – has no effect whatever on the copyright status of a work, and there are no 'registration' forms to complete or additional fees to pay, though the publisher must pay the cost of the book and its delivery.

The publications which must be deposited include (as stated in the 1911 Act) books, and 'every part or division of a book, pamphlet, sheet of letterpress, sheet of music, map, plan, chart or table separately published', and each separate volume or issue of every 'encyclopedia, newspaper, review, magazine, or work published in a series of numbers or parts'. Works first published abroad but imported into the UK are also subject to the deposit regulations when published in the UK. Original microtexts may be deposited, although at present the requirement is not compulsory.

Copies need only be deposited the first time a work is published; any 'second or subsequent edition', whatever its format and whoever its publisher, need not be deposited unless it 'contains additions or alterations either in the letterpress or in the maps, prints, or other engravings'. Thus newly edited versions of public-domain works should be deposited.

The copy deposited 'shall be a copy of the whole [work] with all maps and illustrations belonging thereto, finished and coloured in

---

*The publisher of any book first published in the Republic of Ireland must also comply with these regulations.

the same manner as the best copies of the book are published, and shall be bound, sewed, or stitched together, and on the best paper on which the book is printed'.

Deposit is not required for reproductions of Artistic works (other than maps, plans and charts) when they have no accompanying text. Publications in the following categories need not be deposited except upon written demand:* 'trade advertisements; timetables of local passenger transport services; calendars; blank forms; posters produced for the purpose of elementary instruction'.

The publisher may also have to provide up to five more copies. 'He shall also if written demand is made before the expiration of twelve months after publication, deliver within one month after publication, to some depot in London named in the demand a copy of the book for' the Bodleian Library, Oxford, the University Library, Cambridge, the National Library of Scotland in Edinburgh, the Library of Trinity College, Dublin and the National Library of Wales. The agent for the Copyright Libraries, Mr A. T. Smail (100 Euston Street, London NW1 2HQ) is responsible for requesting such copies.

The copies delivered to these libraries 'shall be on the paper on which the largest number of copies of the book is printed for sale, and shall be in the like condition as the books prepared for sale'.

Failure to comply with these regulations exposes a publisher to 'a fine not exceeding five pounds and the value of the book' for each copy not delivered.

Since the Theatres Act 1968 came into force (on 26 July 1968) the **scripts of some plays** must also be deposited. When 'there is given in Great Britain a public performance of a new play, being a performance based on a script, a copy of the actual script on which that performance was based shall be delivered to the Trustees of the British Library [Department of Manuscripts] free of charge within the period of one month beginning with the date of the performance; and the Trustees shall give a written receipt for every script delivered to them'. Failing delivery, the person who presented the performance will be liable to a fine of up to £5.

A 'play' is '(a) any dramatic piece, whether involving improvisation or not, which is given wholly or in part by one or more persons

---

* This list comes from the pamphlet 'Legal Deposit in the British Library' issued by the Legal Deposit Office.

actually present and performing and in which the whole or a major proportion of what is done by the person or persons performing, whether by way of speech, singing or action, involves the playing of a role; and (b) any ballet given wholly or in part by one or more persons actually present and performing, whether or not it falls within paragraph (a) of this definition'.

The regulations apply only to 'new' plays. A play is new if it has never before been publicly performed in Great Britain. It is not new if it is based (a) 'on a script substantially the same as that on which a previous public performance of a play given there was based' or (b) 'substantially on a text of the play which has been published in the United Kingdom'.

The 'script' which must be deposited is 'the text of the play (whether expressed in words or in musical or other notation) together with any stage or other directions for its performance, whether contained in a single document or not'.

It is not necessary to deposit a script if the play is performed 'solely or primarily' for the purposes of rehearsal, or to enable a recording or film to be made, or to enable a performance to be broadcast or diffused by radio or television.

46 Composing the Copyright Notice

To give 'notice' to a person is to inform him of essential facts. Most often these will be connected with legal matters, and the purpose of the notice will be to prevent him pleading ignorance if he does something illegal. If he picnics under a sign which says 'Trespassers will be prosecuted' he cannot later claim to have thought he was picnicking on common land. On the other hand if he has a legal right to picnic at that spot the mere fact that someone has nailed up a 'No Trespassing' sign does not turn him into a trespasser. (Thus the 'disclaimer' which insists that a novel has no connection with any person living or dead does not prevent the author being sued for libel, and a statement that no part of a book may be quoted without permission is subject to the legal fact that less than a substantial part of a work may freely be used in a number of ways.)

A notice of copyright contains two elements:

(1) *the copyright line, e.g.:*
© Mary Brown 1993

(2) *the general copyright notice, e.g.:*
All Rights Reserved. Except as
permitted under current
legislation no part of this work
may be photocopied, stored in a
retrieval system, published,
performed in public, adapted,
broadcast, transmitted, recorded
or reproduced in any form or by
any means, without the prior
permission of the copyright
owner. Enquiries should be
addressed to [the publishers and
their address].

The General Copyright Notice

The general copyright notice above is one which we personally sug-
gest for books (and, with simple obvious adaptations, for other
works), but there is no 'standard' form. Individual publishers and
different branches of publishing all have their own favourite wording. The Publishers Association has no current preference, though
it used to recommend this one:

> All Rights Reserved. No part of this publication may be reproduced,
> stored in a retrieval system, or transmitted, in any form or by any means,
> electronic, mechanical, photocopying, recording or otherwise without
> the permission of [the publishers and their address].

The words 'All Rights Reserved' must *always* appear, to protect
works in countries (mainly South American) whose copyright laws
only protect material bearing a 'notice of reservation of rights'.

In the suggested forms above you may prefer to highlight different restrictions, or to delete, add or alter others. For instance,
where 'photocopied' is not relevant, 'copied' probably will be. The
list of 'means' in the Publishers Association form can be expanded
to include 'electrical, chemical or optical'. After 'All Rights
Reserved' you can insert some variation of 'Apart from any fair
dealing for the purpose of private study, research, criticism or

review, as permitted under the Copyright, Designs and Patents Act 1988 . . .'

You can add specific details to help readers who want to perform the work, or photocopy it, and you can put in other notices of a non-copyright nature, such as restrictions on hiring, lending, resale or rebinding.

The Copyright Line

The words '© Mary Brown 1993' constitute what is called the 'copyright line' or 'UCC line'. The symbol © is read aloud as 'copyright' or, when it is necessary to distinguish between word and symbol, as 'C-in-a-circle'.

The C-in-a-circle line is the form required by the text of the Universal Copyright Convention which the United Kingdom ratified on 27 September 1957. Article III of the Convention says:

> 1. Any Contracting State which, under its domestic law, requires as a condition of copyright, compliance with formalities such as deposit, registration, notice, notarial certificates, payment of fees or manufacture or publication in that Contracting State, shall regard these requirements as satisfied with respect to all works protected in accordance with this Convention and first published outside its territory and the author of which is not one of its nationals, if from the time of the first publication all the copies of the work published with the authority of the author or other copyright proprietor bear the symbol © accompanied by the name of the copyright proprietor and the year of first publication placed in such manner and location as to give reasonable notice of claim of copyright.*

Copyright protection within the United Kingdom and other Berne Convention countries is not affected by the presence or absence of a copyright line. But the line is essential for protection in countries which are not members of Berne but are signatories to UCC.

The only wise course, then, is to print a copyright line (and the general copyright notice given above) on all newly published works. No notice of any kind is required on unpublished works (but see

---

*Contracting States remain free to make their own rules for works either first published in their territory or by their own nationals, for court procedures and for the protection of unpublished works; and 'if a Contracting State grants protection for more than one term of copyright and the first term is for a period longer than one of the minimum periods prescribed in Article IV, such State shall not be required to comply with the provisions of paragraph 1 of this Article III in respect of the second or any subsequent term of copyright'.

page 160). A new copyright line cannot update the copyright status of older work, nor should one be added to a work previously published without it. But the general copyright notice should certainly be added to all works still in copyright.

Each piece of copyright material which is separate or easily separable from its parent package (e.g. wall charts associated with a children's reader, or prints sold loose in a folder) should bear a copyright line and, if possible, a general copyright notice.

On sound recordings the symbol ℗ should be used instead of ©. See page 125.

Where Should the Line Be Printed?

According to UCC a copyright line should be 'placed in such manner and location as to give reasonable notice of claim of copyright'.

It is common in most countries to place the copyright line and general copyright notice for a book on the title page verso (or 'copyright page'): the reverse of the page upon which the title of the book and the names of author and publisher appear. If the book has no title page, the next best place is probably inside the front cover.

The beginning of any text (back or front according to which way the language of the text reads) would seem to be the best place for a copyright line, legally speaking, but design considerations have their effect: thus common UK practice is to relegate the notice on newspapers to the bottom of the last page.

The general notice and copyright line on each issue of a periodical, or at the front of a book, do duty for all the material in it; but any article whose copyright vests in an owner different from the owner of the whole should probably carry its own notice, where the article itself begins, as a footnote at the bottom of the first column, or at the end of an article provided the whole article appears on a single page.

Requirements for the Copyright Line

UCC requires that a copyright line should include three things: 'the symbol © accompanied by the name of the copyright proprietor and the year of first publication'. It does not insist that the three should appear in that same order, but it happens that this order lends itself best to the additions that are sometimes necessary, and the most generally favoured form is:

© Jo Smith 1993

The line should be kept as short and simple as possible but it is sometimes very helpful to preface it with a brief explanation:

This edition © UK Publishers Ltd 1993

On the other hand it is not good practice to mix extraneous matter with the copyright line (e.g. © 1990 UK Publishers Ltd, 310 Witherspoon Street, Thamesford, England).

The presence or absence of punctuation in the line is immaterial. It is sometimes felt that the symbol © may not be meaningful to the 'innocent' infringer and that a little interpretation is safer. Those who feel this way must not drop the symbol, but they can expand the line to read:

Copyright © Jo Smith 1993

When to Print a New Copyright Line

Any original material (text or illustrations) first published on or after 27 September 1957 (when the UK joined UCC) should have an appropriate line to cover it. The line must appear on every copy, from the beginning. Material for sale in the USA may sometimes carry a UCC line with a date earlier than 1957[p. 165] and in some cases reissues may have one.[p. 165]

One must distinguish between material which needs what can be called a 'main' copyright line and material which should be covered among the acknowledgements. In general, anything which has been previously published by itself or as part of another work and is now reused in the new work in a subsidiary fashion will have an acknowledgement line. (For acknowledgement of text see page 85, of illustrations, page 185.) The main body of the new work – perhaps only the editorial arrangement – will be covered by a new line. But if an undifferentiated part of the new work itself has previously appeared (as in the case of a book which was first published in instalments in a newspaper), the main copyright line should include the year(s) of the serialization with, if necessary, a descriptive line. If the copyright owners of the two appearances are different, then two lines will have to appear one above the other. (See 'The Date' below.)

Revisions must be 'original' within the meaning of the Act [p. 20] before a new line can be added to cover them.

When an item in an anthology or other work is published for the first time in that work the item should have a new line of its own. See below.

There are cases when it may be wise to add a copyright line to work which the author may regard as being still in draft form. If a sufficient number of copies are circulated to a sufficient number of people this may constitute legal publication, [p. 25] and if some of these copies are sent abroad it is doubly important to add a full-blown UCC notice to them. The date on a line used on the draft will have to be repeated when the text is properly printed and published, but as long as further work has been done on the draft before it is finally published there will also be a date for publication in book form.

Mistakes

The significance of a mistake in the copyright line varies from country to country. Omitting it, or getting the symbol, name or date wrong scarcely matters within the United Kingdom or Berne Union countries generally, since copyright protection in them does not depend on it.

However, for protection in countries which adhere to UCC but not to Berne, a correct UCC line is essential. In countries where protection depends on formal registration (for which the UCC line is a substitute) virtually any mistake may invalidate the copyright unless it can be shown to have occurred on a few copies only.

Total omission of the line is the worst mistake, since it could be equivalent to a declaration that the work is in the public domain. Its effect can only be overcome by inserting it on new copies and by complying with registration and deposit formalities in all countries which require them.

Putting the wrong name in a copyright line does not transfer ownership from the true owner to the person named. However, in countries where registration is necessary this might cause considerable muddle and may result in loss of protection. It is conceivable, too, that a court might accept a statement about ownership in a printed copyright line in the absence of other evidence.

It must be borne in mind that in the vast majority of cases mistakes only become significant when the validity of a copyright has to be proved in a court of law – most commonly in the course of an action against an infringer.

The Symbol

The letter C enclosed by a *circle* must be used, thus: ©. For UCC protection the word 'copyright' is not enough.

The Name

When a work is first published the name in the copyright line should be the name of the copyright owner at the time it is published (or, since publishers cannot be omniscient, when it is printed). It need not be a full name – 'J. Smith' will suffice, though obviously it is better to include a forename. It is not illegal to use a pseudonym in a copyright line but for practical reasons[p. 99] it is much better to avoid this unless the author insists on keeping his identity a total secret, and for purposes of litigation anywhere it is desirable to use the name of a real person or firm.

Do not automatically assume that the author (or publisher) is the copyright owner. Check the author–publisher contract. If it does not have a clause devoted specifically to the copyright line, remember that in an assignment[p. 201] the copyright belongs to the assignee (usually the publisher); in a licence[p. 200] the copyright remains with the licensor (usually the author).

If the author is the owner, ascertain whether he contracted in his own name or whether he has incorporated himself. If so, the name in the notice must be that of the corporation.

Copyright owners may of course be corporations, governments, heirs of the author, or almost any person or firm, but *not* unincorporated bodies. If in doubt about the ownership of a copyright, *Who Owns the Copyright?* (page 28) may be helpful.

Since copyright is divisible, the owner at one time or place may not be the same as the owner at another time or place. In particular, the copyright owner may differ as between the UK and USA territories, and will almost certainly be different as between a translation and its original. It is also possible for an author to assign part of his copyright (e.g. film rights) but not the rest, so that the owner of the copyright in the rights assigned will be some other person or firm, and the owner of the rights retained will be the author. The name given, then, should be the one appropriate to the place where the work is to be sold and to the form in which it is sold. It may even be advisable to print two names, with an appropriate explanatory phrase.

Between one edition of a work and the next the copyright may be assigned (or revert) from one owner to another. Opinions differ about what to do in such a case; the safest course is to keep the original name.*

If there is more than one copyright proprietor all the names must appear. For joint works[p. 15] the names of all the authors should appear together on the same line:

© Jo Smith, M. Brown and Black Enterprises Ltd 1993

For collaborations where various authors have contributed distinct pieces and have not assigned them to a single person or firm there may have to be several lines:

Chapters 1, 3 and 7 © Jo Smith 1993
Chapters 2, 4 and 6 © M. Brown 1993
Chapters 5 and 8 © Black Enterprises Ltd 1993

In publications with a supervisory editor (encyclopedias, anthologies, etc.[p. 149]) you must consider three types of copyright: that in the arrangement as a whole; that in any material published in the publication for the first time (do not forget an editor's Introduction or notes); and that in quoted pieces which have been previously published. These last will of course be relegated to the Acknowledgements.[p. 85] It is most common for the copyright in the first two to vest in the same person (or, more usually, firm) so one copyright line will cover both, and no explanatory wording is needed. Very occasionally, however, and especially in anthologies of contemporary work, a piece in which the author retains the copyright will have its first publication in the anthology. Such a piece will deserve a copyright line of its own:

---

*In the USA the assignee's name can only be substituted when the assignment has been registered with the Copyright Office. (See also page 208.)

Editor's Introduction and this arrangement © UK Publishers Ltd 1993

The poem 'Margarita' © U.R. Poet 1993

The Date

Since the United Kingdom did not ratify UCC until 27 September 1957 a UCC line cannot usually be used for material published before that date (but see 'UK Reprints and Reproductions' below).

The date given in a UCC line must be the year in which the material was first published. To show a later date will at the least amount to misleading the public and in some countries might put a work into the public domain. Revisions, translations and new versions generally, being newly copyrightable, will have later dates than the parent work.

If different sections of a text have been published in different years, the usual rule is that all the dates must be shown. If a book was first published in 1993 but one chapter appeared as an article in a magazine in 1991, the copyright line might read, according to varying circumstances:

© Jo Smith 1991, 1993

or:

© Jo Smith 1993
Chapter Three © Travel Publications Inc. 1991

or:

© Jo Smith 1993
Chapter Three is reprinted by kind permission of *Italy Magazine*, © Travel Publications Inc. 1991

If a book published in 1993 has already been serialized word for word in a magazine during 1991, the copyright line can only carry the 1991 date.

Revisions present an awkward problem. As long as the changes are extensive enough to be 'original'[p. 20] each revision will qualify for a new copyright of its own, and a new date. If a work is likely to be revised only once or twice, the easiest course is to show all the dates:

© Jo Smith 1970, 1987, 1993

or:

First Edition © Jo Smith 1970
Second Edition © John Bull and Sarah Smoggins 1987
This Edition © Sarah Smoggins 1993

However, one can imagine this sort of line stretching to infinity as the years go by. It has been held that in works like almanacs the whole qualifies for a new copyright each year, so if there are revisions throughout a work only the latest date and the latest copyright owner need appear in the copyright line.

It may be that only a clearly distinguishable portion of a work has been revised, and the rest remains the same. A second edition of a book on engines might have the line:

© UK Publishers Ltd 1970, 1993

or more clearly:

© UK Publishers Ltd 1970
Nuclear Powered Engines © UK Publishers 1993

If an otherwise out-of-copyright work is republished with new footnotes (and/or other new material) a new line must be run for the new material, and although one can simply put '© Jo Smith 1993' a more honest version would be:

Introduction and footnotes © Jo Smith 1993

If the text itself of an out-of-copyright work has been revised in a sufficiently original[p. 20] way it will qualify for a new copyright and the line will cover the entire new version. Again the simple line '© Jo Smith 1993' will do but a more explicit one would be:

Abridgement © Jo Smith 1993

Translations

An agreement for the sale of translation rights should include a clause binding the purchasing publisher to print a UCC line in his edition – as long as his country is a UCC member.[p. 218] If the English edition also carries a UCC line he should at a minimum print:

Original English-language edition © Jo Smith 1991
This translation © Purchasing Publishers 1994

Any other copyright notices in the English edition (e.g. for illustrations) should also reappear, and a commendable custom is to mention the original title and the name of the original publisher as well. Of course, these rules apply equally to a UK publisher issuing a work which has been translated into English.

UK Reprints and Reproductions

A reprint (whether in the same format as the original or a different format) should simply repeat the relevant copyright line shown in the previous edition unless newly protectable material has been added. If a UCC line or All Rights Reserved did not appear in the previous edition, do *not* put them in the new edition unless new material has to be covered, subject to the remarks in the next paragraph.

The UK did not ratify UCC until 27 September 1957 so material published in the UK before that date will not have a C-in-a-circle line. The United States ratified UCC on 16 September 1955, so if an American edition of your book carries a UCC line it can be added to the UK reprint. *However* there is one bothersome point to watch for: the USA invented the C-in-a-circle line for its own internal use long before UCC, so one may well appear with a date before 1955; if so it should *not* be copied.

When a UCC line cannot be printed one can simply print nothing, but on works which are still in copyright it is often preferable to put in some positive fact, for future reference, or for the sake of the 'notice' it gives to potential infringers, or because there is a UCC line covering later material and to run it alone might be misleading. In such circumstances use a general copyright notice[p. 156] and some variation of:

First published 1933
First revised edition published 1949
Second revised edition © UK Publishers Ltd 1993

(For lines covering revisions see also 'The Date' above.)

Opinions differ as to whether, in this situation, the line 'Copyright under the Berne Convention' is useful, since this statement is unlikely to be completely accurate. A work will only be copyright in countries which were adherents of Berne when it was first published, and it may be copyright in countries which are *not* signatories to Berne.

When giving permission for quotations, the quoting publisher should be asked to include in his acknowledgements the UCC line (if any) which covered the extract and also 'All Rights Reserved', if this appeared on the original material.

Reproductions of parts of a work (e.g. single-sheet maps, or a pamphlet containing one chapter from a book) should carry as much of the complete original copyright notice as is relevant and possible.

Material for Sale in the United States

When a UK publisher sells film, sheets or bound copies to an American publisher it is most important that they should agree on the form of notice which is to appear. Occasionally the owner of the copyright in the USA will not be the same person as the UK owner. The copyright may have been renewed[p. 211] and the American publisher may want to add a line to this effect. He may want to print a Library of Congress Catalog Card Number. The preferred wording of the general copyright notice is bound to differ, though 'All Rights Reserved' should certainly appear. If the work is in the public domain in the United States, the American publisher may ask for the copyright line to be omitted altogether.

The United States ratified UCC on 16 September 1955, but until it also ratified the Berne Convention with effect from 1 March 1989, some form of copyright notice was legally essential there on any work in which the American copyright had not expired. Although not now essential for copyright protection, the Copyright Office advises the following:

> The notice for visually perceptible copies should contain all of the following three elements:
> 1.   *The symbol* © (the letter C in a circle), or the word 'Copyright', or the abbreviation 'Copr.'; and
> 2.   *The year of first publication* of the work. In the case of compilations or derivative works incorporating previously published material, the year date of first publication of the compilation or derivative work is sufficient. The year date may be omitted where a pictorial, graphic, or sculptural work, with accompanying textual matter, if any, is reproduced

in or on greeting cards, postcards, stationery, jewelry, dolls, toys, or any useful article; and

3. *The name of the owner of copyright* in the work, or an abbreviation by which the name can be recognized, or a generally known alternative designation of the owner.

Example: © 1989 John Doe

The 'C-in-a-circle' notice is required only on 'visually perceptible copies'. Certain kinds of works, e.g. Musical, Dramatic and Literary works, may be fixed not in 'copies' but by means of sound in an audio recording. Since audio recordings such as audio tapes and phonographic disks are 'phonorecords' and not 'copies', the 'C-in-a-circle' notice is not used to indicate protection of the underlying Musical, Dramatic or Literary work that is recorded. But they do need a ℗ notice. (See page 125.)

47 A Checklist for the Copyright Page

The back of the title page ('copyright page', 'imprints page' or 'title page verso') has become the repository for all kinds of legal, quasi-legal, bibliographical and trade information. There may be more to put on it than will conveniently fit there, including:

> the full name(s) and address(es) of the publisher(s) – unless these appear on the title page
> the country in which the book was printed
> the name and address of the printer (if the book was printed in the UK)
> the copyright line(s) [p. 157]
> a general copyright notice [p. 156]
> an assertion of the author's moral right of paternity [p. 101]
> International Standard Book Number(s) – see below
> Library of Congress Catalog Card Number – see below
> British Library Cataloguing-in-Publication data – see below
> the dates of first publication and of subsequent reprints or new editions
> statements required by existing contracts (e.g. 'published in association with Tympany Television')

acknowledgementsP. 159
the previous title, if the title has been changed, or if the work
is a translation

The first three items above are required by UK law. Of course,
individual publishers may add many other items of an editorial and
design nature.

International Standard Book Numbers ('ISBNs') have been in use
since 1967, at first as SBNs, without the first digit (see below). They
are not legally required but are very important in the trade and for
Public Lending Right. The system also extends to software for sale
by retail. Originally of most help to booksellers and computerized
order systems, ISBNs and their bar codes now identify titles in
library computers, in the PLR computer, in bibliographies and in
reprography licensing. Getting the ISBN absolutely correct is very
important indeed.

The ISBN should also appear on the bottom of the back jacket
or cover. It is also advisable to include on the jacket a European
Article Number (EAN). This is a 13-digit bar code number including
the ISBN and a prefix book code.*

ISBNs are allocated in the first instance by the Standard Book
Numbering Agency; many publishers thereafter assign their own
numbers.

An ISBN consists of 10 digits divided into four groups separated
by hyphens or spaces, e.g. 0 304 32635 6. The first group (the 'group
identifier') denotes the language, geographical or other area in
which the book is published (0 or 1 means the UK, the USA,
Australia, Canada, Eire and South Africa). The second group (the
'publisher prefix') identifies the publisher and the third (the 'title
number') identifies not only the title but the precise edition and type
of binding. (If there is more than one volume there is a number for
each volume and a number for the complete set.)

The number of digits in each of these three groups may vary, but
they always total nine. The tenth (1 to 9, or X, for 10) is a single
'check digit' which helps computers recognize any error in transcription. (The check digit has to be recalculated for the EAN.) The
computer multiplies the first digit by 10, the second by 9, and so on,

---

*Full details are available in a booklet *Machine Readable Codes for the Book
Trade*, available from the Publishers Association.

---

and then adds the answers together. The check digit is chosen so that the final total will be divisible by 11, and if it is so divisible the computer will assume the number is valid.

It is sensible to print all your own relevant numbers in each copy; for instance a two-volume paperback should carry ISBNs for the set and for each volume, plus the relevant numbers for the hardback version, each version being identified by an appropriate descriptive phrase. When printing with another publisher, his numbers should appear on his copies unless you share the same copyright page, in which case both sets of numbers should appear.

Further information may be obtained from the Standard Book Numbering Agency Ltd, 12 Dyott Street, London WCIA 1DF, and in their publication *International Standard Book Numbering*, which includes guidelines for software publishers.

International Standard *Serial* Numbers (ISSNs) for magazines are obtainable through the UK National Serials Data Centre, The British Library, Boston Spa, Wetherby, West Yorkshire LS23 7BY. Some publications (e.g. yearbooks) may carry both an ISSN and an ISBN.

Cataloguing in Publication (CIP) is a voluntary scheme run by the British Library, separately from the library deposit required by law, to provide librarians and suppliers with similar standardized information for selecting, ordering and cataloguing titles but *before* publication. The publisher provides advance information and may receive in return a block of copy to be printed on the copyright page. This gives the author, title, cross-reference headings, various systems of library subject-classification numbers and the ISBN.

CIP data is published in the *British National Bibliography,* on cards, magnetic tape and CD-ROM and on-line via BLAISE. Information is obtainable from the agents responsible for the collection of material on behalf of the British Library: J. Whitaker & Sons Ltd, 12 Dyott Street, London WCIA 1DF.

Library of Congress catalog card numbers should be printed in any books destined for sale in the United States. The American CIP programme is similar to the British Library one (above), but antedates it by a quarter of a century. The entry in a book is similar, or may be only a single line, e.g. 'Library of Congress catalog card number: 84–90326'. The first two digits are the year the number was applied for, which is not necessarily the same as the year of first publication. Further information is obtainable from the Cataloging in Publication Division, Library of Congress, Washington, DC 20540.

48 Copyright in Artistic Works

Artistic works are the fourth category of original creative works protected by the Act. They can be divided into:

1 PHOTOGRAPHS
A photograph is 'a recording of light or other radiation on any medium on which an image is produced or from which an image may by any means be produced, and which is not part of a film' (a frame from a film would be protected as part of the film). A photocopy, having no element of originality, does not qualify as a photograph for copyright purposes, although works not immediately thought of as photographs, such as holograms and X-rays, would be included.

2 GRAPHIC WORKS
'Graphic works' include 'any painting, drawing, diagram, map, chart or plan, . . . engraving, etching, lithograph, woodcut or similar work'. They also include drawings made in connection with industrial designs and typefaces.

3 ENGRAVINGS
Engravings are now included in the definition of graphic works at 2 above, but under the 1956 Act they were entitled to a different period of protection from other Artistic works. In the 1956 Act engravings were defined as 'any etching, lithograph, woodcut, print, or similar work, not being a photograph'. Pictures (such as photographs) which merely happened to be reproduced by a printing process resembling engraving were not part of this group.

4 SCULPTURE OR COLLAGE
Sculpture includes 'a cast or model made for purposes of sculpture'.

5 WORKS OF ARCHITECTURE
These include buildings or models for buildings. A building 'includes any fixed structure, and a part of a building or fixed structure'. It

could even cover, for instance, a landscaped garden that included structures such as walls. (Architectural plans are drawings.)

6   WORKS OF ARTISTIC CRAFTSMANSHIP

This category is undefined by the Act but is presumably intended to include such things as china figurines, pottery and jewellery. Its protection has been invoked (though without success) for dresses and furniture, and its application depends very much on interpretation in individual cases.

The law takes much the same attitude to Artistic works as it does to the Literary, Dramatic and Musical works already described, but there are of course differences in detail.

The legal **author** of an Artistic work is the person who created it. However, until 1 August 1989, the author of a **photograph** was the person or firm who, at the time when the photograph was taken, was the owner of the film or other material upon which it was taken (this also applies to photographs commissioned before, even if not taken until after, 1 August 1989). The author of an **engraving** is the person who designs it. The author of a **drawing** is the person whose hand does the drawing (not the person who suggests the idea). The authors of **paintings, works of architecture, sculpture** and other works of **artistic craftsmanship** are respectively the painter, the architect, the sculptor and the artist.

To **qualify for UK copyright protection** an Artistic work must first of all be 'original'. The criterion of originality in copyright law is of a very low order, requiring little more than that a work should not be a direct copy of another.[p.52] Accordingly, most Artistic works are specifically protected 'irrespective of artistic quality', but this phrase is not used in connection with **architecture** or **works of artistic craftsmanship**. It must be assumed, therefore, that a house, say, or a piece of jewellery, will not qualify for protection unless its design is truly original in the popular sense.

Bank notes, coins and postage stamps are all protected by copyright, and special regulations apply.*

---

*Bank notes: apply to the Principal, Issue Office, Bank of England, London EC2R 8AH; Coins: apply to HM Treasury, Parliament Street, London SW1P 3AG; Stamps: apply to Royal Mail Stamps, 76–86 Turnmill Street, London EC1M 5NS.

Note that **maps** are very much in copyright. The Ordnance Survey, in particular, enforces its rights with vigour, and provides maps in many forms, including microfilm and digitized versions for computers.*

Unpublished original works are protected if the author[†] was a qualified person[p. 23] at the time when the work was made or, when the making extended over a period, a qualified person for a substantial part of that period.

Published original works are protected if the first authorized publication took place in the UK or another acceptable country[p. 8] OR if the author was a qualified person at the time the work was first published OR if the author died before first publication but was a qualified person immediately before his death. However, works published before 1 June 1957 will only be protected if first publication took place in acceptable territory.

Both published and unpublished works made under the direction or control of a government department or House of Parliament[p. 24] or a recognized international organization (since 1 June 1957)[p. 23] will be protected even if they do not otherwise qualify. But any Artistic work made before 1 June 1957 which 'was used, or intended to be used as a model or pattern to be multiplied by any industrial process' and which was capable of registration under the Registered Designs Act, is not protected by copyright.[p. 178]

Publication of an Artistic work is a fairly rare event. A work is published when, and only when, copies of it are issued to the public (including making them available by means of an electronic retrieval system). Exhibition is not publication. Issuing copies of a graphic work representing, or photographs of, a work of architecture, sculpture or artistic craftsmanship, is not publication. The inclusion of an Artistic work in a film, broadcast or cable programme is not publication. However, a work of architecture or any Artistic work incorporated into a building is considered 'published' when it is constructed. The issue to the public of authorized graphic works or photographs of a painting, or casts or miniatures of a work of sculpture, would constitute publication of the painting or sculpture.

---

*Maps: apply to Copyright Branch, Ordnance Survey, Romsey Road, Maybush, Southampton SO9 4DH.

[†]In a work of joint authorship, 'author' means any one or more of the authors (see page 15).

The **first owner of the copyright** is the legal 'author' (see above) unless:

1. He has assigned his prospective copyright to someone else in an agreement made on or after 1 June 1957. The owner is then the assignee.

2. He has made the work since 1 June 1957 in the course of employment.[p. 30] The copyright owner is then the employer. If a work was made between 1 June 1957 and 1 August 1989 by an employee of a periodical, there are some qualifications to this.[p. 31]

3. He was commissioned, before 1 August 1989, to take a photograph, to make an engraving (which includes any etching, lithograph, woodcut, print or similar work) or to paint or draw a portrait. When the person commissioning such a work paid or agreed to pay for it in money or money's worth, and the work was made in pursuance of that commission, the person who so commissioned the work was entitled to the copyright, unless he and the artist made an agreement to the contrary, even if the work was not actually made until after 1 August 1989. (When *other* Artistic works were commissioned before 1 August 1989, and for all Artistic works commissioned since then, the copyright remains with the artist unless he has agreed otherwise.)

4. He made the work as an officer or servant of the Crown in the course of his duties or under the direction or control of Parliament. The owner will then be the Crown or a House of Parliament.[p. 31]

5. He made the work after 1 June 1957 under the direction or control of a recognized international organization and was not a qualified person. The owner will then be the organization.[p. 23]

The **term of copyright protection** for most Artistic works (published or unpublished) continues until 50 years from the end of the year in which the author* dies (see also *Europe*, page 203). The exceptions to this general rule are as follows:

---

* In a work of joint authorship the relevant author is the one who dies last, unless some or all of the authors are pseudonymous or anonymous, in which case it is the one who dies last among those whose identity has been disclosed (see page 42).

1. A **photograph** is now protected for 50 years from the end of the calendar year of the death of the person who took it. However, a photograph taken before 1 June 1957 will only remain in copyright for 50 years from the end of the calendar year in which it was taken. Photographs taken and published between 1 June 1957 and 1 August 1989 are protected for 50 years from the end of the calendar year in which they were published. Photographs taken between 1 June 1957 and 1 August 1989, and still unpublished at 1 August 1989, are protected until 1 January 2040.*

2. For an **engraving** still unpublished when the author died, if the author died before 1 August 1989 the term of protection is until 50 years from the end of the calendar year in which the engraving is published, or until 1 January 2040, whichever is the sooner.*

3. Under the 1911 Act **maps, charts and plans** were entitled only to a term of 50 years from publication. Those still in copyright at 1 June 1957 are presumably entitled to the longer term described above.

4. **Artistic works that are Crown copyright** and which were made since 1 August 1989 are protected for 125 years from the end of the year in which they are made or, if commercially published[p.27] within the first 75 years, until 50 years from the end of the year of such publication. Crown copyright Artistic works, other than photographs and engravings, made before 1 August 1989 are protected until 50 years from the end of the year in which the work was made. Crown copyright photographs and engravings made before 1 June 1957 are protected until 50 years from the end of the year in which they were made. Crown copyright photographs and engravings made between 1 June 1957 and 1 August 1989 and published before 1 August 1989 are protected until 50 years from the end of the year of publication. Crown copyright photographs and engravings made on or after 1 June 1957 and existing but unpublished at 1 August 1989 remain in copyright until 1 January 2040.

5. For **Artistic works that are Parliamentary copyright** and which existed, unpublished, at 1 August 1989, and for those created since then – whether published or not – the term of protection is until 50 years from the end of the year in which the work was created.

---

*See also *Europe*, on page 203.

The **Acts Restricted by the Copyright** in all Artistic works are:

1. Copying a substantial part[p. 45] of the work 'in any material form' (including the making of a three-dimensional model of a two-dimensional work or vice versa).
2. Issuing copies of a substantial part of the work to the public.
3. Broadcasting a substantial part of the work or including it in a cable programme service.

Note that exhibition is not a restricted act, so a work can be exhibited without obtaining permission from the copyright owner. A work cannot, however, be exhibited against the wishes of the person who owns it as a physical property.

Indirect infringements are as described on page 48 for Literary, Dramatic and Musical works.

Exceptions from protection, when an Artistic work may be used without permission from the copyright owner, are as follows:

1. Fair dealing for purposes of research or private study.[p. 54]
2. Fair dealing for purposes of criticism or review, whether of that work or another work, as long as the use is accompanied by sufficient acknowledgement.[p. 54]
3. Fair dealing for the purpose of reporting current events[p. 55] (with sufficient acknowledgement as required) – with the important exception of photographs (which of course often have particular news value) for which permission *must* be obtained.
4. The incidental inclusion of an Artistic work in another Artistic work, film, broadcast or cable programme.[p. 121]
5. Reproduction for purposes of public administration.[p. 55]
6. The making of a subsequent Artistic work by the same artist, even if part of the earlier work is reproduced in the new one, so long as the artist does not repeat or imitate its main design.
7. The reproduction of a work for examination purposes, and for educational instruction, or preparation for instruction, provided the copy is not made by a reprographic process.[p. 62]
8. Illustrations that appear along with 'old unpublished works' or with anonymous or pseudonymous works may be published under special circumstances.[p. 66]
9. Reproducing illustrations to Literary and other works copied in libraries.[p. 58]

10. Making an article to a design (or copying an article made to that design) which is embodied in a design document[p. 179] (such as a drawing, written description or photograph) or in a model, unless the article is itself an Artistic work or typeface. (See page 180.)

11. Making and issuing copies to the public of a graphic work or photograph of a building or including it in a film, broadcast or cable programme service.

12. Doing anything in relation to a building for the purpose of reconstructing it does not infringe the copyright in the building or in any drawings or plans in accordance with which it was constructed.

13. If a sculpture, or anything which comes under the heading of 'works of artistic craftsmanship',[p. 171] is permanently situated in a public place, or in premises open to the public, it is permissible to make and publish a graphic work or photograph of it, or to include it in a film, broadcast or cable programme service, without permission from the copyright owner or the owner of the physical work. (However, museums and public galleries, and other organizations such as the National Trust and English Heritage, do impose their own restrictions as landlords.[p. 183])

14. An Artistic work may be copied, and copies may be issued to the public, for the purposes of advertising its sale (the reproduction cannot then be reused for other purposes without permission).

15. Articles of cultural or historical importance or interest that cannot lawfully be exported unless a copy is made and deposited in a library or archive may be copied for that purpose.[p. 94]

The **ownership** of an Artistic work as a piece of physical property constitutes no claim, by itself, to copyright in the same work. (See also page 183.) Artists generally sell a physical work (e.g. a painting) but not the copyright in it, so the owner of a painting may hang it on the wall in Chicago while the copyright continues to be owned by the artist in Paris. This means, among other things, that if you own a painting (or any other Artistic work) you have no right to allow anyone to copy, publish, film, or televise it unless you have a document proving that the copyright has been transferred to you, or the circumstances are such that the permission of the copyright owner is not necessary (see preceding paragraphs).

A **copyright notice** is as necessary on a published Artistic work as on any other kind of copyright material (see page 156).

Moral Rights

An artist is protected against the use of his name on something which is not his own work. The rules against **passing off**[p. 98] are equally applicable to Artistic works. For works created since 1 August 1989, the moral rights of **integrity** (the right not to have the work subjected to derogatory treatment) and **paternity** (the right to be credited as the author of the work) apply equally to Artistic works (see page 100). The right **not to have work falsely attributed** applies to artists and has done since 1 July 1957. During his lifetime and for 20 years after his death, the artist or his heirs can sue anyone who **alters** a work, or deals with the altered version as though it were the unaltered work of the artist. This would probably include, for example, the colouring of a black and white photograph. It is also illegal to pretend that **reproductions** have been made **by an artist of his own work** if in fact they have not.

There is a moral right of **privacy** in certain photographs and films. Since 1 August 1989 the person who commissions a photograph or film for private and domestic purposes has the right not to have copies of any part of it issued to the public, exhibited or shown in public, broadcast or included in a cable programme service. However, the right does not apply to photographs taken or films made before 1 August 1989. Furthermore, the right is not infringed if the work is incidentally included[p. 121] in an Artistic work, film, broadcast or cable programme service, or if it is used in connection with public administration.[p. 55] It is also not an infringement of the right of privacy to do anything with the work to which the person who has the right has consented. The right can be waived altogether, or waived for use of the work in specified circumstances. The right of privacy lasts for as long as the work remains in copyright, and can be assigned to the owner's heirs on his death.

Droit de suite, under which authors and their heirs in some countries (but not the UK) can continue to claim a financial interest in the disposal of their work even after they have sold it themselves, applies especially to Artistic works. (See page 93.)

Registered Designs and the Design Right

It is not within the scope of this book to cover designs in detail, but the following brief summary of previous legislation and the provisions introduced by Parts III and IV and Schedules 3 and 4 of the Copyright, Designs and Patents Act 1988 might be helpful.*

Between 1 July 1912 and 31 May 1957 the law of copyright did not apply to 'designs capable of being registered under the Patents and Designs Act 1907, except designs which, though capable of being so registered, are not used or intended to be used as models or patterns to be multiplied by any industrial process'.

Between 1 June 1957 and 24 October 1968 an owner whose work qualified for the protection of copyright law could register a 'corresponding design' under the contemporary Registered Designs Act. His industrial rights in the registered corresponding design then lasted for 15 years. During that time and afterwards, any industrial application of his design which he had specifically registered could be made without infringing his rights under copyright law. This rule also applied if he had authorized his work to be used industrially, even when he had not formally registered it, as long as the use to which it was put would have fallen within the scope of a registered corresponding design. (If his work was used or registered without his authorization these rules did not apply.) A design was taken to be 'applied industrially' if it was applied (a) to more than 50 articles all of which did not together constitute a single set of articles† or (b) to goods manufactured in lengths or pieces, other than hand-made goods.‡

---

* A full discussion of copyright and industrial designs can be found in chapter 20 of *Copinger and Skone James on Copyright* (see *Bibliography*).

† A 'set of articles' is 'a number of articles of the same general character ordinarily on sale or intended to be used together, to each of which the same design, or the same design with modifications or variations not sufficient to alter the character or substantially to affect the identity thereof, is applied' (Registered Designs Act, 1949).

‡ Copyright (Industrial Designs) Rules, 1957.

The following designs were excluded from registration and therefore from its effects: '(1) works of sculpture, other than casts or models used or intended to be used as models or patterns to be multiplied by any industrial process; (2) wall plaques and medals; (3) printed matter primarily of a literary or artistic character, including book jackets, calendars, certificates, coupons, dressmaking patterns, greetings cards, leaflets, maps, plans, postcards, stamps, trade advertisements, trade forms, and cards, transfers, and the like'.*

From 25 October 1968 when the Design Copyright Act 1968 came into force, until 1 August 1989, the position was roughly the same except that, even during the 15-year period while his exclusive industrial rights lasted, an author could claim full copyright protection as well.

The Copyright, Designs and Patents Act 1988 introduced a number of changes in relation to designs which may now be protected in one or more of three ways:

1. If a work created since 1 August 1989 qualifies as an Artistic work, it is entitled to full artistic **copyright**, whether or not it is also entitled to design right protection.
2. The **design right**, which like copyright is a property right not dependent on formal registration, protects original non-commonplace designs. A 'design' is defined as 'the design of any aspect of the shape or configuration . . . of the whole or part of an article' other than surface decoration. The design right comes into existence if and when an article has been made to the design or the design has been recorded in a 'design document'. A design document is 'any record of a design, whether in the form of a drawing, a written description, a photograph, data stored in a computer or otherwise'. Design right does not apply to a method or principle of construction (although that may be patentable). There are also what are known as the 'fit and match' exceptions: the right does not apply to the features of an article which '(i) enable the article to be connected to, or placed in, around or against, another article so that either article may

---

* Designs Rules, 1949.

---

perform its function, or (ii) are dependent upon the appearance of another article of which the article is intended by the designer to form an integral part'.

3. The features of shape, configuration, pattern or ornament applied to an article by any industrial process may be registered as **Registered Designs**. The finished article must have features which 'appeal to and are judged by the eye'. Registration involves the payment of a fee per five years for protection of up to 25 years from the date that the design was registered.

The first owner of the design is its designer. If the work is commissioned or done in the course of his employment, the first owner will be the commissioner or employer. Protection begins when the design is first recorded in material form and it lasts for 15 years or, if the work is first marketed within 5 years from when it is first recorded, for 10 years from the date of its first marketing (i.e. there is a maximum period of protection of 15 years from when the design is first recorded).

There is inevitably a large area of overlap between Artistic works and designs. If an act is an infringement of the copyright in the design, it cannot also be held to be an infringement of the design right. In other words, there cannot be two prosecutions – one under copyright and one under design right – for the same infringement. Where an Artistic work has been commercially exploited, with the permission of the copyright owner, by the marketing of articles which are copies of the work, protection of those articles (rather than of the original work) lasts for 25 years from the end of the calendar year in which the articles were first marketed. After 25 years it is not an infringement to do anything in relation to those articles although copyright in the original Artistic work will remain otherwise valid for the full period of protection.

It is not an infringement of the copyright in a design document[p. 179] or a model recording or embodying a design (although it may be an infringement of a design right) to make or copy an article to the design – unless the design document is an Artistic work or a typeface. For further information about the copyright in **typefaces**, see page 107.

Export Control of Works of Art

Anyone who wants to export photographs or works of art over 50 years old, or archaeological material buried for more than 50 years, must apply to the Department of National Heritage for an export licence. Permission for export may be refused on the grounds of the national importance of the object. (See page 93 for more details.)

---

49 Commissioning and Copying Artistic Works

Illustrations and artwork are a costly part of many publications. Artistic works of all kinds appear either directly* or as photographed, not only in books and periodicals but also in television programmes, video recordings and films. They can appear in the advertising for innumerable products; on book jackets and covers; in point-of-sale material. Quite often they are not illustrations to a text at all but are reproduced by themselves: on postcards or as separate, frameable colour prints or photographic slides.

Before an Artistic work can legally be reproduced it is sometimes necessary to get permission from as many as four or more different sources, though most cases are not so complex. The notes below are addressed mainly to book publishers illustrating books, but the same rules should be observed by anyone intending to reproduce an Artistic work in any way or in any medium.

Any person or firm who, for instance, buys a painting to hang on a wall, or commissions a portrait or a piece of sculpture, should be aware that he does not also have copyright in the work unless there is a written assignment to that effect.

---

* Here and in all the notes below the actual printing process is irrelevant and is ignored.

Newly Commissioned Works

New, original artwork and photographs are only too often commissioned by publishers in a completely casual manner, over the telephone or the lunch table, with no written agreement whatsoever. It may be that in many cases the 'intention of the parties' is that all rights in the resulting work, or an exclusive licence to exploit it, should belong to the publisher, but this is not automatically the case and irritating (and sometimes very costly) disagreements do arise. For instance, the artist may believe he is free to sell the same work to another buyer; the publisher may believe that he can sell the artist's work all over the world in any form without further payment to the artist. In the absence of any clear agreement between the two, the law will side sometimes with one and sometimes with the other.

When the illustrator does a considerable quantity of work (especially if the task is complicated by having to make special arrangements with museums, or in similar cases) he should be asked to sign a full-scale agreement. *Publishing Agreements*[p. 222] contains a specimen Illustration and Artwork agreement between publisher and illustrator which covers in detail the often complex arrangements in this situation. Ideally, every person who contributes *any* original artwork should be asked to sign a short, standard form so that everyone is clear as to the rights being transferred. It is usual for illustrators to retain ownership of their artwork or negative and generally, though not always, the copyright in it.

It should be noted that an artist's work may not be altered without his permission.[p. 102]

When an artist has, say, been commissioned to draw, paint, engrave or photograph existing subjects, permission to do so will have to be obtained by him or his publisher from the owner of the object and also, if the copyright has not yet expired, from the owner of the copyright in the object. (See 'The Object Reproduced', below.)

Permission to Reproduce Existing Artistic Works

No one may reproduce or publish an Artistic work which is still in copyright without permission from the copyright owner unless the use of it is one of the 'Exceptions from Protection' listed on page 175.

If you wish to use an illustration you should make certain that you have all four of the following types of permission whenever they are relevant:

1. Permission to reproduce **the illustration itself** (e.g. a photograph):
    (a) from the copyright owner of the illustration, if the illustration is still in copyright[p. 173] and
    (b) from the owner of the physical illustration, if this person is different from the copyright owner, whether or not the illustration is still in copyright.
2. Permission to reproduce the **object in the illustration** (e.g. in a photograph of a painting the object is the painting; in a drawing of an Egyptian mask the object is the mask):
    (a) from the copyright owner of the object if the object is in copyright; and
    (b) from the owner of the physical object, if this person is different from the copyright owner, whether or not the object is still in copyright.
    In some cases this type of permission is not necessary. See 'The Object Reproduced', below.
3. Permission from the landlord of the **premises** where the object of the illustration is available, for setting up the equipment necessary to make a copy of it. For instance, if a painting hangs in a museum, the museum can charge for permission to photograph it even if the museum owns neither the painting itself nor the copyright in it. Similarly, a landowner may charge a television crew for permission to set up its cameras on his land no matter what it is filming. (The National Trust and English Heritage can be strict about photographers on their property.)
4. If a photograph was commissioned for an individual's **private use,** his permission must be obtained to ensure that any use of the picture is not a breach of his moral right of privacy.[p. 104] With certain photographs (for instance, of medical cases) care should be taken that the patient who is the subject of the picture cannot be identified, which could be a breach of confidence.

A great many transparencies and illustrations are bought from agencies on a non-exclusive basis, and in these cases you should ensure that the rights you are paying for are what you need. (See 'Giving Permission and Charging Fees', below.)

Many agencies and museums are prone to ignore the distinctions between owner and copyright owner, and between the illustration and the object illustrated. Quite often they do not know whether the illustration they are dealing with has or has not been published before. If there is any doubt, the prospective publisher of the illustration should try to make certain that the source from which he obtained the illustration did in fact have the legal right to give all the necessary permissions, and that it supplies him with a copyright line (where relevant for works first published after 1 June 1957), a moral rights line (for works created after 1 August 1989) and in any case with all the relevant information for composing proper captions and acknowledgements.

The Object Reproduced

Many Artistic works (especially photographs, but also paintings, drawings and engravings) do themselves reproduce other objects. This results in a Chinese-box effect which needs especially clear thinking when applying for permissions. Objects commonly reproduced in this way are:

1 SCENERY AND SIMILAR NATURAL SUBJECTS
There is no need to get permission, obviously, if the object of an illustration is a mountain or a wild flower, or anything else of this description.

2 PEOPLE
Unless and until more stringent laws are passed to protect the privacy of the individual, photographs and other pictures may be freely made of anonymous crowds. If a portrait was made on commission before 1 August 1989 the copyright may vest in the person who commissioned it.[p. 171] Pictures commissioned since 1 August 1989 for a person's private use are subject to their right of privacy.[p. 104]

3 FACSIMILES OF TEXTS AND MANUSCRIPTS
There may be a typographical copyright[p. 105] in a printed text, necessitating permission from its publisher before it can be reproduced. Permission to reproduce a manuscript in facsimile must be obtained from its owner. If the printed text or manuscript is still

in copyright permission will probably have to be obtained from the copyright owner. (See *Reprinting Extracts,* page 81.)

4   WORKS OF ARCHITECTURE
It is legal to make and issue copies to the public of a graphic work[p. 170] or photograph of a building or the model for a building, or to include it in a film, broadcast or cable programme service, without having to obtain permission from the owner.

5   SCULPTURES AND 'WORKS OF ARTISTIC CRAFTSMANSHIP' [p. 171] IN PUBLIC PLACES
Anyone may make and publish a graphic work or photograph of such objects, and include them in a film, broadcast or cable programme service, without permission from the owner, provided the object is 'permanently situated in a public place, or in premises open to the public'. (Note that a statue, say, which is simply on loan to a museum from a private collection may *not* be reproduced without permission.)

6   PAINTINGS, DRAWINGS, ENGRAVINGS AND PHOTOGRAPHS, AND SCULPTURE AND 'WORKS OF ARTISTIC CRAFTSMANSHIP' NOT IN PUBLIC PLACES
Except in the special cases mentioned among the 'Exceptions from Protection' on page 175, no one may make or publish a painting, drawing, engraving or photograph of any of the above objects without permission from the owner of the copyright (if the object is in copyright) and in any case from the owner of the physical object.

The Copyright Line, Moral Rights Assertion and Acknowledgements

From the point of view of the copyright notice, illustrations are of two kinds: those which have been published before and those which have not.

The copyright line for the text of a book will probably protect any new illustrations but it is better to say clearly, e.g. 'Text and illustrations © I. M. Author 1993'. When the owner of the copyright in the illustrations is not the same person as the owner of the copyright in the text, the illustrations must have a line to themselves. For instance, in a book where the copyright in the text belongs to the author, and the copyright in the (new) illustrations belongs to the artist, and an employee of the publisher drew some maps, the notice should be along the following lines:

> Text © Jane Smith 1993
> Maps © UK Publishers Ltd 1993
> Line drawings © I. M. Artist 1993

When illustrations are issued separately (e.g. as prints for framing) each separate sheet should carry its appropriate copyright notice, moral rights assertion[p. 101] and/or acknowledgements of the permissions given by all interested parties.

If in doubt about the copyright status of illustrations, see *Copyright in Artistic Works* (page 170). For notes on copyright lines in general see *Composing the Copyright Notice* (page 155).

Previously published illustrations such as those obtained from agencies can carry a credit line to the owner of the illustration (and/or a copyright line and moral rights assertion) directly above or below the bottom line of the picture. Alternatively such credits can be included in the acknowledgements or other list of illustrations if this seems preferable.

In addition to the copyright and moral rights lines (for new illustrations) and the credit line (for old ones) there will usually be a great many other facts which must appear somewhere, especially if notes on such things as the provenance and present whereabouts of the work are included. If only a few illustrations are used this information may all fit on the copyright page. Alternatively all information except the copyright lines for first-published illustrations can be included in the captions accompanying the illustrations. Alternatively again, all the information except the copyright lines for first-published illustrations can be printed in a separate acknowledgements section.

Giving Permission and Charging Fees

Like other 'permissions', artwork which has already been used in a publication is usually sub-licensed on a non-exclusive basis.[p. 201] First of all it is, of course, important to make sure that the rights are yours to license (i.e. that you did not get them from someone else on a non-exclusive basis yourself). Next check the agreement with the illustrator to discover whether you can sub-license the pictures and, if so, whether there are any restrictions as to time, territory, division of the proceeds, etc.

Realistic fees for artwork permissions must take a large number of factors into account: the territory for which permission is requested; the size in which the illustration is to be reproduced; whether it is in black and white or colour; where it is to be used (inside or on a jacket or cover); what the new publication is (magazine, hardback, paperback, calendar, slide); the purpose of the use (educational, encyclopedia, novel, advertising); the print run of the licensee publication; the reputation of the illustrator; the number of pictures used from a single source; whether the use will compete with your own publication. Sometimes an access or lending fee for the physical transparency or artwork may be added.

Many publishers, and all agencies, have their own scales of fees worked out on these bases. *Publishing Agreements* by Charles Clark [p. 222] contains a very helpful Appendix on fees for illustrations other than photographs, and the Association of Photographers* will give advice on using photographs.

If you sub-license many illustrations a form letter is useful. Any permission should include: (1) a statement that the rights granted are non-exclusive; (2) an exact identification of the pictures; (3) territory (US, UK, etc.); (4) size or approximate size of the intended reproduction; (5) black-and-white or colour use; (6) place used (e.g. cover); (7) limit of use (e.g. one edition, hardback, magazine); (8) fee; (9) who pays, and how much, if the artwork is lost or damaged; (10) if insurance is necessary, whose responsibility it is to get the policy; (11) access fee, if any; (12) credit line(s) desired.

*The Association of Photographers, 9/10 Domingo Street, London EC1Y 0TA.

50 **If a Copyright Owner Dies**

Copyrights are treated by the law in the same light as any other personal and moveable property. A copyright owner can will his copyrights and the benefit of them to others or in trust for others. If you die intestate, copyright, PLR and the physical work will pass to whoever inherits your other property. In the case of joint works and other collaborations, your share does not pass to your co-author(s) but to the heirs of your other property – unless of course you have left contrary instructions. Inheritance tax may be payable on the capital value of copyright.*

A manuscript or Artistic work, any entitlement to PLR, and the copyright in the work are separate objects of ownership[p.92] and may be willed or devolve separately. However, section 93 of Part I of the 1988 Act states:

> 'Where under a bequest (whether specific or general) a person is entitled, beneficially or otherwise, to –
> (a) an original document or other material thing recording or embodying a literary, dramatic, musical or artistic work which was not published before the death of the testator, or
> (b) an original material thing containing a sound recording or film which was not published before the death of the testator,
> the bequest shall, unless a contrary intention is indicated in the testator's will or a codicil to it, be construed as including the copyright in the work in so far as the testator was the owner of the copyright immediately before his death.'

These provisions are very similar to those obtaining under the 1956 Act.

For deaths occurring on or before 30 June 1912 inheritance of a

---

* Inheritance tax is considered, in some detail, in *Copinger and Skone James on Copyright*, paras. 16-31–16-34 (see *Bibliography*).

manuscript had no legal relevance to the inheritance of the copyright in it. For deaths occurring on or before 31 May 1957 the statutory rules were somewhat different from those today. The legatee of the manuscript would inherit the copyright (in the absence of an expressed contrary intention or contrary ruling of a court) only if the will in question was made by the actual author of the work and if the work had not been published, performed or delivered in public.

The assignment of future copyrights [p. 202] permitted since 1 June 1957 gave rise to a further provision in the 1956 Act (applying to agreements made before 1 August 1989 but repealed by the 1988 Act):

> Where, at the time when any copyright comes into existence, the person [i.e. the assignee of a future copyright] who, if he were then living, would be entitled to the copyright is dead, the copyright shall devolve as if it had subsisted immediately before his death and he had then been the owner of the copyright.

Authors and other owners of copyright would do well to deal separately in their wills with their copyrights (and PLR) – and also, though this is less important, with their manuscripts. In particular an author may wish to appoint a literary executor,* who ought to be someone who understands the author's business.

There is often confusion about what is meant by a 'literary executor'. The task of executors is to assemble assets, meet any outstanding liabilities and then retain or distribute what is left as directed by the will. If you want someone to act as a trustee of your literary properties and to manage them for your beneficiaries, you should bequeath manuscripts, copyrights and PLR to the literary executor in trust for the beneficiaries. If you have an agent and want him to continue dealing with your work for the benefit of your heirs, you need only express a wish in the will that the executors and beneficiaries continue to use the services of the agent. If you do not have an agent, your heirs are entitled to join and receive the benefits of membership of the Society of Authors in the same way as a living author (but the Society will not generally take on the role of literary executor). Burdening an ordinary family solicitor with the problems

---

*The Society of Authors, 84 Drayton Gardens, London SW10 9SB, issues a very helpful Quick Guide leaflet *Your Copyrights After Your Death*, which is free to members and available to non-members at a small charge.

of a business of which he has no experience may well be more of a hindrance than a help.

It may be important to recall that rights licensed or assigned by authors between 1 July 1912 and 31 May 1957 may revert to their heirs 25 years after their death.[p. 34]

Publishers should remember that the name in the copyright line[p. 161] on a work not yet published when an author dies may, if practicable, be changed to that of the new owner of the copyright, as long as it is certain who this is to be.

An ordinary publishing agreement for a completed work continues despite the death of the author or other copyright owner, the author's obligations (unless they are of a personal nature) and earnings passing unchanged to the appropriate heir. If a work is unfinished by an author at the time of his death, a publisher or other firm to whom he has agreed to deliver it cannot compel the executors to finish the work, even in cases where this might be artistically possible. A copyright contract is one for the personal services of the author and cannot be transferred.

Both executors and licensees of the deceased should check all relevant contracts to ascertain whether there are any clauses bearing on the problems – financial or otherwise – which crop up at such a time.

51 Composing a Contract

The object of a contract for a copyright work is to transfer a degree of control of the copyright in the work from one person to another, typically from the author of the work to a publisher. The person who controls the copyright can use the work to make money, so the publisher will pay the author for it.* The contract (or 'agreement') will state the amount of this payment, and if the author is to share in later earnings it will specify what his share is to be. Differing methods of transfer and payment are discussed in more detail below.

---

*Money matters are left to individual negotiation. The 1988 Act does not concern itself with them and the Copyright Tribunal can arbitrate on (but not set) fees within its province.

It is not always legally necessary for a contract to be in writing, but written ones are always preferable. Never depend on the unsupported word or goodwill of an individual. He may change his mind, or his job, and the memory of even the most honourable man is frequently unreliable. Furthermore, the clauses (numbered paragraphs) in a written agreement serve to emphasize facts of which the parties may be ignorant.

You do not have to be a lawyer to write a legal contract. In the publishing business, indeed, an experienced executive will probably produce a more sensible document than any solicitor except one versed in copyright law and accustomed to the intricacies of the industry. But it is essential to seek experienced professional advice if you find yourself negotiating in an area whose technicalities you do not fully understand.

In any case, very important points can be overlooked, so an existing model should be followed or used for comparison whenever possible. Every UK publisher should have a copy of *Publishing Agreements: A Book of Precedents* by Charles Clark,[p. 222] which contains model contracts between publisher and author for general and educational books, plus agreements for paperback rights, the writing of translations, the sale of translation rights, electronic rights, book club rights, illustrations and artwork, merchandising rights, 'packaging' sales, United States rights, and option and assignment agreements for film, television and other rights. With its detailed advice and abundant information on all kinds of relevant topics Mr Clark's book is indispensable for anyone preparing or receiving such agreements. Covering similar ground, but viewed from the author's rather than the publisher's perspective, is *Understanding Publishers' Contracts* by Michael Legat.[p. 222] Authors are also advised to have any contract vetted by an agent or their appropriate organization.*

Many authors, illustrators and even publishers pay far too little attention to the contract they sign, forgetting that the way it is worded can make or lose them considerable amounts of money. This attitude is perhaps due to the regrettable fact that all too often

---

*The Society of Authors, 84 Drayton Gardens, London SW10 9SB (which also publishes a *Quick Guide* to publishing contracts); or the Writers' Guild of Great Britain, 430 Edgware Road, London W2 1EH. The Society and the Guild have negotiated Minimum Terms Agreements with a number of publishers.

the document they sign does not accurately reflect the business they have discussed. This should not be so. Ideally a contract should be tailored to the individual case. Standard agreements are useful time-savers, but they should leave plenty of scope for additions and alterations.

A publishing agreement cannot be put away and forgotten when it has been signed (though the original should be carefully preserved like any other valuable document). The information it contains will be in continual demand by all departments, so the more easily comprehensible it is, and the more it takes into account the individual needs of those departments, the better and more useful it will be.

A good contract is clear. 'Ordinary' language, like that of a good business letter, is preferable to unfamiliar legalese, but it is essential that only one meaning can be extracted from it. (Consider the multiple disasters inherent in a sentence like 'The principal illustrations shall be selected by the Author in consultation with the Editor and he shall be responsible for all fees payable.') It is wise to punctuate as little as possible and, where punctuation is used, to ensure that the sentence will mean the same with or without it. This straining after a single interpretation is the chief reason for the turgid sound of legal documents.

Careful definition is necessary. Such phrases as 'net receipts', 'after deduction of all expenses', 'revised editions' can cause much confusion, and so can the use of a term (such as 'the Smith edition') whose meaning is so clear to the original signatories of the agreement that they overlook the necessity of explaining it for the benefit of future business generations. Trade terminology cannot be expected to survive unchanged, so a phrase like 'second serial rights' should be further defined.

A good contract covers all likely eventualities. Constant renegotiation to deal with situations which should have been foreseen is a nuisance and causes untold confusion. It is true that 'a contract can always be modified' – but only as long as both sides are willing to modify it.

A good contract should be self-explanatory, containing 'the whole understanding of the parties'. It should mention all relevant facts and should ideally be immediately comprehensible to someone quite unfamiliar with the original negotiations, 50 years or more after it has been signed.

A contract is itself a copyright work, owned by the publisher or agent who drafts it.

The Basic Contract

A contract can be a lengthy document with many clauses, referring to the signatories in the third person ('. . . and the Publisher shall . . .') or it may be a letter ('. . . and you have undertaken to . . .'). In either case every party to the contract should be supplied with one copy of it signed by the other parties.

Before an agreement is signed there will be a period of negotiation varying from a short telephone conversation to bargaining lasting for months. It is during this time that the essentials of the contract should be settled. There is no point in signing an agreement until all or nearly all of these essentials have been agreed. A mere 'agreement to agree' is unenforceable.

Most contracts concerned with copyright works transfer the effective control of some or all of the copyright from the existing copyright owner to a buyer. Typically the copyright owner of a Literary work is an author and the buyer is a publisher, but often both copyright owner and buyer are publishers. There are also profit-sharing agreements (author–publisher and publisher–publisher) and commission agreements, where no rights change hands. A transfer of copyright can also take place for other purposes when the person acquiring the copyright cannot exactly be described as a 'buyer'. The notes below are written mainly from the point of view of an author–publisher contract, but the principles involved apply to any agreement relating to a copyright.

It will be obvious that besides the questions listed here, there are a great many others of a legal or practical nature which should be answered by a contract of any complexity. These will vary very much, depending on the type of copyright work being sold, the requirements of the industry involved and the individual arrangements made.

In general, however, the essential questions to be answered by the terms of any contract are these:

1 WHO ARE THE 'PARTIES TO THE AGREEMENT' (THE BUYER AND SELLER)?
Their names and addresses must be given, and a brief identification of their roles (author, publisher, editor, etc.). If there are more than two parties to the agreement their relationship to each other must be clear. Joint authors can contract jointly but it is easier if they agree that one of them shall be responsible for any decisions that

have to be taken. All of them should, however, sign the contract. A person should contract under his real name, but pseudonyms may be added in parentheses after an author's real name (or elsewhere) if this seems useful. If it is absolutely necessary to conceal his identity an author can sign contracts with his pseudonym only (provided his bank and the Inland Revenue are aware of his dual identity) but this can cause difficulties in other respects (see page 41).

An agreement with a limited company must clearly be with that company and signed 'for and on behalf of' it by an appropriate officer, otherwise the agreement may turn out to have been a personal one with, say, one of the directors. An unincorporated body cannot enter into a contract except via a personal one signed by one of its members.

A buyer who acquires rights under an exclusive licence[p. 200] or any form of assignment[p. 201] can pass these rights on to a further buyer. However, the buyer cannot do this if the copyright owner has only signed the agreement because of the buyer's unique reputation or skill. An exclusive licence on royalty terms may be held to be of this personal character anyway, but an author may wish to include a statement that the agreement is not assignable by the publisher,[p. 34] while a publisher's interests lie in the opposite direction.

As for an author, a publishing agreement is almost always one for his personal services. He cannot hand on his obligations to someone else to perform, and if he dies before his work is complete no buyer can force his executors to have it finished, unless there are contractual terms to this effect. A reference in an agreement to 'the Author's executors, administrators and assigns or successors in business' will, however, be applicable to transactions *after* the complete work has been delivered.

2   WHAT PRECISELY IS THE WORK COVERED BY THE CONTRACT?

Whether the contract is concerned with an existing work or is a 'commission' for a future copyright, an exact description should be given. For a manuscript this will mean at a minimum its working title and its approximate length; an outline of its subject-matter or a full-length synopsis may be added. If other items such as an index or illustrations accompany the text, these too should be described.

A description of illustrations should specify their number, the text (if any) which they are intended to illustrate, and as many other facts as possible which will enable them to be identified later: e.g. whether they are photographs, line drawings, water-colours, engravings; in black and white or colour; their titles; their subject-matter.

3   WHEN MUST THE COPYRIGHT OWNER DELIVER THE WORK TO THE BUYER?

4   WHAT MEASURE OF CONTROL IS TO BE TRANSFERRED?
In a commission agreement or profit-sharing agreement the present owner of the copyright may continue to keep full control of it. If this is the situation the contract should say so. But if a buyer is to acquire any legal power to make his own decisions about the work he is paying for, the owner of the copyright must give him this power via a non-exclusive licence, an exclusive licence, a partial assignment or an outright assignment. See 'Licences and Assignments', below.

5   MORAL RIGHTS
The author should assert his moral right of paternity if the work is one to which moral rights apply (see page 102).

6   WHAT STEPS MUST BE TAKEN TO PROTECT THE COPYRIGHT?
The copyright owner should ensure that the buyer will, if legally possible, print a UCC copyright line[p. 157] on all copies of the work. Special care must be taken when a work is published in the United States[p. 208] or in translation.[p. 117] An actual example of the intended copyright line should appear in the contract. Whether it is in the name of the buyer or the seller will depend on the answer to Question 4 above. Besides being invaluable to the person responsible for setting the copy, such an example expresses the essence of the contract in a way which only the most careless signatory can miss.

7   SHOULD OTHER CONTRACTS BE TAKEN INTO ACCOUNT?
Consider the agreement you are drafting 'in the round'. For instance, if the new work is part of a series, or one contribution among many, should all authors sign identical terms? When sub-licensing, check previous agreements for undertakings which should be passed on (preferably in identical wording) to new buyers; do

not inadvertently sell the same rights, or conflicting rights, to different buyers.

8 WHAT RIGHTS IS THE BUYER ACQUIRING?

The Acts Restricted by the Copyright look strange to anyone familiar with the 'rights' sold by authors to book publishers and other buyers. The Act deals with generalizations intended to be applicable to as many individual cases as possible: publication, for instance, is publication however it is effected. But to an author, serial rights sold to a periodical and volume rights sold to a book publisher are quite separate ways of earning money. The customs, technology and business structure of each medium are different enough to obscure the essential similarity of the two methods of reproducing a text.

The Act's divisions are no direct help to a copyright owner trying to sell his work. It would do him no good to offer his reproduction rights to one company, his publication rights to another and his translation rights to a third. What he actually does is to divide his copyright into a number of saleable packages, each package containing limited slices from several different 'restricted acts'. Thus a novelist may sell a package loosely called 'television rights' which includes slices from the restricted acts of broadcasting, performance and adaptation of a non-dramatic work into a dramatic one.

A contract should not only make clear what rights are being transferred but also (if this is the case) that all others are retained by the copyright owner. If the intention is to transfer all rights and if there is no reason (e.g. varying shares of the proceeds from sublicences) for mentioning them separately it is best simply to say 'all rights'.

9 HOW LONG WILL THE BUYER KEEP THESE RIGHTS?

The agreement may remain in force for a stated number of years and terminate on a stated date. Or termination may depend on some particular occurrence: for instance, the rights in books commonly 'revert' to the author (a) when the book is out of print* and the publisher does not reprint it within a certain time after receiving

---

* A book is said to be out of print ('o/p') when no copies are left or not enough copies are available from stock to satisfy reasonable public demand.

appropriate notice from the author, or (b) if the publisher goes into liquidation or (c) fails to comply with the terms of the agreement. An agreement may be terminable by one side giving the other, say, a year's notice. An 'outright' assignment has no provisions for termination: all rights are assigned for the full term of copyright. (See also 'Reversion of Rights under the 25-year Proviso' on page 34.)

10 IN WHAT LANGUAGES MAY THE BUYER USE THESE RIGHTS?
This question is not strictly relevant in the case of Artistic works, nor to Musical works without accompanying words, but it is sometimes prudent to ensure that a work may be used 'in connection with' all languages. For a discussion of translation rights in Literary and Dramatic works see page 117.

11 WHERE MAY THE BUYER USE THESE RIGHTS?
The buyer may control the rights throughout the world where copyright subsists or in certain countries only. Our copyright law does not recognize any territorial division smaller than a country, and though smaller divisions may be agreed as a matter of contract only, it is important to remember that sales in the European Community are subject to the Treaty of Rome, which insists upon free circulation of goods within the European Economic Area.[p. 207] The only safe course is to grant (or retain) rights in any one language for the whole of Europe.

When selling English-language rights to the United States, markets are individually negotiated for each title.* A schedule of territories, usually divided by continent and then alphabetically by country, must be attached to every such contract – and indeed to *all* contracts which grant some markets and withhold others – specifying where the buyer has exclusive distribution rights and where rights are exclusively reserved to the seller, and noting that in the remainder (the 'open market') both buyer and seller have a non-exclusive right of distribution. Canada is often a particular bone of contention between US and UK publishers.

With effect from 24 December 1991 Australia amended its

---

*The old semi-automatic division into the 'British publishers' traditional market' and an exclusive American market was outlawed by the anti-trust decree of the US Department of Justice in 1976.

Copyright Act so that, in order to secure Australia as an exclusive market, a work must be published in Australia within 30 days from when it is first published elsewhere. In addition, for titles first published overseas before 24 December 1991, and for titles for which Australian exclusivity has been established by publication within the 30-day limit, the importers within Australia must also fulfil orders by booksellers within 90 days from the placement of the order – failing which copies can legally be imported direct from somewhere else.

12 WHEN MUST THE BUYER EXERCISE HIS RIGHTS?

In the case of assignments, especially, it is not at all clear whether the purchase of a copyright work obliges the buyer to make use of it. In any situation where the copyright owner wants the buyer to publish, display, perform or otherwise use a work the agreement should include an undertaking by the buyer to do so by a given date.

13 HOW MUCH (AND WHEN) WILL THE BUYER PAY FOR THE RIGHTS?

There will usually be a principal payment for the rights of greatest use to the buyer and which the buyer will in most cases exercise himself. Thus the central question in a book contract (and similarly in any contract dealing mainly with a right which is expensive to exercise) is the amount of the royalty and of the advance against royalties. A royalty is usually a percentage of the retail price of a book, but this should be explicitly stated. If a publisher agrees to pay an author a royalty of 10 per cent of the published price and his book is sold in the shops at £10 a copy, the author will receive £1 for every copy sold. The advance is the sum commonly paid before copies of the book are ready to sell and is calculated on the likely sales of the first print run. If an author receives a £1,000 advance he will not receive any more money until the royalties earned by the sales of his book amount to £1,000. (Legally, the advance is usually returnable to the buyer if the work contracted for is not delivered.)

Some agreements, especially those for short articles or commissioned illustrations, are concerned only with one 'lump-sum' payment after which no further money changes hands. The agreement should make this very clear.

Any attempt to relate payments to 'net profit' (in, for instance, a profit-sharing agreement) creates a minefield of ill-feeling and administrative difficulties, if nothing worse. In such situations payments should be related to actual (or, in publishing parlance, 'net') receipts (i.e. invoice value).

It is important to describe exactly *when* the buyer must pay any sums due to the seller. Common book-publishing stages for advances are on signature of the contract, on delivery of the completed work, on publication; royalties are paid once or twice a year on stated dates.

The buyer not only acquires rights from the copyright owner but often hopes to resell these same rights to other purchasers. If the copyright owner is to share in earnings from these sales the amount and basis of his share under different circumstances should be clearly stated. Such earnings come from two main sources: sales of the physical work other than those covered by the principal payment (e.g. sales of sheets or bound copies of a book to overseas publishers or to book clubs, in addition to the royalty-earning retail sales), and sales of rights alone (e.g. the sub-licensing of translation rights, film rights, American rights). If the copyright owner is not entitled to a share in these earnings this too must be made clear. Conversely, it may be agreed that the buyer will share in the earnings from rights retained by the copyright owner.

Other financial points to be covered include whether Value Added Tax should be added to the payments; in what currency payments should be made and in what form (e.g. irrevocable letter of credit); and whether withholding tax may be deducted.

14 WHO PAYS THE NECESSARY EXPENSES?

It is always wise, and sometimes vital, to ensure that the buyer will bear the whole cost of exercising the rights he has bought (e.g. that a publisher will bear all expenses in connection with the production, publication and advertisement of a book). On the other hand, an author is expected to pay his own permission fees,[p. 86] travel expenses and similar costs unless he expressly arranges otherwise. It is essential to spell out who is to pay for large contributions such as an index or illustrations.

This situation will be reversed in a commission agreement, and in a profit-sharing agreement expenses will be split on a percentage basis. In both these cases an exact definition of 'expenses' can be the longest and most important part of the contract.

15 WHOSE LAW APPLIES?

Copyright and contract law, and therefore the interpretation of a contract, vary from country to country. If the signatories to a contract are based in different countries the contract should include a statement that it is to be construed in accordance with the law of one country or the other (or of an individual state in the USA), and that any action concerning it is to be brought in the courts of that country. The country specified should be the one where the contract is drafted.

Licences and Assignments

For the sake of clarity the following notes assume that the copyright owner who is selling his work is a book author, and that the buyer is a book publisher, but whoever owns a copyright and whoever buys it the same principles apply.

Licensing a copyright resembles letting a house. If a book is published under licence from the author, he retains the copyright and it is his name which appears in the copyright line when the book is published. He usually has a continuing interest in the sales of his book (e.g. he receives royalties) and the agreement should include some kind of termination clause.

An author who grants rights to a publisher in an **exclusive licence** cannot then grant the same rights to anyone else (nor can he exercise them himself) though he may retain other rights which remain saleable elsewhere. For instance, he can give a London publisher an exclusive licence to publish his book in the English language, and then give a Paris publisher an exclusive licence to publish his book in French. Most royalty contracts are exclusive licences.

Exclusive licences must be in writing.

An author who licenses his book to one publisher exclusively gives him a considerable amount of control over the rights covered by the contract. For instance, if the rights include serial rights, the publisher will be able to arrange serialization of the book without consulting the author. Even if the contract specifies that the author's consent must be obtained before serial rights are sold, it is the publisher, not the author, who must negotiate with the interested periodical and sign the necessary agreement. A publisher who is an exclusive licensee can sue an infringer by himself, although the author may have to become a party to the action unless the court decides otherwise.

When an author grants rights to a publisher in a **non-exclusive licence** he retains the power to sell the same rights to as many other publishers as may be interested, and the publisher cannot sub-license the rights he acquires to anyone else. Consequently book rights will almost never be the subject of a non-exclusive licence. On the other hand, for smaller items like photographs or single poems, it will usually be in the author's interest to grant non-exclusive licences only, leaving himself free to sell the same rights as often as he can. 'Permissions'[p. 81] to reprint extracts or short items are non-exclusive licences. The payment involved in a non-exclusive licence may be either a lump sum or a royalty.

A non-exclusive licence need not be in writing (though a written one is always preferable). It can be made orally, or implied from circumstances.

Rights granted by a non-exclusive licence should be tied to one particular situation. A photographer, for instance, would be foolish to give a publisher the right simply to 'reprint' his photograph, since even in the unlikely event that he was to receive a royalty on every use, such a wide licence might prevent him entering into a more lucrative exclusive licence or assignment later on.

Assigning a copyright resembles selling the freehold in a house. An author who assigns his copyright to a publisher gives up all control over the rights covered by the agreement. The copyright line will be in the publisher's name, and the publisher, who is now the sole owner of the copyright in the rights transferred, can deal with the book as he pleases.*

All assignments must be in writing.

All assignments (and licences) in the United States can usefully be registered with the Copyright Office.[p. 208]

Typically an author assigns his rights for one single lump sum or 'outright' payment, but the monetary arrangements under an assignment can be as varied as they are under licences. Authors are usually advised not to accept a continuing royalty and at the same time

---

*The author continues to have some protection against alterations to his work. See 'Moral Rights', page 100.

---

assign their rights because if the publisher reassigns the copyright to someone else the author may have difficulty getting paid.

Since 1 June 1957 it has been possible to assign the copyright in a work which does not exist when the agreement is signed, so that the publisher (not the author) is the owner of the copyright from the moment any part of the work is 'made'. This is called an assignment of 'prospective' or 'future' copyright and is now a common sort of agreement for many kinds of work.

A publisher to whom an author assigns his copyright can sue an infringer without making the author a party to the action, and he can even in extreme circumstances sue the author himself.

An **outright assignment** is one in which the author transfers his copyright to the publisher for all time. An outright assignment includes all the rights which comprise the copyright. It is rare these days for a book to be the subject of an outright assignment, but articles written for newspapers, commissioned artwork and the like may well be sold on this basis.

Authors should be particularly wary of signing anything (including the backs of cheques and receipts if there is no pre-existing contract) which refers simply to 'the copyright' or 'an assignment of copyright' since in the absence of further definition these phrases will most probably be interpreted as an assignment of all rights whatever in perpetuity.

A partial assignment transfers complete control of the copyright to the publisher in the same way as an outright assignment, but the transfer is for only a limited time (e.g. after a certain period all rights revert to the author) or territory (the agreement is concerned with rights in the United States only) or language (only rights in English) or by the rights granted (the author assigns his television and film rights but retains all the others). Some partial assignments can be almost indistinguishable from exclusive licences.

If a contract is carelessly drawn it may be very difficult to tell whether it should be interpreted as an assignment or a licence. Obviously the actual words 'licence' or 'assignment' should appear, though if they are wrongly used and are plainly contradicted by the rest of the agreement a court may still hold that the intention of the parties was different.

It is important to bear in mind that no one can pass on a greater measure of control than he himself owns: an exclusive licensee can sub-license rights but he can never assign them. An author cannot grant rights which he has already granted exclusively to someone else.

52 **Europe – Changes on the Agenda**

In 1988 the European Commission published a *Green Paper on Copyright and the Challenge of Technology*[p. 1] as part of a programme to harmonize and strengthen copyright protection throughout the Community. Arising from the *Green Paper* the EC is drafting a number of directives which will directly and indirectly affect publishing in the UK:

Directive on the Duration of Copyright

At the time of writing, the Directive on 'The Harmonization of the Term of Protection of Copyright and Certain Related Rights' is still only a draft. However, a common position on the draft Articles has been reached by the EC internal market ministers, although it still has to be approved by the Council of Ministers. You should consult your professional association for further information.

The draft Directive states that, from 1 July 1995, the duration of copyright for all **Literary, Dramatic, Musical** and **Artistic works**[p. 40] will be extended to 70 years from the end of the year in which the author dies, whether or not the work was made available to the public[p. 37] within that time. The extended period of protection will apply to any work which is in copyright anywhere within the European Community on 1 July 1995. This will mean that some works which had gone out of copyright in the UK before that date may go back into copyright, because some EC countries (e.g. Germany) have longer periods of copyright protection for works first published there and some have curious exceptions, such as the extension to protection given by France to some works during World War II.

Works of **joint authorship**[p. 15] will be protected until 70 years from the end of the year in which the last surviving author dies. For **anonymous and pseudonymous works**[p. 41] where the identity of the authors is unknown, copyright protection will last until 70 years from the end of the year in which the work was created or, if authorized copies are made available to the public[p. 37] within that time, until 70 years from the end of the year it was first made available to the public.

The draft Directive makes clear that these provisions are 'without prejudice to any acts of exploitation performed before [1 July 1995]' and that 'Member States should adopt the necessary provisions to protect particular acquired rights of third parties'.

Films[p. 133] will be protected until 70 years from the end of the year of the death of the last surviving of the following four people: the principal director, the author of the screenplay, the author of dialogue, the composer of music specially written for the film. In addition, unlike the present position in the UK, the principal director will be held to be the **author**, or one of the authors, of a film (as opposed to the script).

Sound recordings[p. 122] (called phonograms in the draft Directive) will be protected for 50 years from the end of the year of first fixation unless lawfully published or made available to the public[p. 37] within that time, in which case protection will last until 50 years from the end of the year they are first made available to the public.

The copyright in **broadcasts**[p. 133] will last for 50 years from the end of the year of first transmission, whether by wire or over the air and whether by cable or satellite.

The **performer's right** is described on page 118. Under the draft Directive, the performer's right will last until 50 years from the end of the year of the first performance of a work, unless a fixation (e.g. a film) of the performance is first lawfully published or made available to the public[p. 37] within that time, in which case it will last until 50 years from the end of the year it is first made available to the public.

The producers of the first fixation of a film (defined as 'a cinematographic or audiovisual work or moving images, whether or not accompanied by sound') will have a right (presumably similar to the performer's right) for 50 years from the end of the year of first fixation of the film unless it is lawfully published or made available to the public in that time, in which case protection will last until 50 years from the end of the year it is first made available to the public.

Out-of-Copyright Works

The draft Directive proposes an entirely new right in **unpublished works that have gone out of copyright**. The person who first makes available to the public[p. 37] such a work will have 'a protection equivalent to the economic rights of the author' for 25 years from the end of the year in which the work is first made available to the public.

In addition, Member States *may* (but probably will not have to) protect critical and scientific editions of works which have gone out of copyright. The protection would last for a maximum of 30 years from the end of the year the critical or scientific edition was first published.

The draft Directive contains further provisions, for example covering the treatment of works from non-EC countries. Expert, up-to-date advice should be sought where necessary.

The Software Directive

A Directive on the copyright protection of computer software was adopted by the Council of Ministers in May 1991 and took effect on 1 January 1993. The UK already gave copyright protection to computer programs as Literary works (one of the specifications of the Directive). The UK Act already also provided for the rental right in computer software.[p. 109]

Under the Directive the copying of software is permitted in limited circumstances if it is for the making of back-up copies. 'Reverse engineering' is also permitted in order to correct errors in a program or to study or test it but not to make improvements or upgrade it. (See page 137.) At the time of writing, amendments are being ratified by Parliament so that UK law complies with the Software Directive.

Directive on Rental and Lending Rights

A Directive on Rental and Lending Rights was adopted by the Council of Ministers in November 1992 and gives authors, performers, and the producers of sound recordings and films the exclusive right to permit and be remunerated for the rental of their works. This right would cover, for example, the renting of Literary works on tape or CD-ROM. The Directive will affect works protected by copyright at 1 July 1994 although countries will be allowed to delay implementing a number of the provisions until 1 July 1997.

There are PLR schemes in Denmark, Germany, the Netherlands and the UK. However, the provisions of the Directive concerning a Lending Right met stiff opposition and have been greatly diluted. It seems that countries probably will be obliged at some time to introduce either a right to control lending or a scheme remunerating authors for the lending of their works. However, it seems that categories of lender, which could include school, university and even public libraries, will be able to opt out and the level of remuneration to writers may be determined according to the individual country's 'cultural promotion objectives'. There may be renewed pressure for existing PLR schemes, and any new ones, to treat all European authors equally. The EC has undertaken to produce a report on the implications and effects of lending right schemes by 1 July 1997.

Directive Requiring Adherence to the Latest Versions of the Berne Convention (Copyright) and the Rome Convention (Neighbouring Rights)

This has been agreed as a Resolution of the Council of Ministers and would extend to the countries in the European Economic Area. The UK is a signatory to the latest version of the Berne Convention but not at the time of writing to the latest text of the Rome Convention (covering rights of performers, producers of sound recordings, and broadcasting organizations).

Directive on the Legal Protection of Databases

The main standards that are needed are a definition of originality and of term of protection and the draft Directive proposes that the maker of a database should be protected, even if the database is not sufficiently original to qualify for copyright protection. Separate from any copyright in the database, its maker would have an 'unfair extraction right', i.e. the right (with various exceptions) to prevent wholesale copying. This right would last for 10 years from the end of the year in which the database was first made publicly available.

Directive on Reprography

Some countries impose a levy on photocopying equipment[p. 64] and the number of collective licensing schemes[p. 64] is growing, but there is no doubt that a vast amount of illegal copying goes on. At the time of writing, the EC is undertaking studies on ways to control reprography and to remunerate rights holders.

Directive on Moral Rights

The moral rights conferred on authors vary widely in Europe. For years the French have been proud of their *droit moral* and in the 1988 Act the UK introduced moral rights.[p. 100] Whether the Commission has competence in the area of moral rights (which are not strictly economic rights) and, if so, how they could be harmonized are, at the time of writing, under examination by the Commission.

Directives on Cable and Satellite Transmissions, the Collective Administration of Copyright, and **Data Privacy** are all on the agenda.

Authors, publishers and agents should consult their professional associations for up-to-date information regarding developments on European Directives.

The Single European Market

The European Community and those countries that make up the European Economic Area are subject to the Community's rules on the free movement of goods. This means that a copyright owner cannot prevent the movement of a work between member countries if authorized copies have been put onto the market anywhere within the single market. This would override, for instance, an exclusive licence to national territorial rights, so an American edition of a work lawfully sold in, say, Germany may equally lawfully be sold in the UK, even if that means it is directly competing with the UK edition.

It is therefore sensible to ensure that the whole European Economic Area is treated as a single territory when licensing rights.

---

53 Copyright and the United States

After more than 20 years of study the United States of America passed a Copyright Revision Act* in 1976, the bulk of which came into effect on 1 January 1978. The United States joined the Universal Copyright Convention on 16 September 1955 and much more recently joined the Berne Union, on 1 March 1989.

Anyone taking more than a passing interest in American copyright should consult *Entertainment Law and Business* by Harold Orenstein and David E. Guinn (see *Bibliography*). Here we can only glance at the points of most importance to British book publishers and authors.

Under the 1976 Act **copyright is divisible,** as it is in the UK, and parts of a copyright can be assigned or licensed in the way we have always been accustomed to. (Under the old law, when an author wanted to assign part of his copyright, he had to go through the rigmarole of assigning the whole of it and then leasing back the rights he wanted to keep.) All transfers of copyright may be recorded with the Copyright Office, but this is no longer obligatory. However, recordation (of, for instance, exclusive licences or assignments) must be effected before a transferee can bring an action for infringement, and by and large a recorded transfer will take precedence in the courts over one which has not been recorded.

A published work qualifies for copyright protection (subject to the other requirements described in this chapter) if at the time of its

---

*USA Code 1976, Title 17. The 1976 Act is reprinted in *Copinger and Skone James on Copyright* (see *Bibliography*). Much of the new Act is intended only as a guide, and on many points interpretation can be obtained direct from the Copyright Office, Library of Congress, Washington, D.C. 20559. Their pamphlet *R1 – Copyright Basics* is particularly helpful.

first publication at least one of its authors 'is a national or domiciliary of the United States, or is a national, domiciliary, or sovereign authority of a foreign nation that is a party to a copyright treaty to which the United States is also a party, or is a stateless person' *or* 'the work is first published in the United States or in a foreign nation that, on the date of first publication, is a party to the Universal Copyright Convention or the Berne Copyright Convention' *or* 'the work is first published by the United Nations or any of its specialized agencies, or by the Organization of American States' *or* the work is specially protected by Presidential proclamation.

All unpublished works which exist in tangible form are now protected under the Act (not, as before, under the common law of individual States) without regard to the nationality or domicile of the author. Unpublished works may be registered with the Copyright Office.

Protected works are now 'original works of authorship fixed in any tangible medium of expression, now known or later developed, from which they can be perceived, reproduced or otherwise communicated, either directly or with the aid of a machine or device'. These include '(1) literary works; (2) musical works, including any accompanying words; (3) dramatic works, including any accompanying music; (4) pantomimes and choreographic works; (5) pictorial, graphic, and sculptural works; (6) motion pictures and other audiovisual works; and (7) sound recordings'. Computer programs are regarded as Literary works. Most works by officers and employees of the US Government are specifically excluded from copyright protection.

Note, however, that until 1 March 1989 full protection was only given to works which, in addition, bore the proper copyright notice and were registered with the Copyright Office. Until 1 July 1986 they also had to comply with the requirements of the 'manufacturing clause' when applicable. These points are discussed more fully below.

With these provisos it is safe to say that virtually every new book you have handled since 1 January 1978 will be protected by United States law. The further back you go, however, the more cloudy the situation becomes. Although the UK has had copyright relations with the USA for the whole of this century these have varied considerably, and have been particularly bedevilled by the manufacturing clause. Until 27 September 1957, when the United Kingdom joined the Universal Copyright Convention, the two countries never belonged to the same copyright union; one result of this was that, to establish protection for a UK book within the Berne Union (to which the UK and most leading countries belonged, but the USA did not), books had to be published first in the UK, or 'simultaneous' publication of a US edition had to be arranged in Canada. Consequently, establishing the exact status of an old work is, in practical terms, often impossible. In years gone by many US publishers developed the most estimable habit of treating all works which were in copyright elsewhere as if they were in copyright in the USA, and this is a good precedent to follow.

Copyright vests initially in the author or, in the case of a work made for hire, in the employer, who is then the author for copyright purposes. **A work made for hire** is now defined as '(1) a work prepared by an employee within the scope of his or her employment; or (2) a work specially ordered or commissioned for use as a contribution to a collective work, as part of a motion picture or other audio-visual work, as a translation, as a supplementary work, as a compilation, as an instructional text, as a test, as answer material for a test, or as an atlas, if the parties expressly agree in a written instrument signed by them that the work shall be considered a work made for hire . . .'

The term of protection is now based partly on the old and partly on the new law. The term for works created on or after 1 January 1978 is now generally the author's life plus 50 years, or in the case of joint authors, 50 years from the death of the last surviving author. Anonymous, pseudonymous and 'for hire' works have a term of 75 years from publication or 100 years from creation, whichever is shorter.

The old law provided for a term of 28 years (to the day) from the date of first publication wherever that took place (or in the case of a work which was registered while still unpublished, from the date of that registration) plus a 'renewal' term of another 28 years. Renewal had to be applied for during the last 12 months of the first 28-year term or its protection would be lost. The application had to be made by the author himself or his closest relations if he was dead, except that the copyright in composite works (encyclopedias, anthologies) and in works made for hire could be renewed by the proprietor.

On 26 June 1992 the Copyright Act was amended so that for works in which copyright was originally secured between 1 January 1964 and 31 December 1977, protection is automatically extended for a further 47 years (making a total of 75 years). Failure to renew copyright does not forfeit protection, although renewal (with a filing fee of $20) is still advisable. The Authors' Guild of America tells us that the Copyright Office is the primary source of information for film producers and others tracing the rights holders of works that are out of print, if they are seeking to exploit rights. A Copyright Office circular also explains that renewal will vest copyright in the name of the renewal claimant (e.g. the inheritor of the copyright if the original author is dead); it constitutes prima facie evidence as to the validity of the facts stated in the renewal certificate; and that 'the right to utilize a derivative work in the extended term is affected' (for example, if the author is dead, the renewal claimant may be able to terminate an assignment of rights in the exploitation of a derivative work). If a work was not registered with the Library of Congress in the first place, this can be done along with the application for renewal for the single $20 fee.

Until 1992, if a work was still in its *first* 28-year term on 1 January 1978 it had to be renewed in the old way, and then qualified for a total term (including the first 28 years) of 75 years from registration. If it was not renewed, it lost copyright protection. If a work was in its *second* term on 1 January 1978, it received an automatic extension to the same 75 years. While Congress was debating the new copyright bill, temporary extensions were granted to works which were already in their second 28-year terms and whose protection would otherwise have expired between 19 September 1962 and 31 December 1977; these also now qualify for the 75 years from first registration. Works that are in the public domain cannot retrospectively get copyright protection. This applies to works that had gone into the public domain on 1 January 1978, those that had not been renewed before 1992, or which had not qualified for protection under UCC requirements before the USA joined the Berne Convention. All term calculations (and the termination calculations below) now extend to the last day of the calendar year in which they would otherwise have expired.

Some contracts may be terminated after a certain number of years, though not if the work was made for hire. If the work was in either its first or renewal term on 1 January 1978, contracts signed by the author or (in general) his heirs before that date may be terminated by notice in writing 'at any time during a period of five years beginning at the end of fifty-six years from the date the copyright was originally secured, or beginning on January 1, 1978, whichever is later'. Similarly, a contract made on or after 1 January 1978 may be terminated 'at any time during a period of five years beginning at the end of thirty-five years from the date of execution of the grant'. 'If the grant covers the right of publication of the work, the period begins at the end of thirty-five years from the date of publication . . . or at the end of forty years from the date of execution of the grant, whichever term ends earlier.' The notice must be served not more than 10 years and not less than 2 years before the required date of termination. The requirements of these sections (203 and 304) are detailed, and although rights in the original work revert, rights in 'derivative' works (i.e. adaptations[p. 47]) do not revert.

Until 1 March 1989, no published work qualified for copyright protection in the USA unless it bore a **copyright notice**. The obvious notice on books today is the UCC line ('© Jo Smith 1992'), plus All Rights Reserved.

Omitting a copyright line, or printing an incorrect one, does not, since the USA joined the Berne Convention, mean that copyright protection is forfeited. Between 1 January 1978 and 1 March 1989 omission of the copyright notice was not usually fatal (at least in the circumstances described at Section 405(a) of the Act). Under the old Act, omission of the correct notice invalidated copyright protection.

Registration of published works with the Copyright Office is not now mandatory, but in fact remains central to full protection. Failure to register does not void a copyright, but it is necessary to rectify errors in or omission of the copyright notice and is usually a prerequisite to legal action. Registration may be made at any time during the life of a copyright but it should be arranged within three months of first publication, if at all possible, since this secures a claim to statutory damages and attorneys' fees in court actions. Registration within five years from publication establishes certain prima facie evidence for a court.

Registration does not confer copyright. The Copyright Office will, for a fee, conduct a search to discover whether a particular work has been registered, but, as elsewhere, whether a given work is legally entitled to protection can only be finally decided by a court.

For a book first published outside the United States, registration involves sending to the Copyright Office a special application form, a fee (currently $20) and one complete copy of the first edition. (There are slight variations for works not precisely of this description, e.g. if a book is first published in the USA two copies must be sent.)

Deposit with the Library of Congress is mandatory for all works published in the USA. (Note that distribution is, of course, publication.) Two copies must be deposited within three months of US publication. Failure to deposit may result in fines but does not void the copyright.

Registration and deposit are best handled by an American publisher or agent who is familiar with the process. The two requirements can, for instance, be combined, thus saving on the cost of the books. Any agreement with an American publisher should bind him to take the necessary steps. A UK publisher distributing his own edition in the USA should certainly register it, and if it is essential to handle the business from abroad the Copyright Office will supply forms and information. (See the footnote on page 208.)

The Manufacturing Clause

This onerous complication of US copyright law had originally provided that books published in the English language had to be published from type set, and be printed and bound, within the USA. Until the United States joined the UCC this meant that a large proportion of British books were not protected in America, although there were provisions for 'ad interim' protection. The Manufacturing Clause was modified by the 1976 Copyright Act so that it only affected 'copies of works consisting preponderantly of nondramatic literary material that is in the English language' and which had been manufactured outside the USA or Canada and where the author of a substantial part of the work was a US national or a foreigner domiciled in the USA (but not if he had been domiciled outside the USA for a continuous year before the importation or distribution of the work). Failure to comply with the clause no longer invalidated copyright and allowed the importation of up to 2,000 copies of a work. Furthermore, individual authors could arrange for first publication and manufacture abroad as long as the publisher was not 'a national or domiciliary of the United States or a domestic corporation or enterprise'.

The Manufacturing Clause was abolished completely on 1 July 1986.

Further information on the provisions and implications of the manufacturing clause are given in Chapter 18 of *Copinger and Skone James on Copyright*.[p. 222]

54 Copyright and the Countries of the Former USSR

Although the USSR was a signatory to the UCC[p. 217] it does not automatically follow that the independent countries that have emerged from it are likewise signatories. In 1992 the Russian Federation established the Russian Agency on Intellectual Property (RAIS) which replaces the former USSR's similar agency VAAP (see below) and which is drafting a new copyright law and aims to combat piracy and develop publishing in the private sector. At the time of writing the future is unclear, so we thought it best to reproduce here the relevant chapter from the second edition of this book. For up-to-date information, you should consult your professional association.

The Soviet Union became a member of the Universal Copyright Convention on 27 May 1973, adhering to the 1952 (Geneva) version of the Convention. This was the first time that the Soviets had joined any international copyright convention, and there appears to be little likelihood of their joining the Berne Union, which has much stricter standards.

Most authorities agreed at the time that the main purpose of their joining was to give the government full control over dissemination of Soviet literature in the West – what the *New York Times* called 'effective international censorship'. If any Western publisher now translates a protected Soviet text without permission he can legally be sued in the courts of his own country. Among many others[p. 218] the United Kingdom and the United States are members of UCC.

WORKS FIRST PUBLISHED BEFORE 27 MAY 1993

Soviet law used to permit the free reprinting or translation of foreign works without remuneration to their authors. Occasionally, however, the Soviets would in their uniquely random manner agree to pay some roubles to a Western author, though the roubles were 'blocked' and had to be personally collected in the USSR by the author or his fully authorized representative. He was more likely to be paid if he was famous, or if he had cooperated in preparing the Soviet edition of his work. This situation has not changed: foreign works are in the public domain in the USSR if they were first published[p. 27] outside it before 27 May 1973. But if a substantially updated version of such a work has been produced since that date it will most likely qualify for protection.

However, the position is not so clear-cut the other way round. Works by Soviet nationals first published in the USSR before it joined UCC do not qualify for protection in the West. But if a Soviet author arranged, as many did, for a translation or same-language edition of his book to be first or simultaneously[p. 27] published in a Berne or UCC country his book will be in copyright in any country belonging to the appropriate convention. Permission to publish such a book, or to retranslate from it into another language, must be obtained from the copyright owner.

WORKS FIRST PUBLISHED ON OR AFTER 27 MAY 1973

Works by Soviet authors first published in the USSR or in any other UCC country on or after the date the USSR joined UCC are in copyright in all UCC countries. Similarly, Western authors of works first published with UCC protection after that date now have the protection of Soviet copyright law. A Soviet translation of their work can only be made and published with their consent, and they will be paid for it.

NEGOTIATIONS WITH THE USSR

Shortly after Soviet adherence to UCC the All Union Copyright Agency of the USSR (VAAP) was established to participate in the international publishing field. It promotes Soviet books abroad and organizes book fairs in the USSR – though woe betide any foreign publisher if he or his books are judged unacceptable for any reason. VAAP is also, and most importantly, the final clearing-house for foreign book contracts, and has dealt with many thousands since 1973.

A great deal of very hard work, first by individual agents and publishers and then by formal groups, has gone into bridging the wide gap between Soviet publishing customs (and law) and our own, and in 1982 the Publishers Association and VAAP agreed on a basic model contract. To mention a few points: translations by a Soviet publisher can be into any one of many different languages (the USSR speaks over a hundred); all payments are made in ·

sterling, whether the publisher is Soviet or British; a British publisher pays royalties in the way we are accustomed to, but the Soviets
pay lump sums calculated on a complex statutory basis which takes
account of the physical length of the book and/or text and/or illustrations, the number of editions, the category of book (e.g. fiction,
scientific, political) and sometimes the reputation of the author.
Initial negotiations can be handled by individual British and Soviet
publishers, but the final contract must go through VAAP.

55 International Copyright Conventions

The first copyright laws gave no protection to foreign works at all.
Gradually, however, a maze of unilateral arrangements was made
in which the signatory countries would agree on the protection each
could offer works originating with the other.

It became evident that some standard international code was very
necessary and in 1886 several of the leading European powers agreed
at Berne on a text called the International Convention for the Protection of Literary and Artistic Works, which was ratified by the
United Kingdom on 28 November 1887. Since that time the Berne
Convention (or 'Berne Union') has extended its membership to
include most of the leading countries of the world. The USA joined
in 1989 and the People's Republic of China in 1992.

The original text of the Berne Convention has been revised at
conferences in Paris (1896), Berlin (1908 and 1914), Rome (1928),
Brussels (1948), Stockholm (1967)* and Paris (1971). These revisions
are often mentioned without any reference to 'Berne' ('the Brussels
Convention', 'the Paris Act'), to the confusion of the uninitiated.

---

*The Stockholm text is now a dead letter, since (because of opposition to the
latitude offered developing countries in its Protocol) it failed to achieve the
necessary five signatures for ratification. It does, however, form the basis of the
greater part of the text agreed at the 1971 Paris conference. The Brussels text
(Cmnd 361) may be obtained from HMSO. *Copinger and Skone James on
Copyright* (see *Bibliography*) reprints the Paris text.

When any particular revision has been agreed, each signatory country undertakes to incorporate it in its own national copyright law. Before a revision can be actually ratified by any country the copyright law of that country must be rewritten to conform to it. The 1956 UK Act was passed to enable the UK to ratify the Brussels revision, and the 1988 Act to ratify the 1971 Paris proposals.

Because of this lapse between agreement in committee and ratification by government, and also because some countries prefer to adhere to a revision other than the latest, the members of the Berne Union are not at any given time all signatory to the same text. There are also some points which the Convention leaves to the individual discretion of its members. On the whole, however, any author who is a citizen of a Berne Union country or who is domiciled in one, or who first publishes in one, will find his works protected in all Berne Union countries to much the same extent, and without the necessity for formal registration in any of them.

The United States and countries in Central and South America have from time to time set up conventions based upon their own hemisphere, to none of which the UK or any English-speaking country (other than the USA) belongs. The most important of these Pan-American Conventions is the Buenos Aires Convention of 1910, and the inclusion in a copyright notice[p. 156] of the words 'All Rights Reserved' (or the Spanish equivalent 'Todos los derechos reservados') is principally intended to protect rights in BAC countries.

The Universal Copyright Convention ('UCC')* was formulated in 1952 in Geneva under the auspices of UNESCO to bridge the gap between the Berne Convention countries and, in particular, the United States, whose domestic copyright law then prevented its adherence to Berne. UCC is a much less detailed text than Berne and imposes less stringent regulations on its members. The minimum term of protection is, for most works, 25 years from first publication or the life of the author plus 25 years. However, it differs from Berne in extending protection to works by nationals of contracting states wherever they are published, as well as to works published within contracting states.

---

* The Geneva and Paris texts of the Universal Copyright Convention are obtainable from HMSO. Both texts also appear in the Appendices to *Copinger and Skone James on Copyright* (see *Bibliography*).

The most far-reaching effect of UCC in practical terms has been the introduction of the 'C-in-a-circle' copyright line[p. 157] for international protection. UCC member countries accept this line in lieu of any deposit and registration otherwise required by their local law, although they may impose special regulations on their own nationals, on works first published in their territory, or as a prerequisite to litigation.

Heroic efforts to make the provisions of Berne and UCC more compatible, especially for developing countries, resulted in the Paris Acts of 1971: revised texts for both Conventions which included identical regulations for the compulsory licensing of translations and reprints.[p. 68]

UCC and Berne cover copyright for writers, composers, artists and films, but not sound recordings, performers, broadcasts or the newer technologies. Attempts to deal with these have been made with varying success by such international agreements* as the European Agreement (Strasbourg 1960) on the Protection of Television Broadcasts; the Convention (Rome 1961) for the Protection of Performers, Producers of Phonograms and Broadcasting Organizations (the 'Neighbouring Rights Convention'); the Convention (Geneva 1971) for the Protection of Producers of Phonograms Against Unauthorized Duplication of their Phonograms (the 'Anti-Piracy Convention'); the Vienna (1973) Agreement for the Protection of Type Faces and their International Deposit; and the Convention (Brussels 1974) Relating to the Distribution of Programme-Carrying Signals Transmitted by Satellite.

Countries adhering to UCC and/or Berne at the time of writing are as follows:

Country	Member of
Algeria	UCC
Andorra	UCC
Argentina	both
Australia	both
Austria	both
Bahamas	both

---

*These are all reprinted in *Copinger and Skone James on Copyright* (see *Bibliography*).

Bangladesh	UCC
Barbados	both
Belgium	both
Belize	UCC
Benin	Berne
Bolivia	UCC
Brazil	both
Bulgaria	both
Burkina Faso	Berne
Cambodia	UCC
Cameroon	both
Canada	both
Central African Republic	Berne
Chad	Berne
Chile	both
China	both
Colombia	both
Congo	Berne
Costa Rica	both
Côte d'Ivoire	Berne
Croatia	both
Cuba	UCC
Cyprus	both
Czech Republic	both
Denmark	both
Dominican Republic	UCC
Ecuador	both
Egypt	Berne
El Salvador	UCC
Fiji	both
Finland	both
France	both
Gabon	Berne
Gambia	Berne
Germany	both
Ghana	both
Greece	both
Guatemala	UCC
Guinea	both
Guinea-Bissau	Berne
Haiti	UCC

Holy See	both
Honduras	Berne
Hungary	both
Iceland	both
India	both
Irish Republic	both
Israel	both
Italy	both
Japan	both
Kazakhstan	UCC
Kenya	UCC
Korea (South)	UCC
Laos	UCC
Lebanon	both
Lesotho	Berne
Liberia	both
Libya	Berne
Liechtenstein	both
Luxembourg	both
Madagascar	Berne
Malawi	both
Malaysia	Berne
Mali	Berne
Malta	both
Mauritania	Berne
Mauritius	both
Mexico	both
Monaco	both
Morocco	both
Netherlands	both
New Zealand	both
Nicaragua	UCC
Niger	both
Nigeria	UCC
Norway	both
Pakistan	both
Panama	UCC·
Paraguay	both
Peru	both
Philippines	both
Poland	both

Portugal	both
Romania	Berne
Russian Federation	UCC
Rwanda	both
St Vincent & the Grenadines	UCC
Senegal	both
Slovak Republic	both
Slovenia	both
South Africa	Berne
Spain	both
Sri Lanka	both
Surinam	Berne
Sweden	both
Switzerland	both
Tajikistan	UCC
Thailand	Berne
Togo	Berne
Trinidad & Tobago	both
Tunisia	both
Turkey	Berne
United Kingdom	both
United States of America	both
Uruguay	Berne
Venezuela	both
Yugoslavia	both
Zaire	Berne
Zambia	both
Zimbabwe	Berne

Bibliography

Bagehot, Richard, *Music Business Agreements*, Sweet & Maxwell, 1989

Bainbridge, David I., *Intellectual Property*, Pitman, 1992

Brophy, Brigid, *A Guide to Public Lending Right,* Gower Publishing, Aldershot, 1983

Butcher, Judith, *Copy-editing: the Cambridge Handbook for Editors, Authors and Publishers,* Cambridge University Press, 3rd edition, 1992

Clark, Charles (ed.), *Publishing Agreements: a Book of Precedents,* Butterworths, 4th edition, 1993

Clark, Charles, *Photocopying from Books and Journals*, British Copyright Council, 19 Berners Street, London W1P 4AA, 1990

Clark, Charles and Hadley, Colin, *Collective Administration of Reprographic Reproduction Rights. Principles and Practice: the British Experience*, Copyright Licensing Agency, 90 Tottenham Court Road, London W1P 9HE, 1992

Cornish, W. R., *Intellectual Property: Patents, Copyright, Trade Marks and Allied Rights,* Sweet & Maxwell, 2nd edition, 1989

de Freitas, Denis, *The Law of Copyright and Rights in Performances,* British Copyright Council, 1990

Dorner, Jane, *Writing on Disk*, John Taylor Book Ventures, Stevenage, 1992

Dworkin, G. and Taylor, R.D., *Blackstone's Guide to the Copyright, Designs and Patents Act 1988*, Blackstone Press, 1988

Flint, Michael F., *A User's Guide to Copyright,* Butterworth, 3rd edition, 1990

Laddie, H. I. L., Prescott, P. R. K. and Vitoria, M., *The Modern Law of Copyright*, Butterworth, 2nd edition, 1993

Legat, Michael, *Understanding Publishers' Contracts*, Robert Hale, 1992

Orenstein, Harold and Guinn, David E., *Entertainment Law and Business*, Butterworth USA, 1989

Phillips, Jeremy J., Durie, Robyne and Karket, Ian, *Whale on Copyright*, ESC Publishing, Oxford, 4th edition, 1993

Skone James, E. P., Mummery, J. F., Rayner James, J. and Garnett, K. M., *Copinger and Skone James on Copyright*, Sweet & Maxwell, 13th edition, 1991

Sterling, J. A. L., *Intellectual Property Rights in Sound Recordings, Films and Videos*, Sweet & Maxwell, 1992

Stewart, S. M., *International Copyright and Neighbouring Rights,* Butterworth, 2nd edition, 1989

Sumsion, John, *PLR in Practice, a Report to the Advisory Committee,*

PLR Office, Prince Regent Street, Stockton-on-Tees, Cleveland TS18 1DF, 2nd edition, 1991

Tapper, Colin, *Computer Law*, Longman, 4th edition, 1990

The Copyright, Designs and Patents Act 1988, HMSO

The Public Lending Right Act 1979, HMSO

The Public Lending Right Scheme 1982 (Commencement of Variations) Order 1988, SI 1988 No. 2070, HMSO

Annual Reports, by the Secretary of State for National Heritage are laid before Parliament annually and are available from HMSO

The Photographers' Guide to the 1988 Copyright Act, The British Photographers Liaison Committee, 9–10 Domingo Street, London EC1 OTA, 1989

The Writers' & Artists' Yearbook, A. & C. Black, annually

The Writer's Handbook, Macmillan, annually

Quick Guides on *Copyright and Moral Rights, The Protection of Titles, Permissions, Publishing Contracts, Your Copyrights After Your Death* and other subjects are published by the Society of Authors, 84 Drayton Gardens, London SW10 9SB

Leaflets on *Cable Retransmission, The Photocopying Licensing Scheme, Educational Recording, German PLR* and *Rights Collectively Administered* are published by the Authors' Licensing & Collecting Society, 33–34 Alfred Place, London WC1E 7DP

Leaflets on *Copyright Concerns, The CLA, Copying in Schools and Colleges* and *Fair Dealing and Library Privilege* are published by the Copyright Licensing Agency, 90 Tottenham Court Road, London W1P 9HE

The Net Book Agreement and *Book Club Regulations* are published by the Publishers Association, 19 Bedford Square, London WC1B 3HJ

Index

abridgements 13
  duration of copyright 43
  originality 21
  of quotations 83
abstracts 56
'acceptable territory' 7-9, 18
  qualification for protection 22
acknowledgements
  copyright line 86
  quotation in anthologies for
    educational use 62
  sufficient 54, 62
  by supervisory editors 162
Act of Parliament, copying authorized
  by 56
acts restricted by copyright, *see*
  restricted actions
ad interim copyright 213
adaptation
  computer programs 48, 137
  musical works 48
  strip cartoons 48, 119-20
  of substantial part 47-8
  in United States 212
  see also dramatization; translations
advertising
  copy 12
  originality 21
  slogans 96
agreements, *see* contracts
aircraft, copyright aboard 9
'all rights reserved' 156, 166, 217
  US requirement 212
All Union Copyright Agency of
  USSR (VAAP) 215-16
almanacs 11, 13
  see also reference works
annuals 11
anonymous works 23
  copying by libraries 60
  copying permitted 55
  copying without permission 67-8
  duration of copyright 41-2, 204
  ownership of copyright 30
anthologies 13
  duration of copyright 43
  for educational use 61-2

originality 20
  see also literary works
Anti-Piracy Convention 218
apprenticeships 30, 31
architectural works 170-1
  author 171
  copying in artistic works 185
  moral rights 100-5
  see also artistic works
archives 6, 59-60
argument development
  copying 96
  submission for publication 143
  see also ideas
arrangements of musical works 48
artistic craftsmanship, works of 171
  author 171
  copying in artistic works 185
  moral rights 100-5
  in public places 176, 185
  see also artistic works
artistic works 4, 10
  alteration of 182
  assertion of moral rights 102
  author 171
  commissioning 182
  copying of 181-4
    illustration itself 183
    object in illustration 183
    permission 182-4
    photography privacy right 183
    premises where object
      available 183
  copying in the work
    architectural works 185
    natural subjects 184
    people 184
    scenery 184
    sculptures 185
    texts and manuscripts 184-5
    works of artistic craftsmanship 185
  copyright line 185-6
  copyright notice 177
  Crown copyright 174
  design right 178-80
  drawings 13
  droit de suite 93, 177-8

duration of copyright 173-4
exceptions from protection 175-6
export control 181
false attribution 177
fees for use 187
giving permission 186-7
infringements 175
library deposit 154
moral rights 100-5, 177-8, 186
movement of 93-4
ownership of copyright 173, 181
ownership of work 176-7, 181
Parliamentary copyright 174
passing off 177
publication 172
qualification for protection 171
'qualified persons' 172
recognized international
    organizations 172
registered designs 178-80
restricted actions 175
signatures 92-3
see also individual types, e.g.
    architectural works; sculpture
assignments
Copyright Office registration
    (US) 201, 212
exclusive licence 3, 33, 200
future copyright 32-3, 189, 202
moral rights 105
outright 3, 202
partial 33, 202
payment 201-2
prospective (future) copyright 32-3,
    189, 202
Public Lending Right 142
reversion 33
in writing 201
Association of Photographers 187
audio recording(s), *see* sound
    recording; sound recordings
author's name
malicious falsehood 99
moral rights 98
passing off 98-9
pseudonyms 98-100
authors
anonymous works 23
architectural works 171
artistic works 171
broadcasts 130
co-authors 15, 29-30
collaborators 15
computer programs 136
computer-generated works 15-16

contributors 15, 30
dictation 15
duration of copyright 40
editors 30
employers 30-1
engravings 171
false attribution 19, 98, 104
films 133, 204
first owner 29-30
    in US 210
'ghosts' 15
joint authors 13-14, 15, 23, 30,
    162, 203-4
meaning 15-16
mediums dictated to by spirits 15
name of, *see* author's name
ownership of copyright 29-30
photographs 171
pseudonymous works 23
quotations 15
revised text submission 148
sculpture 171
single author 15
sound recordings 122-3
translators 30
typographical arrangements 16
untraceable 41-2, 84
works of artistic craftsmanship 171
see also ownership of copyright
Authors' Guild of America 211
Authors' Licensing and Collecting
    Society 110
authorship, false attribution 19, 98,
    104

ballet choreography 15
banknotes 171
see also artistic works
bankruptcy, reversion of rights
    on 33-4
Belgium, collecting society in
    (SABAM) 129
bequests 92, 188
Berlin Convention 216
Berne Convention 1, 17, 23, 27, 93,
    100, 122, 206, 208, 216-17
copyright line 157
countries adhering to 218-21
USA as member 208
Bible 79-80
Authorized Version 28, 79-80
liturgical texts 80
perpetual copyright 28, 79
Scottish Bible Board 79

blank forms 12
blasphemous works 19
blind persons
    Braille 10, 12
    talking books 121
books 10, 12
    common-source 13
    see also literary works
booksellers' copies 26
Braille 10, 12
breach of confidence 57, 95–6
breach of contract 95–6
British Broadcasting Corporation 127
British Copyright Council 59
British Library 28, 58, 153
British sphere 9, 24, 38–9, 106
broadcasting 126–8
    'broadcast' defined 126
    cable, *see* cable television
    ephemeral right 127, 131
    fees 127
    hospital radio 127
    satellite 127–9
    sound recordings 124
    substantial part 47, 127
    television rights 3, 126, 132
broadcasts as subject of copyright 10, 129–32
    author 130
    cable programme 129–30
    duration of protection 130, 204
    exceptions from protection 131–2
    fair dealing 131
    first owner 130
    infringements 131
    restricted acts 130
    satellite transmission 130
Buenos Aires Convention 217
buildings 10
    see also artistic works

C-in-a-circle 157, 161, 167, 218
cable television 26, 127–9
    broadcasting substantial part 47
    cable programme service defined 126
    copyright on programmes, *see* broadcasts as subject of copyright
    dishonestly receiving encoded broadcasts 50
    licensing 128–9
    programmes 10

sound recordings as subject of copyright 124
    television rights 126
calendars 12
captions for pictures 12
cartoons 48, 119–20
catalogues 10, 13
    fraudulent 19
    see also literary works
Cataloguing in Publication (CIP) 169
CD-I 135, 139
CD-ROM 135, 139
Central Board of Finance of the Church of England 80
characters
    character right 96
    in strip cartoons 120
    as trade marks 97
charts 10
    see also artistic works
choreography 15
circulars 12
    see also literary works
CLA, *see* Copyright Licensing Agency (CLA)
clearing permissions 81, 149
co-authors 15, 29–30
codes 4, 10
coins 171
    see also artistic works
collaborations
    collaborators 15
    duration of copyright 43
collective licensing 107–11
    alternatives 109
    arrangement of 108
    Copyright Tribunal 109, 110
    lending right 109–10
    licensing body 108–9
    organizations 110–11
    reprography 64–5
collective works 13–14
comic strips, *see* strip cartoons
commercial publication 27
commissioning
    artistic works 183
    contributors 150
    pictures 184
    sound recordings 123
common-source books 13
compilations 10, 13
    compilers' Public Lending Right 142
    databases 13
    electronic storage 13

originality 20
see also literary works
compulsory licence 56, 68-9
computer programs
  adaptation 48, 137
  authors 136
  duration of copyright 136-7
  EC Software Directive 205
  infringements 137
  meaning 135
  moral rights 138
  ownership of copyright 136
  protection 136-8
  restricted acts 137
  see also literary works
computer-generated works 138
  authors 15-16
  originality 21
computers
  CD-I 135, 139
  CD-ROM 135, 139
  Data Protection Act 140
  databank or database 13, 138-9,
    206-7
  electrocopying 139-40
  electronic publishing 139
  manuscript delivery on disk 140
  multi-media packages 139
  print-outs 12
  word processing 135-6
  works in electronic form
    135-40
condensations 13
  originality 21
  see also abridgments
consideration, *see* payments
contracts
  assignments 201-3
  basic contract 193-200
  composition 190-203
  consideration of other contracts
    195-6
  control to be transferred 195
  definitions in 192
  delivery of work 195
  duration of rights purchased 196-7
  expenses 199
  for services 31
  international law 200
  language of contract 192
  language of works 197
  licences 200-1
  model contracts 191
  moral rights 195
  negotiations 193

  object 190
  of service 30
  parties to 193-4
  payments 198-9
  professional advice 191
  protection of copyright 195
  pseudonyms 194
  rights purchased 196
  subject of copyright itself 192
  termination in USA 211-12
  territorial limitation 197-8
  timing of exercise of rights 198
  25-year reversion 197
  work covered by 194-5
contributors 15
  assignment of copyright from
    each 150
  authors 15, 30
  commissioning 150
  duration of copyright 43
  ownership of copyright 30
  payment 150-1
control 3
  assignment, *see* assignments
  ownership of copyright and 29
  see also contracts
cookery books 13
copies
  new print, *see* newly printed form
  parodies 53
  permitted, *see* permitted copying
copying
  across national frontiers 57
  entire works 68-9
  illegal 52
  more than one reproduction 26
  new form, *see* newly printed form
  permitted, *see* permitted copying
  republication 68-9
  single copy 26
  substantial part 44, 45, 46-7
  see also reprography *and individual*
    subjects or material, e.g.
    artistic works; public records
copyright
  divisibility 3
  infringement, *see* infringement of
    copyright
  length of protection, *see* duration
    of copyright protection
  meaning 2-3
  ownership, *see* ownership of
    copyright
  perpetual, *see* perpetual copyright
  purpose 2

copyright *(continued)*
  qualification for protection, *see* qualification for protection
  reversion, *see* reversion of rights
  suspension 35
  see also individual aspects and works, e.g. letters; literary works
Copyright Clearance Centre (US) 65
Copyright, Designs and Patents Act 1988 1
  jurisdiction 7–9
  outline 5–7
Copyright Licensing Agency (CLA) 44, 64–5, 111
  licences 106
copyright line 2, 157–8
  acknowledgements 86
  artistic works 185–6
  C-in-a-circle 157, 161, 167, 218
  dates 163–4
  errors 160–1, 212
  name of copyright owner(s) 161–3
  new 159–60
  P-in-a-circle 125, 158
  placement 158
  pseudonymous works 99
  reissues 165–6
  requirements 158–9
  revised texts 148–9
  translations 164–5
  in United States 212
copyright notice
  'all rights reserved' 156, 166, 212, 217
  artistic works 177
  checklist 167–9
  composition 155–67
  elements of 156
  general copyright notice 156–7
  line, *see* copyright line
  material for sale in USA 166–7
  reissues 165–6
  sound recordings 125
  translations 164–5
  in United States 212
Copyright Office (US) 211
  registration 201, 212
Copyright Tribunal 109, 110
  performance 114
corporate bodies
  duration of copyright 40
  ownership of copyright 28
coupons 12
Crown copyright 67

artistic works 174
  duration 39
  ownership 31–2, 39
  permitted copying 56
  reproduction of material 69–73
current event reporting, copying permitted 45, 55

Data Protection Act 140
databanks/databases 13, 138–9
  downloading 139
  EC Directive on protection of 206–7
  moral rights 139
death of owner of copyright 188–90
  bequests 92, 188
  copyright contract 190
  literary executor 189–90
  25-year-rule reversion 190
  wills 189
deposit regulations, *see* library deposits
Design and Artists' Copyright Society 111
design right 178–80
  excluded designs 179
developing countries 35
  compulsory licence 68–9
development of argument
  copying 96
  submission for publication 143
dictation 15
  to mediums 15
digests 13
  copying 95
  see also literary works
directors of films 100–1, 204
directories 13
  see also literary works; reference works
dramatic works 4, 10
  adaptation of 47
  library deposit of scripts 154–5
  lyrics 14
  making 22
  meaning 14
  publication 25
  scenery 14
  screenplays 14
  scripts 14
  stage plays 14
  stage presentation 14
dramatization 47, 132
  duration of copyright 43

fair dealing 116
  of literary work 116–17
  new copyright for 117
  substantial part 116
drawings 13
  see also artistic works
droit de suite 93, 177–8
Duchy of Lancaster records
    77–8
duration of copyright
    protection 35–43
  abridgements 43
  anonymous works 41–2, 204
  anthologies 43
  artistic works 173–4
  authors 40
  broadcasts 130, 204
  collaborations 43
  computer programs 136–7
  contributions 43
  copyright first owned by
    governments 38–9
  corporate bodies 40
  designs 180
  dramatizations 43
  EC Directive 36, 203–4
  editors 43
  engravings 174
  films 134, 204
  foreign origin works 43
  in or out of print 37–8
  joint works 42, 203–4
  letters 43
  maps 174
  ownership and 37
  performers' rights 115, 204
  photographs 174
  posthumous publication 38, 41
  pseudonymous works 41–2, 204
  Public Lending Right 142
  'qualifying foreigners' 40
  republication of out-of-copyright
    works 152
  selections 43
  significance of publication 37
  sound recordings 123, 204
  translations 43
  typographical arrangement 106
  in UK 38
  in USA 210–11
  works created before 1 August
    1989 40–1
  works created since 1 August
    1989 40
duration of moral rights 105

e-mail 139–40
editors 16
  assignment of copyright from
    contributors 150
  as authors 30
  commissioning of contributors
    150
  duration of copyright 43
  name in copyright line 162
  ownership of copyright 30
  payment of contributors 150–1
  Public Lending Right 142
  relationship with publisher and
    copyright 150
  revisions by 16
  supervisory 149–51
educational establishments
  examinations 62
  instruction 62–3
  libraries in 58
  performance 113
  permitted copying 55, 60–3
  privileged establishments 60–1
  publication by 63
  quotation in anthologies for use
    in 61–2
  reprographic copying 63
  reprography collective licences
    65
Educational Recording Agency
    111
electrocopying 139–40
electronic publishing 139
  see also computer programs;
    computers
electronic retrieval system 25
electronic storage 13
employers and employees
  contract for and of service 30–1
  infringement responsibility 48
  letter written by employee 31
  ownership of copyright 30–1
    computer programs 136
encyclopedias 13
  originality 21
  see also literary works; reference
    works
engravings 170
  author 171
  duration of copyright 174
  see also artistic works
Euromark 97
European Commission
  Berne Convention and 206
  Directives

European Commission (*continued*)
  Directives (*continued*)
    duration of copyright 36, 203–4
    legal protection of
      databases 206–7
    lending rights 109, 205–6
    moral rights 207
    out-of-copyright works 205
    rental and lending rights 205–6
    reprography 207
    software 205
  Green Paper on Copyright and the
    Challenge of Technology 1
  movement of works of art 93–4
  Rome Convention 206
  Single European Market 207–8
examination papers 13
  copyright material in 62
exclusive licences 3, 33, 200
exhibitions
  artistic works in public places 176,
    185
  public record material in 76
expenses 199
export control 60
  artistic works 181
extract reprinting 81–92
  acknowledgements 85–6
  fees 87–92
    complimentary copies 91
    future editions 90
    languages 89–90
    pro-rata share of income 90–2
  permission to quote
    application for 85
    document 91–2
    giving permission 87
    notice 83–4
    when to ask 82–5
  translations 84
  untraceable authors 84

fair dealing
  broadcasts 131
  copying 45–6, 54
  dramatization 116
  performance 113
  public records 75
false attribution of authorship 19,
    98, 104
fax (facsimile copy) 52
  infringement of copyright by 49
fees
  artistic works 187

  broadcasting 127
  for quotations 87–8
    basis for charging fees 89–90
  see also payments
fictitious names 96
film as subject of copyright 10,
    133–5
  author 133, 204
  definition of film 133
  duration of protection 134, 204
  exceptions from protection 134
  infringements 134
  ownership of copyright 134
  privacy right 104, 177
  publication 133
  qualification for protection 133
  restricted acts 134
  soundtrack 133
  video recordings 135
filming
  containing text 12
  director's paternity right 100–1
  dramatization 132
  film rights 2, 132, 133
  performance in public 132
  recording 132
  television rights 132
  video recording 132
folksongs 122
forms 12
future copyright assignment 32–3,
    189, 202

Geneva Convention 218
'ghost' writers 15
governments
  in British sphere 24
  ownership of copyright 28
  see also Parliamentary copyright
graphic works 170
  moral rights 100–5
  see also artistic works
graphs 10, 13
  see also artistic works
Great Ormond Street Hospital for
    Sick Children 28, 38, 81, 110
guidebooks 13

handicapped persons, *see* Braille;
    talking books
high seas jurisdiction 9
home territory 8
hospital broadcasting 127

ideas 4
  argument development 96, 143
  copying 95
  submission for publication 143
illegal works 19
illustrations 13, 52, 59, 152
  copying by libraries 59
  as trade marks 97
  see also artistic works
individuals, ownership of
    copyright 28
information copying 95
infringement of copyright 48-50
  artistic works 175
  computer programs 137
  dealing 49-50
  direct 48
  dishonestly receiving encoded
      broadcasts 50
  employer responsibility 48
  films 134
  importation of infringing article
      49
  indirect or secondary 48, 49-50
  permitted copying, *see* permitted
      copying
  permitting place of entertainment to
      be used 50
  pirate publication of unpublished
      work 50
  reprography 64-5
  retrospective legislation 50
  selling copy used for 49
  sound recordings 124-5
  supplying equipment used for
      49-50
  time limits 48
  transmission via telecommunication
      system 49
integrity right 98, 102-4
  exceptions 103-4
intermediate territory 8-9
international conventions 9, 17,
    216-21
  Berlin Convention 216
  Berne Convention 1, 17, 23, 27,
      93, 100, 157, 206, 208, 211,
      216-17
  Buenos Aires Convention 217
  countries adhering to UCC or
      Berne Convention 218-21
  developing countries 218
  Geneva Convention 218
  Paris Convention 216
  place of publication 27

Rome Convention (neighbouring
    rights) 125, 206, 218
Stockholm Convention 216
Universal Copyright Convention 17,
    23, 27, 157, 208, 214, 217-21
International Federation of
    Phonographic Industries 111
International Federation of
    Reprographic Rights
    Organizations 65
International Standard Book Numbers
    (ISBNs) 168-9
International Standard Serial Numbers
    (ISSNs) 169
interviews 115
  copying permitted 55
issuing copies to public 25, 26-7
  copy of substantial part 47
  sound recordings 123-4

joint authors 15, 23
  duration of copyright 42, 203-4
  names in copyright line 162
  ownership of copyright 30
  works by 13-14
jurisdiction
  'acceptable territory' 7-9, 18, 22
  British sphere 9, 24, 38-9, 106
  Copyright, Designs and Patents
      Act, 1988 7-9
  foreign territory 9
  high seas 9
  home territory 8
  intermediate territory 8-9

labels 12
languages
  extract reprinting 89-90
  quotation permission 89-90
  translations into more than
      one 119
leaflets 12
lectures
  delivery of 112
  public record material in 76
legal interest, *see* control
lending rights 109
  Copyright Tribunal 109, 110, 114
  EC Directive 109, 205-6
  see also Public Lending Right
letters 10, 11, 92-3
  duration of copyright 43

letters (*continued*)
  manuscripts 92–3
  written by employee 31
  see also literary works
Library of Congress catalog card
    numbers 169
library copying
  amount copyable 58–9
  archives 6, 59–60
  articles in periodicals 58–9
  educational establishments 58
  export condition 60
  illustrations 59
  one copy only 59
  permitted 55, 57–60
  prescribed 58
  profit-making companies 58
  research or study 45, 46, 54, 59
  subject matter which can be
      copied 59–60
  unpublished works 6
library deposit
  artistic works 154
  British Library 28, 58, 153
  demands for copies 154
  newspapers 153
  publications to be deposited 28, 153
  regulations 152–5
  scripts 154–5
  in United States 212–13
libretti 14
licences 200–1
  collective 64–5
  compulsory 56, 68–9
  developing countries 68–9
  exclusive 3, 33, 200
  movement of works of art 93–4
  non-exclusive 201
  reversion 33
limitation, infringement of copyright 48
lists 12
literary executor 189–90
literary works 4, 10–14
  abridgement, *see* abridgements
  Braille 10, 12
  computer programs, *see* computer
      programs
  dramatization, *see* dramatization
  making 22
  means of recording 10
  part works 11, 13
  publication, *see* publication
  revision, *see* revision of text
  submission, *see* submission for
      publication

  videotape containing text 12
  *see also individual forms of work,
      e.g.* encyclopedias; letters
'lump sum' payments 198
lyrics 12, 14, 83
  see also literary works

magazines 11–12
  see also periodicals/periodical
      articles
malicious falsehood 99
manufacturing clause, in USA 213
manuscripts 92–4
  bequest of 92
  copying in artistic works 184–5
  definition 92
  delivery on disk 140
  export of 93–4
  fee for use 152
  moral rights 140
  ownership of copyright 29, 92
  ownership of script 29, 92
  physical use charge 92
  publication 26–7
  submission, *see* submission for
      publication
  see also letters
maps 13, 172
  duration of copyright 174
  see also artistic works
mathematical symbols 10
Mechanical Copyright Protection
    Society 111, 121
microfiches 12
  copying in newly printed form 51
microfilms of text 12
mime (dumb show) 14
moral rights 5, 100–5
  architecture 101
  artistic works 177–8, 186
  assertion 101, 186
  assignment 105
  author's name 98
  computer programs 138, 139,
      140
  contracts and 195
  databank/database 139
  derogatory treatment 100, 102–4,
      139
  droit de suite 93, 177–8
  duration 105
  EC Directive 207
  false attribution 100, 177
    of authorship 98, 104

moral rights (*continued*)
  integrity 102–4
  manuscripts 140
  paternity 100–2, 195
  prejudicial to honour or
      reputation 100, 102–3
  privacy 104, 177, 183, 184
  revision of text 146–7
  sculpture 101
  translators 100, 118
  waiver 105
multi-author works, *see* editors
multi-media packages 139
musical works 4, 10
  adaptations 48
  arrangements 48
  ballet choreography 15
  libretti 14
  lyrics 12, 14, 83
  making 22
  meaning 14–15
  new arrangements 16
  publication 25
  transcriptions 16, 48

names, fictitious 6, 143–4
negligent misstatement 143
neighbouring rights 36, 206
Neighbouring Rights Convention 125,
    206, 218
'net profit' payments 198–9
new editions, *see* reissues
newly printed form 51–8
  breach of confidence 56
  computer storage 51
  copy meaning 52–3
  copying across national
    frontiers 56
  copyright exceptions 54–6
  microfiche 51
  own words reused 53
  parodies 53
  reference works 53
  translations 53
newspapers 11
  library deposits 153
  see also periodicals/periodical
    articles
non-exclusive licences 201
notice of permission to quote 63–4

old unpublished works
  anonymous or pseudonymous 67–8
  copying 65–7

Ordnance Survey material 71–2, 172
Organization of American States,
    qualification for protection 24
original manuscripts, *see* manuscripts
originality 4–5, 52
  abridgements 21
  advertising copy 21
  anthologies 20
  closely similar works 21–2
  compilations 20
  computer-produced work 21
  condensations 21
  encyclopedias 21
  new versions of existing work 20–1
  new works 20
  qualification for protection 17,
    20–2
  selections 20
out-of-copyright works
  EC Directive 205
  reissues 151–2
  republication, *see* republication of
    out-of-copyright works
  translations 151–2
ownership of copyright 28–34
  active control 29
  anonymous works 30
  artistic works 173, 181
  assignment 33
  authors 29–30, 40
  computer programs 136
  contributors 30
  corporate bodies 40
  corporations 28
  created in course of employment
    136
  death of owner, *see* death of owner
    of copyright
  designs 180
  duration of protection and 37
  editors 30
  films 134
  first owner 29–30
    assignee of prospective
      copyright 32–3
    author 29–30, 210
    broadcasts 130
    Crown 31–2, 39
    employer of author 30–1
    governments in British
      sphere 38–9
    Parliament 32
    recognized international
      organizations 39–40
    in USA 210

ownership of copyright (*continued*)
  government departments 28
  individuals 28
  later owners 33
  limited prerogatives 44
  loss 35
  manuscripts 29
  name in copyright line 161–3
  passive possession of work 29
  pseudonymous works 30
  qualifying foreigners 40
  recognized international
      organizations 28, 39–40
  reversion, *see* reversion of rights
  rights controlled by owner 3–5, 46–8
    control 3, 29
    saleable rights 3
    temporal rights 4
    territorial rights 3–4
  suspension of copyright 35
  transfer of publisher's rights 34
  translators 30
  unincorporated bodies 28
  works existing before 1 July
      1912 29

P-in-a-circle 125, 158
paraphrasing 84
Paris Convention 216
Parliamentary copyright 24, 67
  artistic works 174
  duration of copyright 38–9
  ownership 32
  reproduction of material 69–73
parodies 53
part works 11, 13
passing off 95
  artistic works 177
  author's name 98–9
  false attribution of authorship 98,
      104
  names 96
Patent Office 97
patent originality 4–5
paternity right 100–2, 195
  assertion of 101–2
  exceptions 102
payments
  assignments 201–2
  'lump sum' 198
  'net profit' 198
  royalties 198
  VAT 199
  see also fees

people, in artistic works 184
performance 112–15
  Copyright Tribunal 114
  educational establishments 113
  fair dealing 113
  incidental inclusion 113
  interviews 115
  obtaining permission 113–14
  performers' rights 114–15
  in public 112
  sound recordings 114
  substantial part 47, 112–13
performers' rights 114–15
  duration 115, 204
Performing Right Society 111
Performing Right Tribunal 110
period of protection, *see* duration of
      copyright protection
periodicals/periodical articles 10,
      11–12
  copying 58–9
  employees of periodical 31
  revision of text 147
  submission of 143
  see also literary works
permissions 81–92
  clearing 81
  permission to quote, *see* quotations
permitted copying
  acknowledgment 54
  authorized by Act of Parliament
      56
  compulsory licence 56, 68–9
  by Crown 56
  current event reporting 45, 55
  for educational use 55, 60–3
  fair dealing 45–6, 54, 75, 113, 116,
      131
  interviews 55
  libraries 55, 57–60
  old unpublished works 55
  for private study 45, 46, 54,
      59
  for public administration 55–6
  research 45, 46, 54, 59
  review 45
  for Royal Commissions 58
  for statutory inquiries 58
  typeface use 56
  unknown authors 55
perpetual copyright 28, 38, 68,
      80–1
  Bible 79
  Peter Pan 28, 38, 81, 110
  registration at Stationers' Hall 80

Phonographic Performance Ltd 111, 114
photographs 68, 170
  author 171
  duration of copyright 174
  moral rights 100–5
  privacy right 104, 177, 183
  of typographical arrangement 107
pictures 10
  captions for 12
  see also artistic works
'picturisation' rights 120
place of publication 27
plagiarism 20, 52, 144, 145
plots
  copying 96
  submission for publication 143, 144
poetry 12
  quotation fees 88
postage stamps 171
posthumous publication, duration of copyright 38, 41
precis 95
prequels 96
Prime Minister's letters 77
privacy right 104
  artistic works 177
  commissioned pictures 184
  photographs 104, 177, 183
private study, copying for 45, 46, 54, 59
probate records 78
prospective (future) copyright assignment 32–3, 189, 202
prospectuses 12
protection
  contracts and 195
  illegal works denied 19
  length, *see* duration of copyright protection
  qualification for, *see* qualification for protection
pseudonymous works 23
  contracts for 194
  copying permitted 55
  copying without permission 67–8
  copyright line 99
  duration of copyright 41–2, 204
  ownership of copyright 30
pseudonyms
  choice of 99–100
  passing off 98–9
public administration
  copying material for 55–6
  copyright exception 131

public domain works 82, 83
  see also out-of-copyright works
Public Lending Right 44, 109, 140–3
  assignment 142
  compilers 142
  duration of protection 142
  editors 142
  international schemes 142–3
  payments 142
  qualifications for author 141
  qualifications for book 141–2
  registration 142, 148
  revised editions 148
  see also lending rights
public performance 26
  infringement of copyright 50
  use of premises 50
public records 73–8
  application for permission 75–6
  copying methods 76–7
  exhibitions and lectures 76
Public Records Office 73
publication
  actual text 26
  artistic works 172
  authorized 25–6
  commercial 27
  deposition of copies, *see* library deposit
  duration of protection and 37
  by educational establishments 63
  films 133
  first publication 27
  issuing copies to public 25, 26–7, 47, 123–4
  made available to public 37
  manuscripts 26–7
  meaning 19, 25–8
  more than one reproduction 26
  place of 27
  posthumous 38, 41
  presentation copies 26
  proportion of work reproduced 26
  reassessment of copyright status at 18–19
  review copies 26
  sound recordings 122
  submission for, *see* submission for publication
  typographical arrangement, *see* typographical arrangements
  written proof 28
Publishers Association 127, 156
  negotiations with VAAP 215–16
  quotation fees 88

Publishers Licensing Society 110–11
publishers' rights 2
  transfer of 34
  typographical arrangement, *see*
    typographical arrangements

qualification for protection
  acceptable territory 22
  artistic works 171
  films 133
  formal registration 18
  governments in British sphere 24
  illegal works 19
  international protection 16–17
  making a work 22
  notice 18
  originality 17, 20–2
  published work 17–18
  'qualifying persons' 17, 23, 106,
    172
  recognized international
    organizations 23–4
  sound recordings 122
  UK protection 17–19
  unpublished work 17
  in USA 208–9
  US origin of works 23
'qualifying foreigners' 40
'qualifying person' 17, 23, 106
  artistic works 172
questionnaires 12
quotations 15
  abridged or condensed 83
  acknowledgements 85–6
  fees 87–92
    complimentary copies 91
    future editions 90
    languages 89–90
    pro-rata share of income 90–2
  giving permission 87
  notice 83–4
  paraphrasing 84
  permission to quote 81–92
    application for 85
    document 91–2
    when to ask 82–5
  from reference books 84
  from translations 84

radio rights 3
recipes 84
recognized international organizations
  artistic works 172
  duration of copyright 39–40

ownership of copyright 28
  qualification for protection 23–4
reference works
  newly printed form 53
  quotations from 84
  see also individual works, e.g.
    encyclopedias
register of voters 12
registered designs 178–80
  artistic copyright 179
  design right 179–80
  duration of protection 180
  first owner 180
  typefaces 180
registered trade marks 97–8
reissues 147–9
  copyright line 148–9, 165–6
  copyright notice 165–6
  library deposit 148
  new ISBN number 148
  out-of-copyright works 151–2
  revised text 148–9
  25-year reversion 148
  unaltered reprint 148
rental rights
  EC Directive 205–6
  sound recordings 124
reprints 148
  extracts, *see* extract reprinting
reproduction, *see* copying;
  reprography
reprography 63–5
  collective licences, *see* collective
    licensing
  EC Directive 207
  infringement of copyright 64–5
  levy on hardware 109
  meaning 64
  overseas organizations 65
  public records 76–7
  reciprocal agreements 65
republication 68–9
  compulsory 56, 68–9
  see also reissues
republication of out-of-copyright
    works 151–2, 153
  duration of copyright 152
  library deposit 153
  typographical arrangement 152
  see also reissues
research, copying for 45, 46, 54, 59
restricted actions
  artistic works 175
  broadcasts 130
  computer programs 137

restricted actions (*continued*)
films 134
sound recordings 123–4
retrospective legislation 50
reversion of rights
by agreement 33
on bankruptcy of purchaser 33–4
25-year rule 34–5, 148, 190, 197
reviews
copying for 45
copyright status and 27
review copies not publication 26
revision of text 145–7
contract 146
copy-editing 145
copyright status and 147
derogatory treatment 100, 102–4, 139
house style 145
moral rights of author 146–7
periodical publication 147
referral to author 145
revisions
dates in copyright line 163–4
originality and 20–1
see also reissues
Rome Convention (neighbouring rights) 125, 206, 218
Royal Commissions, copying permitted for 58
royalties 198
rules for games 12
Russian Agency on Intellectual Property (RAIS) 214
Russian Federation
RAIS 214
UCC signatory 214

SABAM, 129
saleable rights 3
satellite broadcasting 127–9
direct-broadcasting systems 128
point-to-point systems 128
as subject of copyright 130
scandalous works 19
scenery (dramatic productions) 14
scenery (natural) 184
schools, *see* educational establishments
Scottish Bible Board 79
screenplays 14
scripts 14
sculpture 10, 170
author 171
copying in artistic works 185

moral rights 100–5
in public places 176, 185
see also artistic works
selections 13
duration of copyright 43
originality 20
sequels 96
serial rights 3
shorthand 10
signatures 92–3
as trade marks 97
Single European Market 207–8
Society of Authors 127, 189
quotation fees 88
software
EC Directive 205
see also computer programs
sound recording 120–2
definition 120
folksongs 122
form 121
soundtracks 120
statutory licence 121
substantial part 121
talking books 121
sound recordings as subject of copyright 10, 122–5
acts restricted by copyright 123–4
authors 122–3
broadcasting 124
cable TV 124
commissioned 123
copyright notice 125
duration of protection 123, 204
illegal copying 125
infringements 124–5
P-in-a-circle 125, 158
performance 114
publication 122
qualification 122
'qualified persons' 122
renting 124
soundtracks 120, 133
Soviet Union
All Union Copyright Agency of USSR (VAAP) 215–16
copyright in former USSR 214–16
negotiations with 215–16
UCC signatory 214
works published on or after 27 May 1973 215
works published before 27 May 1973 214–15
specifications 12
speech not protectable 4

speeches 10, 11
see also literary works
spin-offs 96
stage plays 14
stage presentation 14
Standard Book Numbering Agency
　　Ltd 169
statutory inquiries, copying permitted
　　for 58
Stockholm Convention 216
strip cartoons 48, 119-20
　protection of characters 120
study, copying for 45, 46, 54, 59
submission for publication 143-5
　checking names 143-4
　development of argument 143
　ideas 143
　letter or article to periodical 143
　manuscript of book 143
　negligent misstatement 143
　plots 143, 144
　titles 143
　unsolicited material 143
　see also revision of text
substantial part of a work
　adaptation of 47-8
　broadcasting 47, 127
　copying 44, 45, 46-7
　dramatization 116
　issuing to public 47
　performance 47, 112-13
　permission to quote 83
　playing 47
　showing 47
　sound recording 121
　translations 118
　typographical arrangement 105-6
sufficient acknowledgement 54, 62
supervisory editors, *see* editors
suspension of copyright 35
symposia 13
synopses 95

tables 10, 12, 13
　see also literary works
talking books 121
telegrams 12
Teletext 25
television rights 3, 126, 132
　see also broadcasting; cable
　　television
Telex, infringement of copyright
　　by 49
temporal rights 4

term of copyright, *see* duration of
　　copyright protection
territorial rights 3-4
territories, *see* international
　　conventions; jurisdiction;
　　territorial rights
textbooks 13
time limits for infringement of
　　copyright 48
timetables 12, 13
titles 4
　copying 94-5
　submission for publication 143
　as trade marks 97
trade catalogues, fraudulent 19
trade marks 97-8
transcriptions of musical works 16, 48
translations 48, 117-19
　copyright line 164-5
　copyright notice 164-5
　duration of copyright 43
　more than one language 119
　new copyright 118
　newly printed form 53
　out-of-copyright works 151-2
　quotations from 84
　substantial part 118
translators
　moral rights 100-5, 118
　ownership of copyright 30
　paternity right 100
travel guides 21
25-year reversion 34-5
　contracts and 197
　death of owner of copyright 190
　reissues and 148
typefaces 107, 180
　permitted copying 56
typographical arrangements 10, 47,
　　58, 64, 105-7
　authors 16
　duration of copyright 106
　photocopying 106
　photographs of 107
　republication of out-of-copyright
　　works 152
　substantial part 105-6

UNESCO 23-4
unincorporated bodies 28
United Nations
　qualification for protection 24
　see also recognized international
　　organizations

United States 208-13
  adaptations 212
  'all rights reserved' 212
  copyright line 212
  copyright notice 166-7, 212
  Copyright Office registration 201,
    212
  duration of protection 210-11
  first owner 210
  library deposit 212-13
  manufacturing clause 213
  material for sale in 166-7
  protected works 209-10
  qualification for protection 23,
    208-9
  termination of contract 211-12
  signatory to UCC 208
  unpublished works 209
  works originating in 23
Universal Copyright Convention 17,
    27, 157, 217-21
  copyright line 157, 160, 163,
    164-5
  countries adhering to 218-21
  Russian Federation 214
  UK ratification 23
  USA as signatory 208
  USSR as signatory 214
unpublished works 2
  copying by libraries 60

copying without permission 65-7
  anonymous or pseudonymous
    67-8
  EC Directive 205
  made on or after 1 August
    1989 68
  old 65-7
  out of copyright 205
  pirate publication 50
  qualification for protection 17
  US protection 209
untraceable authors 84
  duration of copyright 41-2
USSR, *see* Soviet Union

VAAP (All Union Copyright Agency
    of USSR) 215-16
Video Performance Ltd 111
video recording of films 132
video recordings
  containing text 12
  as subject of copyright 135
volume rights 3, 196

waiver of moral rights 105
Whitford Report 5-6, 96
will of owner of copyright 189
  literary executor 189-90